GEORGE WASHINGTON
AND
THE WEST

GEORGE WASHINGTON

From the "Virginia Colonel" portrait by Charles Willson Peale, painted at Mount Vernon in 1772 when Washington was forty years of age. The original hangs in the Lee Memorial Chapel of Washington and Lee University at Lexington, Virginia. Courtesy of United States George Washington Bicentennial Commission for the celebration of the Two Hundredth Anniversary of the Birth of George Washington.

GEORGE WASHINGTON
AND
THE WEST

By

CHARLES H. AMBLER
Professor of History
West Virginia University

CHAPEL HILL
THE UNIVERSITY OF NORTH CAROLINA PRESS
1936

COPYRIGHT, 1936, BY
THE UNIVERSITY OF NORTH CAROLINA PRESS

PRINTED IN THE UNITED STATES OF AMERICA BY THE SEEMAN PRINTERY,
DURHAM, N. C., AND BOUND BY L. H. JENKINS, INC., RICHMOND, VA.
THIS BOOK WAS DIGITALLY PRINTED.

PREFACE

FEW of the thousand and more books about George Washington treat exclusively of his western interests and activities. As these were extensive and admittedly determining factors in his career as a soldier and a statesman, the present writer believes there is a place for another work, to present in some detail the high spots in Washington's relations to the West. By many, such a work may indeed be welcomed, not as a feature in the commemoration of the two hundredth anniversary of Washington's birth but as a permanent contribution to history. Certainly this will be true of all those who believe that the West was a determining influence upon American life and institutions and of all those who admit even an element of truth in the statement of the late Herbert B. Adams, that "it would seem as though all lines of our public policy lead back to Washington as all roads lead to Rome."

For assistance in the preparation of this volume the author is indebted to many persons, most of them students in his classes in the West Virginia University. Accompanied by them he visited many points in the Trans-Allegheny region of the upper Ohio Valley associated with Washington legends and traditions; but specific acknowledgments are due Dr. L. D. Arnett, Librarian of the West Virginia University, for his innumerable kindnesses and his personal interest; Robert Merricks, maker of some of the maps used; my wife, Helen Carle Ambler, Dr. William E. Brooks, Pastor of the Presbyterian Church, Morgantown, West Virginia, and Professor Curtis C. Williams, Jr., of the West Virginia University, College of Law Faculty, each of whom criticized the manuscript while it was in process of making; Dr. William B. Hindman, Pastor of the Presbyterian Church and Chairman of the Fort Necessity Memorial Association, Uniontown, Pennsylvania, through whose kindness unexplored data on Washington's western activities of 1754, particularly English contemporary newspaper accounts, were made available to the present writer; Dr. Solon J. Buck, of the National Archives, who read most of the galley proof and through his suggestions saved the author from a number of errors; Charles McCamie, Esquire, Moundsville, West Virginia, who read the page proof and made helpful suggestions; and his secretary, Mrs. Mary Scott Wunschel, for her patience and helpful suggestions in matters of style and format. For whatever errors this book may contain in possible misstatements of fact and interpretation the author alone is responsible.

CHARLES HENRY AMBLER.

West Virginia University
  January 1, 1935

TABLE OF CONTENTS

CHAPTER		PAGE
	PREFACE	v
I.	MAKING A FRONTIERSMAN	3
II.	THE FRONTIER SURVEYOR	18
III.	A GRAND ADVENTURE	30
IV.	JUMONVILLE	50
V.	FORT NECESSITY	73
VI.	BATTLE OF THE MONONGAHELA	92
VII.	DEFENDER OF THE FRONTIER	110
VIII.	THE FRONTIER ADVANCE	132
IX.	IN THE REVOLUTION	152
X.	IN THE CRITICAL PERIOD	172
XI.	IN THE FEDERALIST REGIME	191
	APPENDIX A. THE BATTLE OF FORT NECESSITY	211
	I. Contemporaneous Newspaper Accounts—II. Articles of Capitulation—III. Roster of Virginia Officers and Privates.	
	APPENDIX B. THE BATTLE OF THE MONONGAHELA	222
	I. Contemporaneous Accounts in the *Pennsylvania Gazette* for July 24, 1755—II. Contemporaneous Account in the *Pennsylvania Gazette* for July 31, 1755.	
	NOTES	227
	SELECT BIBLIOGRAPHY	249
	INDEX	261

LIST OF ILLUSTRATIONS

(With the exception of the maps and line drawings, the illustrations face the pages indicated)

THE VIRGINIA COLONEL.....................................*Frontispiece*	
"WAKEFIELD," VIRGINIA, WASHINGTON'S BIRTHPLACE..............	4
CHAIN, COMPASSES, AND SCALE, DRAWN BY WASHINGTON............	9
LORD FAIRFAX	18
COMPASS DRAWN BY WASHINGTON................................	25
WASHINGTON'S JOURNEY TO FORT LE BOEUF.......................	37
WASHINGTON CROSSING THE ALLEGHENY WITH GIST.................	48
WASHINGTON'S MAP OF HIS "JOURNEY TO THE OHIO," 1753.........	51
JUMONVILLE'S GRAVE	64
HISTORICAL MAP OF THE REDSTONE COUNTRY......................	79
SURRENDER OF FORT NECESSITY, JULY 4, 1754...................	86
FORT NECESSITY RECONSTRUCTED................................	87
BRADDOCK'S TRAIL	103
ORIGINAL GRAVE OF GENERAL BRADDOCK..........................	108
BRADDOCK'S GRAVE AND MONUMENT...............................	109
THE VIRGINIA FRONTIER, 1756-1758............................	119
ROADS TO FORT DUQUESNE, 1758................................	127
WASHINGTON'S JOURNEY ON AND ALONG THE OHIO, 1770............	143
WASHINGTON'S MILL NEAR PERRYOPOLIS, PENNSYLVANIA............	154
WASHINGTON'S WESTERN TOUR, 1784.............................	179

GEORGE WASHINGTON
AND
THE WEST

CHAPTER I

MAKING A FRONTIERSMAN[1]

A DIRECT DESCENDANT in the tenth generation from John Washington of Tewithfield, Lancashire, England, George Washington was born February 22, 1732, on his father's estate at Bridges Creek, later named "Wakefield," Westmoreland County, Virginia.[2] He was the eldest child of Augustine Washington by his second wife, Mary Ball, and was christened "George" for Major George Eskridge, his mother's guardian, and not for the reigning king of England as has been claimed. He had three brothers, Samuel, John, and Charles, and two sisters, Mildred, who died in infancy, and Betty, who married Fielding Lewis, and lived at Kenmore on the Rappahannock River, near Fredericksburg, Virginia.

With this large family, which also included for a time two half-brothers, Lawrence and Augustine, children of Jane Butler, his father's first wife, George Washington made his home until he went to live with his half-brother, Lawrence. These early family contacts did much to develop in George the traits of forbearance and consideration which characterized his life to its end and largely determined its success. For each of his brothers and for his sister, he had genuine affection which with his half-brothers ripened into respect and esteem. Another characteristic of the Washington family attachments was sincerity. With George this quality became so habitual that he carried it into other human contacts, winning for himself the respect and admiration of all classes and conditions of mankind.

Authorities generally agree in giving Washington's mother chief credit for his best qualities. The direct descendant of a long line of illustrious ancestors which may have included John Ball, the "Mad Preacher of Kent," and which certainly included

Mary Montague of the extinct house of Salisbury, Mary Ball was born and reared at Epping Forest on the Rappahannock River, the daughter of Colonel Joseph Ball, who died when she was young. As a girl Mary Ball was known as the "Rose of Epping Forest" and the "Belle of the Northern Neck," but, like most girls of her day, she received little formal education. Instead she learned to do housework and to read the Bible. Later she is said to have become somewhat familiar with profound and scholarly writings of the period. More important still she was "gifted with great firmness and constancy of purpose, as well as with clear judgment and remarkable mental independence."[3] These traits sufficed to make her the ruler of her household, respected and esteemed by her intimates rather than fondled and caressed.

Of the many characterizations of this unusual woman, Lawrence Washington of Chotank, one of George Washington's youthful playmates, left an intimate impression. Lawrence feared her ten times more than he feared either of his own parents, because she awed him "in the midst of her kindness, for she was, indeed, truly kind." In his declining years he wrote, "even now, when . . . I am the grandparent of a second generation, I could not behold that remarkable woman without feelings it is impossible to describe"; and he traced to her the "awe-inspiring air and manner so characteristic of the Father of his Country."[4]

Although independent in judgment Mary Washington was not a "new light" reformer. Instead, she drilled her children in the rather stiff and formal etiquette of her day and in the catechism of the Established Church. With each of them she was on all occasions the "Honoured Madam," never given to praise or flattery. Successful achievement of worthy endeavor was accepted by her as matter of fact. She read to her children from the Bible, from the sermons of the Bishop of Exeter, and from Sir Matthew Hale's *Contemplations, Moral and Divine*. Today at Mount Vernon there is a copy of the last named work, a flyleaf of which bears the signature "Jane Washington,"

"WAKEFIELD," VIRGINIA, A REPRODUCTION OF THE BIRTHPLACE OF GEORGE WASHINGTON (GARDEN SIDE). *Courtesy of United States George Washington Bicentennial Commission for the celebration of the Two Hundredth Anniversary of the Birth of George Washington.*

Augustine Washington's first wife, in her own handwriting, and below it the additional words "and Mary Washington," in her hand.[5]

Recent authors portray Washington's mother as a crude and illiterate woman; as having had little to do with George's upbringing, far less than did his half-brothers, Lawrence and Augustine; and as having been an irascible person, increasingly so as she grew older: an irritant to her son and a source of worry to him.[6] She is said to have smoked almost incessantly. It may be significant that George never smoked and that he left home as soon as he could and remained away as long as possible.

Whatever one may think of this rather Spartan yet kind woman, George Washington attributed to her chief credit for what he became.[7] Probably more than from any other source or from all other sources combined, he acquired from her the strength of a philosopher, the truthfulness of a Christian, a fear of God, and a love of liberty and justice. Nor were the forms and conventions which she drilled into him without value. They gave her son poise and bearing and enabled him naturally to spurn familiarity and to command respect. In his subsequent intercourse with statesmen and diplomats these traits also commanded respect for the independent government which he was largely responsible in establishing.

Neither of George Washington's grandfathers was remarkable for talents and achievements, nor did either belong to the highest class of Virginia gentry. Joseph Ball was a colonel and left his daughter, Mary, about two thousand acres in her own right. The Balls came to America as merchants and Joseph's immediate family had English attachments, largely commercial.[8]

Nor was George Washington's grandfather, Lawrence Washington, more distinguished. Like his famous grandson, he was the eldest child of his immediate family, but, unlike him, he did not increase its importance. He is said to have been a quiet, thrifty man who did not seek adventure "either upon land or water." He died leaving a competent estate but nothing to be compared with those left by the Byrds, the Carters, the Fairfaxes, and others of their day.[9]

More can be said for George Washington's great-grandfather, John Washington, the first of his family in Virginia.[10] "He was a man of great personal strength, inclined to war, very resolute, and of a masterful and very violent temper," in whom biographers have found striking resemblance to his great-grandson. Completing a sojourn in Barbadoes, John Washington, came to Virginia in 1657 and soon thereafter came into possession of a large estate in Prince William County, later called Mount Vernon, which was granted to him and Colonel Spencer for transporting "an hundred laborers."

Thus established upon what was then the frontier, John Washington sympathized with Nathaniel Bacon in his difficulties with Governor William Berkeley, resulting in Bacon's Rebellion, which occurred just one hundred years before the American Revolution. In fact, Washington was reprimanded by Berkeley for harsh treatment of Indians. What this treatment was has not been definitely determined, but there is evidence that the Indians feared Washington. For this reason they gave him the name "Conotocarious" meaning the "Destroyer of Villages."

Whatever may be said of the relations existing between the Indians and John Washington, he died enjoying the respect and esteem of his white neighbors. In 1670 he was a member of the House of Burgesses and at other times he held public positions of honor and trust. Throughout his life he was an active churchman, which does not mean that he subjected himself to great denial, as determined by more recent standards. Rectors of his day engaged in fox hunting and gambling, and became so intoxicated that they could not perform baptismal services. He left a legacy to a church in Washington Parish, Prince William County, and provided also for the erection of a tablet therein, on which was inscribed the Ten Commandments and the King's Arms.[11] Consequently some have traced George

Washington's pious and sterling qualities to others than his maternal ancestors.

Most of the traditions regarding George Washington's early education are of uncertain origin and authenticity.[12] At least there is no documentary source available to the present writer to support the claims that Washington, when about six years old, attended a school taught by one of his father's indentured servants, William Grove, nicknamed "Hobby." This school is supposed to have been located near the Washington homestead, Ferry Farm, on the Rappahannock River, almost opposite Fredericksburg, Virginia, to which Augustine Washington moved his family, after an accidental fire in his home at Little Hunting Creek, later named Mount Vernon for Admiral Vernon, where he had been living since 1734 or 1735. It was from Ferry Farm, according to tradition, that George Washington was first sent to school. It is said that as the school was some distance from his home, he went and came on horseback in the company of a Negro, named Peter.

Equally unauthentic, but nevertheless interesting because of its admitted possibilities, is a tradition to the effect that George Washington attended a school in Fredericksburg, Virginia, taught by the Reverend James Marye. Here Washington is said to have received lessons in writing and in business accounting. If he did attend school in Fredericksburg, he probably made there his first contacts with real boys, robust fellows, his equals in wrestling and other sports. One of them, William Crawford, at whose home Washington is said to have lodged during the school week, later surveyed Washington's western lands and in 1782 was burned to death at the stake by Indians at or near what is now Upper Sandusky, Ohio. Others of Washington's companions of this period later fought with him in the French and Indian and other wars.

Another similar tradition regarding George Washington's early education is that his mother wished him to enter the Christian ministry. His aptitude for learning and his alleged piety prompted this desire which, however, may have been unwittingly thwarted by the boy's father, a typical Virginia planter, who took a keen delight in teaching his son George to ride well, to shoot accurately, and to jump and climb with agility. Tradition has it that in recognition of his accomplishments in these boyhood sports the father gave his son George a small sword with which he was greatly delighted. It is said that his attitude toward his toy disturbed his mother, who thus detected in her son greater interest in the career of a soldier than in the career which she had chosen for him. But these stories may be as baseless as those built around the cherry tree and the fiery colt.

Everything considered, particularly the scarcity of schools and the prevailing customs, it is reasonable to assume that George Washington's early education was directed largely by his father with the possible aid of a private tutor or tutors. Confirming this idea and the belief that George's education was directed, after his father's death, by his half-brother Lawrence Washington, are George's school exercise books.[13] These fall into two distinct groups which overlap each other at dates corresponding to those of his father's death and of the marriage of Lawrence, after which the latter presumably assumed greater responsibility for his youthful half-brother. Whatever these facts may have been, at the age of eleven George Washington "could write a fair and legible, if unformed and sprawling, juvenile hand and had made some progress in the elementals of arithmetic."[14]

Enough of Washington's school exercises have been preserved to give a fair idea of his educational equipment. They were "written in ink, in home-made blank books of paper sheets, folded to about nine by eleven inches and stitched with thread."[15] The earliest documents of this kind are devoted to arithmetic and include fractions, decimals, and interest. For a later period they are given up to trigonometry, logarithms, and finally to geometry and surveying in the pursuit of which he drew splendid illustrations of compasses and chains, the instruments he used.

Other exercise books contain copies of business forms and legal instruments. Among these are a promissory note; a bill of exchange; a general release; a servant indenture; a bill of sale; a power of attorney; and still other forms, notably bonds, judgments, transfers, conveyances, and the like. Practically all of these belong to the period following his father's death and were the product of Lawrence's ideas of a practical education. If more generally known, these devices would doubtless commend themselves to modern educators who claim to have found something new and original in the utilitarian idea of education.

Washington's mathematical exercise culminated in self-assigned problems in surveying, thus further demonstrating the practical character of his education. Indeed, it seems probable that he was taught and studied for the attainment of a definite objective. Be that as it may, at an early age he was trying to demonstrate: "How to take an Inaccessible distance at two Stations;" "How to measure any piece of Ground be it never so Irregular and to Cast up the Content thereof in Acres, Roodes

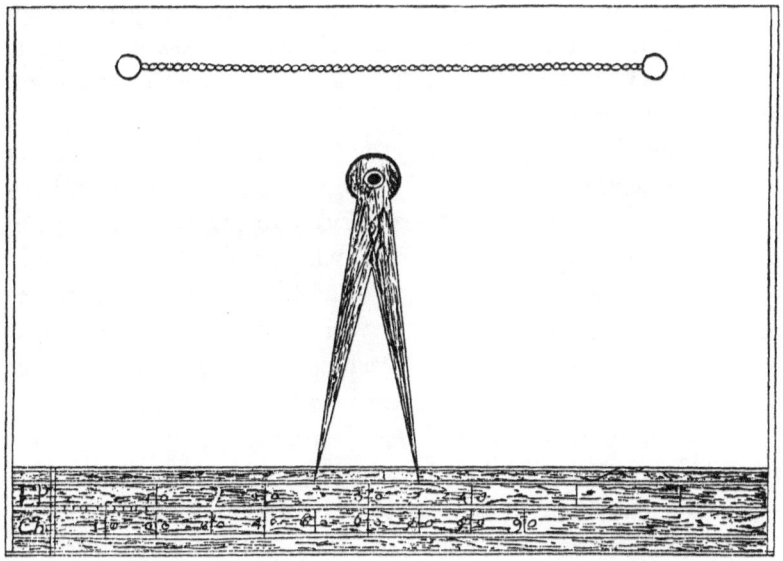

THE CHAIN AND COMPASSES AND SCALE WERE DRAWN BY GEORGE WASHINGTON WHEN HE WAS FOURTEEN YEARS OLD

and Perches."[16] More important still, according to one of his most recent and authentic biographers, "Washington had a natural liking for surveying." Continuing, this author says "the examples are too many, too varied and too carefully inscribed to have been done entirely as tasks."[17]

Washington followed his practical training in mathematics and surveying by equally practical lessons in geography, for which he seems to have had an aptitude. After a fashion somewhat original, his exercise books contained definitions of a continent, a peninsula, a "promatory," climate, and the ocean. For example, "A Climate is a Certain space of Earth & Sea that is included within ye Space of two Parrallels & of them there have been Anciently Accounted Seven," and the earth was "Divided into five Zones."[18] However naïve this phase of Washington's education may seem, it developed him as a map-maker, an art in which he became proficient. As much as any other accomplishment map-making stood him in stead during the rest of his life. Moreover his knowledge of general geography he used almost constantly. It is well known that his ability to judge distances with accuracy approached the marvelous, and that it was next to impossible to lose him anywhere, even in the heart of a trackless forest.

Meanwhile young Washington was making other contacts with the practical side of life.[19] Virginians then led active lives in the open. There were horses to ride; forests contained game in abundance; the broad rivers flowing into Chesapeake Bay were full of oysters, fish, and crabs; and, in season, the marshes paralleling these rivers were favorite haunts for ducks and geese, in the pursuit of which Washington became more or less expert. Another boyhood pleasure was swimming, his favorite resort being "Hobb's Hole, the deepest place in the river." Here he and his companions became past masters in aquatic arts; here they had their clothes stolen; here they played practical jokes on one another; and here they tried the patience of parents by foolhardy darings.

A turning point in the life of this unusual yet quite human

youth came in 1743 with the death of his father. Shortly thereafter, according to the prevailing custom, the Washington estates were divided, the largest ones going to the eldest sons. Thus Lawrence became the owner of Mount Vernon and Augustine of Bridges Creek, while the lands on the Rappahannock, together with a number of Negro slaves and a small amount of personal property, went to the children by his second wife who was to hold and manage the lands specifically willed to each son until he became of age; but in the event that Lawrence died without issue, Mount Vernon was to go to George.

Of greater consequence, the death of George's father is supposed to have caused changes in plans for his son's education. It is reasonable to presume that Augustine Washington had intended to give his eldest son, by his second wife, the same educational advantages which he gave his eldest son by his first marriage and which he himself had received.[20] Such a plan would have taken George to Appleby School in England, but there is no documentary proof that he attended school anywhere. Certainly whatever plans may have been made for his institutional training, they were not carried out following his father's death, and his education continued to be of the practical sort. He was not even sent to William and Mary College in Virginia, a privilege then accorded many sons of first families. Fortunately, both Lawrence and Augustine were in a position to assume a measure of responsibility for their half-brother George.

Because Lawrence was about to be married George did not go to Mount Vernon at once following his father's death but sojourned for a time thereafter with Augustine in his home at Bridges Creek, where George himself had been born. Although he was not able to continue there the training which his father had begun and which Lawrence later continued, Bridges Creek offered George an attractive social life. Augustine Washington had married Ann Aylett, "a kind woman, very orderly and handsome," who brought to her husband a fortune. In her home and under her direction George first met gentle folk and tasted formal society. In these contacts he acquitted himself well and was a favorite with all. Handsome and mature, with a serious manner, he was not lacking in a sense of humor, and his fondness for sports and life in the open made him what would today be called a "good fellow." For a boy on the threshold of adolescence this was indeed a helpful experience.

Even thus early Washington showed evidences of that moderation and restraint that characterized his later life and made him master of himself. The gay life at Bridges Creek, with its race horses and hounds, which would have distracted many another youth, did not banish from his mind the serious purpose of his visit, the furthering of his education. Although he found time to beat his brother and his brother's friends in a fox hunt or two, he lost no opportunity to improve his knowledge of surveying. This was done by continuing his exercises and, when possible, by accompanying surveying parties into the surrounding country. More significant still, George showed as much interest in his brother's large and well-assorted library as in his horses and his hounds. Thus in the midst of what would have been the most unfavorable conditions for a less purposeful youth, George Washington prepared for a career of usefulness, which would in all probability have led him to fame and fortune, had he not achieved them through more important rôles.

Perhaps because of possible reflections upon his limitations in the circle of the socially élite at Bridges Creek, but more probably because of a realization of the facts that he would have to educate himself and that no education is complete without finished manners, Washington early in his teens copied and formulated for his own guidance his famous "Rules of Civility and Decent Behavior in Company and Conversation." These rules had to do with such things as coughing, sneezing, spitting, sighing, and yawning; with the killing of such vermin as "Fleas, lice, &c., in the Sight of Others"; and with the proper care of one's nails, clothing, hair and teeth. They were probably copied from a work by Hawkins, then much used in both France and

England,[21] and throughout were based upon a polite consideration for the rights and feelings of others.

Because of an absorbing attempt on the part of scholars to determine the source of these rules, Washington's reactions to them have been overlooked. It is difficult and sometimes of doubtful value to trace character-forming influences to their sources; but Washington's personality is such a common asset and his conduct parallels so closely some of the rules adopted for his youthful guidance, that the influence of those rules upon his character should not be ignored. For example, the seventeenth rule, "Be no Flatterer," found a living exemplification in him; the thirty-ninth rule, "In writing and Speaking, give to every Person his due title According to his Degree and the Custom of the Place," was observed by him in thousands of letters and otherwise; and the last rule, the one hundred tenth, "Labor to keep alive in your breast that little spark of celestial fire called Conscience," is one which public men have since too frequently ignored. With Washington the obeying of this precept was habitual.

Joseph Addison's tragedy, *Cato*, was also almost certainly a formative influence in Washington's life.[22] To his probable acquaintance with it writers have traced his love of the theater and his knowledge of political philosophy. His friend and adviser, Lord Fairfax, was well acquainted with Addison and several dozen copies of *Cato* were distributed from Williamsburg, Virginia, in 1743. It is thus reasonable to presume that Washington read this work, and, this being granted, that its "high republican principles" left a deep impression upon him. However that may be, "Throughout Washington's entire life the heroics of various lines of *Cato* appear in his letters, and where such lines stuck in his memory, it is safe to say that the philosophy of them lingered."[23]

During the remaining years that Washington resided with his mother he made frequent and extended visits with his half-brothers, Lawrence and Augustine, and with his cousins at Chotank. In this way he continued his informal education and kept in touch with the social life of Virginia. For these purposes he doubtless found Mount Vernon most helpful. Shortly after his father's death Lawrence Washington married Anne Fairfax, daughter of William Fairfax of Belvoir, a near-by estate. William, a cousin of Lord Fairfax and his agent in America, had been educated in England and had seen official service in the English navy, and his accomplished daughter, Anne, brought to Mount Vernon such a gracious hospitality as to make it one of the popular social centers of colonial Virginia. Fortunately for George, the affection Lawrence had always shown him was shared by his new sister-in-law, for whom he developed a strong attachment.

In this new environment Washington learned rapidly. The Fairfaxes were frequent visitors, and doubtless he heard of the romantic adventures of the English navy, in which Lawrence had been an officer, and of British sea power. These accounts must have revived his childhood memories of 1741, when the Washington family, with eagerness and high expectations, though with some concern, sent Lawrence to join Admiral Vernon on an expedition to the West Indies. From his earliest childhood he had also seen strange sailing vessels, some of which belonged to his own father, "Captain" Washington, ascend and descend the Rappahannock; and now similar vessels were appearing in increasing numbers upon the Potomac, all tangible evidence of British sea strength. From the furnace of the Principio Company at Accotink, near Fredericksburg, in which he with others, mostly residents of England, was interested, Augustine Washington transported iron to that country, return cargoes sometimes containing indentured servants, among them convicts.

Out of the mysteries of this situation Washington, just entering his sixteenth year, heeded the call of the sea and decided to become a sailor. Adding to his enthusiasm was the presence of British naval vessels in the Chesapeake and the success of his brother, Lawrence, in securing for him a midshipman's commission. His mother had consented to the appointment, and his clothes and other personal belongings were aboard a ship of his Majesty's navy, when, lo and behold, Mary Washington, according to a well-recognized prerogative of women, changed her mind! As usual, her son obeyed her dictum, and her stepsons were helpless.

Whatever may have been behind this decision, its subsequent effects were momentous. For that reason the following communication from her brother, Joseph Ball, to whom Mary Washington appealed in the matter, confirming his sister's decision, is both interesting and instructive:

STRATFORD-BY-BOW, 19th of May, 1747

I understand that you are advised and have some thoughts of putting your son George to sea. I think he had better be put a prentice to a tinker, for a common sailor before the mast has by no means the common liberty of the subject; for they will press him from a ship where he has fifty shillings a month and make him take twenty-three, and cut and slash and use him like a negro, or rather like a dog. And, as to any considerable preferment in the navy, it is not to be expected, as there are always so many gaping for it here who have interest, and he has none. And if he should get to be master of a Virginia ship, (which it is very difficult to do) a planter that has three or four hundred acres of land and three or four slaves, if he be industrious, may live more comfortably, and leave his family in better bread, than such a master of a ship can. . . . He must not be too hasty to be rich, but go on gently and with patience, as things will naturally go. This method, without aiming at being a fine gentleman before his time, will carry a man more comfortably and surely through the world than going to sea, unless it be a great chance indeed.

I pray God to keep you and yours,

Your loving brother, JOSEPH BALL.[24]

To the credit of the Washingtons, Mary Washington's abrupt and somewhat surprising exercise of authority did not disturb the friendly relations existing between Ferry Farm and Mount Vernon, where George continued henceforth to make his home, to learn the ways of the world, and to develop new interests. Both he and his sister Betty were frequent visitors at

Belvoir, where George met Lord Fairfax and learned from him of his western lands. Young Washington and George William Fairfax, son of the master of Belvoir and eight years George's senior, became fast friends, and to the circle were admitted also George Mason and Richard Henry Lee. In fact, young Washington and "Dicky" Lee are said to have shown greater affection for each other as boys than they later did as men.

But the viewpoint of Americans was rapidly shifting from England and the seas to their own frontiers. Only sixteen years before Washingon was born Alexander Spotswood had made his famous expedition beyond the Blue Ridge mountains, to commemorate which he had established the Order of the Knights of the Golden Horseshoe, whose achievements and purposes were long subjects of interest and conversation. Just before Washington was born, the English, under the leadership of professional fur traders, had penetrated the Ohio Valley, and at the time of his birth Scotch-Irish and German settlers were pushing into the Shenandoah Valley, thus opposing a more or less effective barrier to the expansion of the plantation system of tidewater Virginia. While George Washington was making his first visit to his brother Augustine, following the death of their father, John Howard and John Peter Salling (Salley) were descending the Ohio and the Mississippi rivers all the way to New Orleans, where they were arrested and detained by the French, thus inaugurating a new phase of the pending struggle between the French and the English for supremacy in America, and in the world. To many persons it was already apparent that that struggle would not be determined wholly upon the high seas.

Consequently Washington's decision not to join the British navy was as opportune as it was important. Fortunately he was prepared for the new rôle that was before him. With all the seriousness of a man, with a physical development well beyond his years, at sixteen he was master of those success-commanding traits, modesty, moderation, and self-restraint. From his intimate contacts with nature he had learned to think in terms of things, not words, and the verbal intoxication of the Reformation and pre-Revolutionary periods of European history meant nothing to him. He was already, in fact, one of America's first great realists. Of equal importance, in learning to obey, he had learned to command.

CHAPTER II

THE FRONTIER SURVEYOR

JUST AS George Washington was entering his sixteenth year an arrangement was made whereby he and his friend and companion, George William Fairfax, accompanied beyond the Blue Ridge Mountains a party of surveyors which Lord Fairfax was sending out to prepare his lands for tenantry. So far as available records disclose Washington received no compensation for his services on this journey, if indeed he was expected to perform any. Indications are that it was somewhat of a lark for him, arranged doubtless by his gracious and wise friend, Lord Fairfax.[1]

More than any other person, except his mother and his halfbrothers, Lawrence and Augustine, Lord Fairfax influenced and determined the early career of George Washington. Before 1748 they had met at Belvoir, and Fairfax had become interested in Washington's efforts to learn surveying, in his friends, especially young George William Fairfax, and in their sports and athletic achievements. Here young Washington doubtless learned from Fairfax himself of the history and conventions of the Old World and received first impressions of the comparatively greater opportunities of the New World. In any event, Fairfax's concern for his young protégé was such that he did not hesitate to advise his mother regarding his schooling and other matters pertaining to his welfare.[2]

Through their common interest in the Northern Neck, Washington as a surveyor and Fairfax as owner, the friendship thus formed ripened into an arrangement beneficial and agreeable to both. As finally determined, these lands included all the territory between the Rappahannock and the Potomac rivers, aggregating more than five million acres. In 1649

LORD FAIRFAX

From an oil portrait in the Masonic Lodge Hall, Alexandria, Virginia.

Charles II had granted this vast estate to Lord Culpeper and others as a refuge for Cavaliers, but Culpeper's son, the governor of Virginia, later acquired all the ungranted claims thereto, his father's by inheritance and the others by purchase. His agents managed his estate so badly, however, that repeated efforts were made to dispossess him in the public interest.[3] Consequently when Fairfax inherited his Virginia lands, they were under a ban capable of varied uses in the hands of avaricious lawyers and designing politicians.

Complicating this situation Germans and Scotch-Irish were then pushing into that part of the Northern Neck west of the Blue Ridge Mountains. Ignoring the Fairfax claims, some came as squatters, while others purchased lands from rival claimants, notably Yost Hite. Accordingly Fairfax petitioned the King to determine his rights in the matter, and in 1735 he came to Virginia to give his interests there personal attention. He remained two years. In this time he was able to make a satisfactory arrangement with the Virginia Assembly, which mitigated somewhat the objections to his feudal holdings and brought them into greater favor with the English Privy Council. As a result, but not until 1745, the King confirmed the validity of the Fairfax title to the whole of the Northern Neck but on condition that all legal grants made to others therein prior to that date be respected and confirmed. To determine the legality of a grant to Yost Hite, in 1736 Fairfax instituted a suit which was not finally adjudicated until several years after his death.

The legality of his holdings having been confirmed, Lord Fairfax lost no time in taking possession of them. To this end, in 1746, a company of surveyors ran the famous "Fairfax Boundary Line" which connected the head springs of the Rappahannock and the North Branch of the Potomac rivers.[4] In the same year they planted at the latter "Fairfax Stone." The following year Lord Fairfax emigrated to America and after a sojourn at Belvoir, during which he was in touch with his western interests, he moved permanently to "Greenway Court," a hunting lodge previously built for him but under his direction, on a site about eleven miles from the present city of Winchester, Virginia. To this day the approach of this lodge is indicated by a white post planted on the public highway at a place known as "White Post."

In this retreat this strange man, a tart old bachelor, lived a life that savored somewhat of the American frontiersman of his day. He became a justice of the peace with authority in each county of his proprietary domain, and in 1754, under a commission from Governor Dinwiddie, acted as county lieutenant of militia. As Greenway Court was quite adequate to his needs, his proposed feudal mansion remained only a dream, its would-be lord living instead in the utmost simplicity. Each year he imported new clothes of the latest model but, unlike his protégé, George Washington, Fairfax did not wear them. A titular aristocrat, being the only resident English peer in America, he lived the life of a democrat; an alleged Tory, there is no record of his having raised his voice in defense of English royalty.

Consequently till his death, December 9, 1781, Fairfax was accorded all the privileges of a patriot Virginian, honored and respected even in the bitterest days of the Revolution. Upon being informed of the surrender of Lord Cornwallis at Yorktown, he is reported to have said: "Take me to bed, Joe. It is time for me to die," a statement capable of more than one interpretation. Apropos of this, let it be remembered that Lord Fairfax, the Virginian, was a direct descendant of Lord Fairfax, the Parliamentary leader who, in 1646, vainly commanded Colonel Henry Washington to surrender into his hands Worcester, a Royalist stronghold. The dust of the sixth Lord Fairfax reposes in a crypt beneath Christ Church, Winchester, Virginia.[5]

Even before the ownership of the unappropriated lands in the Northern Neck had been definitely determined, Lord Fairfax had made known his desire to open, to settle, and to develop them. As the first surveying party sent out for these purposes had experienced no mishaps or unusual adventures, young

Washington was allowed to accompany the party going beyond the mountains in the spring of 1748. This party was in charge of James Genn, the county surveyor of Prince William County and a man of many adventures in the wilderness. Accompanied by young Washington, rodmen, chainmen, and other attendants, Genn set out March 11. Going by way of Ashby's Gap and Greenway Court he made his first important stop on the South Branch of the Potomac where that stream intersected the "Fairfax Boundary" which had been determined two years previously.[6] Washington kept a diary of his experiences and adventures.

On March 30, after making a few surveys on or near the Shenandoah River, where they were delayed by swollen streams, over which they swam their horses and conveyed themselves in canoes, the party reached its destination and began its "Intended Business of Laying off Lots," which was not allowed to become monotonous. Hardly a day passed that someone of the party did not kill a wild turkey or two. They cooked meat by holding it over the fire on forked sticks and used bark for dishes. They had scarcely become settled before a "bolstering" night wind carried away their tent, making it necessary for the entire party "to Lie ye Latter part of ye night without covering," drenched by the rain. A few days later they were surprised by "a great Company of People Men Women and Children," who came to inspect their strange operations and to attend them "through ye Woods."[7]

Despite their solicitude for his welfare and their efforts to help him, Washington's first impressions of these people—"Pennsylvania Dutch"—were not very favorable. Fresh from his comfortable living quarters, his wholesome and generous repasts, and his formal and proper contacts, he had not yet developed those traits which, when acquired later, permitted him to go to school anywhere and to learn as long as he lived. He was only a boy, and these strange people apparently annoyed him, for, said he, "they would never speak English but when spoken to they speak all Dutch," which, together with their "Antick tricks," led him to conclude that they were "as Ignorant a Set of People as the Indians."[8] It was not with great regret therefore that the party, April 6, prepared to leave "ye. Branch." Going by way of Henry Van Meter's, they came the next day to Peter Cassey's, where Washington had his first night's rest "in a House since I came to ye Branch."[9] Six days later they were at home.

In other ways than those just indicated, this initiation to the wilderness prepared Washington for the trying ordeals which were before him. March 23, while sojourning with Colonel Thomas Cresap at Old Town on the Potomac at the mouth of the South Branch, he first saw wild Indians near their native haunts, when a band of thirty odd warriors stopped there. They had only one scalp and seemed somewhat dejected; but, when given "Liquor," their spirits revived, and they executed a war dance which Washington described in these words: "They clear a Large Circle and make a Great Fire in y. middle then seats themselves around it y. Speaker makes a grand speech telling them in what Manner they are to Daunce after he has finished y. best Dauncer jumps up as one awaked out of a Sleep and runs and Jumps about y. Ring in a most comical Manner he is followed by y. Rest then begins there Musicians to Play ye. Musick is a Pot half [full] of Water with a Deerskin Stretched over it as tight as it can and a goard with some Shott in it to Rattle and a Piece of an horses Tail tied to it to make it look fine y. one keeps Rattling and y. other Drumming all y. while y. others is Dauncing."[10]

More disillusioning was the knowledge which this journey brought to Washington of the actual living conditions of people of his own race. Horrible as their language must have been to one of his contacts, their manner of living was worse; but it enabled him to see for the first time how the other half of the world lived. As no improvement can be made upon his naïve manner of recording this discovery, Washington will speak for himself: "we got our Supper and was lighted into a Room and I not being so good a Woodsman as ye rest of my Company striped myself very orderly and went in to ye Bed as they called it when to my Surprize I found it to be be nothing but a Little Straw-Matted together without Sheets or any thing else but only one thread Bear blanket with double its Weight of Vermin such as Lice Fleas &c I was glad to get up (as soon as y. Light was carried from us) I put on my Cloths and Lay as my Companions. Had we not been very tired I am sure we should not have slep'd much that night I made a Promise not to Sleep so from that time forward chusing rather to sleep in y. open Air before a fire as will appear hereafter."[11] Two days later he reached Frederick Town [Winchester], where he found his baggage and bathed himself, thus getting "Rid of y. Game we had catched y. Night before."[12]

The novelties and vicissitudes of these experiences were not their only important features. True to the traditions of the man in the making, Washington never lost sight of the beauties of the country through which he passed, particularly its rich lands. As he approached his Lordship's quarters on his way out, he was struck by the "beautiful Groves of Sugar Trees" and spent "ye. best part of y. Day in admiring ye. Trees and richness of ye. Land."[13] The confidence and hope in the expanding West thus inspired, together with the example of his benefactor, were doubtless in a measure responsible for Washington's decision at this time to invest in western lands. Although the sum then expended was not large, it was the first step in the acquisition of that vast acreage later owned by Washington in the West. The payment was an initial one on a tract of 550 acres located on Bullskin Creek in Frederick County, near Greenway Court.[14]

Elated by the thrills that came to most normal persons of the earlier period of American history because of the consciousness of being landowners in their own rights, Washington nevertheless was not satisfied. His interest in surveying continued to appeal to Lord Fairfax who shortly after Washington's initial journey beyond the Blue Ridge gave him more or less regular employment as a surveyor. But preoccupation in this did not keep him from using the library at Greenway Court; at odd intervals he also studied military tactics; he lost few opporrunties to take a turn at the broadsword with soldiers who visited Major Washington at Mount Vernon; and at no time did he neglect his mother who was as accessible from Greenway Court as from Mount Vernon. During the surveying seasons of 1749-1751 he was in the field, far and near, incidentally increasing his knowledge of and acquaintance among the newly arrived settlers, as his business opened their doors to him. Consequently, it has been truthfully said: "the engaging mixture in him of man and boy, must have become familiar to everybody worth knowing throughout all the Northern Neck."[15]

In November, 1749, he wrote of his experiences on the frontier: "since you receid my Letter in October Last I have not sleep'd above three Nights or four in a bed but after walking a good deal all the Day lay down before the fire upon a Little Hay Straw Fodder or bairskin whichever is to be had with Man Wife and Children like a Parcel of Dogs or Catts and happy's he that gets the Birth nearest the fire there's nothing would make it pass of[f] tolerably but a good Reward a Dubbleloon is my constant gain every Day that the Weather will permit my going out and sometime Six Pistoles . . . I have never had my cloths of but lay and sleep in them like a Negro except the few Nights I have lay'n in Frederick Town."[16]

Meanwhile young Washington graduated from the school of experience, and, strange as it may seem, the documentary evidence thereof was conferred by William and Mary College. Through its charter that institution was given the office of surveyor general of Virginia, which carried with it the right to appoint all county surveyors and to retain one-sixth of all fees collected for their services in laying off new lands. The college took its rights and privileges in this matter seriously, all surveyors being appointed by its faculty, usually after a preliminary examination. After only a little more than one year of practical experience Washington, July 20, 1749, passed the required tests and was duly licensed as a county surveyor.[17]

DRAWN BY GEORGE WASHINGTON IN 1750

Shortly thereafter, July 20, 1749, Washington was made surveyor of Culpeper County, Virginia, at an annual salary of approximately fifty pounds. Thus at the age of seventeen he became a public official. Before entering upon the discharge of his duties, "he took the usual oaths to His Majesty's person and government, and took and subscribed to the adjuration oath and test, and then took the oath of surveyor."[18] Fortunately the duties of the office did not occupy him completely, and he continued, from time to time, in the employ of Lord Fairfax and others, making his headquarters at Winchester, where he had an office which he later used as a military headquarters.[19]

Washington's professional career was temporarily interrupted in 1751, when, at the age of nineteen, it became his duty and privilege to accompany his half-brother, Lawrence, to Barbadoes in a quest for health.[20] Never robust, Lawrence's constitution had suffered during those long months spent in the torrid South with Admiral Vernon's fever-stricken fleet, and a fatal consumption had fastened itself upon him. Neither a trip to England nor to the waters of Berkeley Springs, to which George accompanied him, brought relief, and his physicians ordered a sojourn in a tropical climate. George, whom Lawrence loved and trusted, was asked to accompany him on what proved to be the only journey of the former beyond his native land. As if it had been a request from his mother, he consented, thus entering a new field of service generally conceded to belong to women of the most delicate and considerate qualities.

Upon his return from Barbadoes Washington was engaged professionally on several occasions. During the latter part of March, 1752, he undertook a surveying expedition of a month's duration along the waters of Lost River, the Bullskin, Capon River, Dillon's Run, and other streams. The following spring found him again on the frontier making surveys in what are now Hardy, Hampshire, and Jefferson counties, West Virginia. In January, April, and August, 1753, he made trips to Frederick County, apparently in connection with matters related to his profession, but there is meager evidence of surveys which he made that year. Although his short professional career soon came to a close, his journals and papers enumerate over two hundred people for whom he made surveys or transacted business during his four years as a surveyor on the frontier.

Lawrence Washington's death, July 26, 1752, had, in fact, changed the course of George's life, putting "a final term to his youth," and bringing him into man's responsibilities in advance of his years. Before setting out for Barbadoes, Lawrence had arranged to transfer to George his place in the militia and had obtained for him the promise of a commission. Governor Dinwiddie, newly arrived in Virginia, kept this promise by dividing Virginia into four military districts and assigning one of them to young Washington with the rank of adjutant of militia.[21] This was not only a tribute to the deceased Lawrence, but was also a recognition of George's accomplishments as an engineer. At first, November, 1752, he was assigned to the "Southern District" composed of counties south of the James River, but in November, 1753, he was given the adjutancy of the Northern Neck which embraced his home.[22]

In private affairs also Lawrence's death effected a great change in his half-brother's plans. By Lawrence's will, confirming a provision of their father's will, George became residuary legatee of Mount Vernon, in case Lawrence's only surviving child died. As this child, Sarah, survived her father only a few weeks, George came shortly into possession of his brother's estate, except for a life interest belonging to his sister-in-law who married George Lee and accepted an annual allowance in tobacco in lieu of formal possession. Thus, just as he was rounding twenty, George Washington became a large landholder in his own right. Moreover, many things other than his profession demanded attention. Most important of all, he was the executor of his brother's estate; and his mother's affairs could not be neglected. It was at this time that he sojourned at his mother's home, surveyed lands for his brother-in-law, Fielding Lewis, and supervised home affairs, possibly with a view to taking over, the following year, the estates which his father had bequeathed to him on the Rappahannock River.

Despite these forced changes, Washington remained a surveyor and an engineer. Had his brother lived, George would doubtless have continued in the active practice of his profession and would have spent more time upon the frontier. As it was, these experiences rounded out his character, heightened his realistic objectives, and perfected his efficiency and method. His "Book of Surveys" shows his extreme care for detail and his considerable skill. Many of his surveys still exist, unquestioned as to their accuracy.

Although Washington's vocation was not the first choice of his parents, his brothers, or himself, it is doubtful whether he could have chosen one that would have fitted him better for the course before him. The hardships and dangers that he encountered in surveying a virgin forest wilderness of swamps, rivers, and mountains, were comparable to those one would now encounter on a journey to the heart of Africa or on the plains of Manchuria, and they fitted him for still other adventures upon the frontier and in command of armed forces. In addition to informing him regarding the extreme hardships and ever-present dangers besetting the scattered and isolated pioneers residing beyond the mountains and on the outskirts of other settlements, begetting patience and confidence, Washington's experiences in surveying taught self-reliance and resourcefulness. Thus he was able to combine the functions of military leader and executive with those of surveyor and architect. For instance, while assembling and rescuing the shattered remnants of Forbes's army, he did actual construction work on Fort Pitt, and tradition has it that he had previously used his own blacksmith to aid and hasten the construction of Fort Loudoun, near Winchester.

Throughout his life Washington made frequent use of the chain and the compass. As previously indicated, they served him well as a military engineer. Because of the knowledge thus gained, he appreciated the value of maps and charts to the armies of the Revolution and secured the appointment of Robert Erskine as the first geographer of the army. His knowledge of surveying was of material benefit in the numerous enterprises with which he later became associated. For instance, he aided L'Enfant in laying out the grounds for the Federal Capital. After retiring from the presidency Washington made a number of surveys, and as close to his death as November, 1799, he surveyed some of his own lands south of Potomac Falls, making his own notes and transcribing them with the care which he gave to his work while in the employ of Lord Fairfax.

More important still, as has been truthfully said: "Washington's observations [as a surveyor] ... strengthened and deepened his conviction that landownership was the most important factor of colonial development."[23] As a consequence he early became a landowner in his own right and added to his landed possessions, rarely parting with any, until well along in life. His familiarity with Lord Fairfax's large holdings and his contacts with numerous smaller owners and their rivalries only confirmed the fact that "landownership seemed the most important thing in the daily life of the gentlemen around him." It was therefore with real zest and enthusiasm that he entered upon the next phase of his life, that of asserting England's ownership to the Ohio Valley.

CHAPTER III

A GRAND ADVENTURE[1]

WHILE George Washington was surveying lands for Lord Fairfax and others, pursuing fruitless and impossible affairs with his "Lowland Beauty" and others, and trying to nurse his favorite brother to health, the stage was being set for a contest between the French and English for ownership of the Ohio Valley, and between the Pennsylvanians and Virginians for control of "the Forks" of the Ohio, including the surrounding territory. So far as England and France were concerned this contest had been on for more than half a century, and it continued even longer. Beginning in 1689 with King William's War, or the War of the English Succession, echoes of the French and English struggle for North America ceased to be heard only with the overthrow of Napoleon; all the important intervening wars entailed loss of life and destruction of property in America. The impending conflict was only one of several in what has been fittingly called the "Second Hundred Years War," but it marked a turning point in world events and gave birth to the British Empire, child of William Pitt, the Elder.

At this stage the French took the initiative. Although their claims under the alleged discovery of the Ohio River by La Salle (1669-1670) have long since been exploded,[2] they were then seriously asserted. More effective still were their permanent settlements in the Illinois Country and along the lower Mississippi River and the fact that a more or less uninterrupted commerce had long been maintained between these settlements. In the meantime French traders had penetrated the Ohio Valley carrying the fruits of their activities to Great Lake posts and other points.[3]

Finally, stimulated by counter activities of the English,

particularly the Pennsylvanians, in 1749, one Celoron in behalf of the French, had planted leaden plates at several points on the Ohio River, to assert their claims to exclusive ownership. At the same time they warned the Governor of Pennsylvania to keep his traders out of French territory, since "our Commandant-General would be very sorry to be forced to use violence."[4] In preparation for such a contingency, they, nevertheless, began to build a line of forts all the way from Lake Erie to the lower Mississippi. Already they had arrested English traders and carried them to Canada, while others, notably John Frazier located at Venango, were driven from their posts.

In the counter movement on the part of the English, the Pennsylvanians took the lead and that too despite the early warnings of Governor Spotswood and other Virginians, including William Byrd, the Elder, of impending trade dangers to their colony. With the city of brotherly love and its peace-loving traditions as a base of operations and with Benjamin Franklin and Samuel Wharton to aid financially and otherwise, George Croghan, Conrad Weiser, and other traders and agents penetrated the upper Ohio country while George Washington was yet a youth.[5] Before Washington was ten years old Croghan owned a farm of twelve hundred acres on the Pennsylvania border, where he built a house which became a rendezvous for Indian and white traders. Thence, aided by Croghan's intimate knowledge of Indian diplomacy the English penetrated the Indian country to and beyond the Ohio River.

Under these benign influences Pennsylvanians were pushing into the region about the upper Ohio,[6] and but for the flat refusal of their colonial government, under traditional Quaker influences, to build a fort at "the Forks" for the protection of traders, settlers, and friendly Indians, the story of the conquest of the Ohio Valley might have been differently told. Indeed, the whole course of American history might have been altered.

In the meantime the Virginians were not indifferent to developments beyond the mountains, but their suspicions of Pennsylvanians were greater stimuli to immediate action than was their concern for French pretentions. Under a Charter of 1609 to the Virginia Company, Virginia claimed most of the country in dispute. It was also maintained that Batts and Fallam, Virginians, were the first explorers of record to discover waters flowing into the Ohio. In quest of furs Virginia traders had reached the Ohio, possibly before either Croghan or Weiser, and the undetermined location of the common boundary line between Pennsylvania and Virginia west of the mountains, had already given rise to uncompromising claims regarding the ownership of the Monongahela Valley.[7]

In a very real way the early eighteenth-century movement of Virginia planters beyond the Blue Ridge Mountains was a part of the larger westward movement which soon followed into the Trans-Allegheny. Not satisfied with acquiring choice lands in the former region for themselves and locating Pennsylvania Dutch and Scotch-Irish settlers upon the refuse, Lord Fairfax and his young surveyor had little difficulty in inducing friends and relatives in tidewater Virginia to become original patentees of lands west of the mountains and to settle there. This was notably true of Washington's brothers, Samuel and Charles, each of whom settled in the Shenandoah Valley upon lands originally purchased from Lord Fairfax in 1747, by their half-brother, Lawrence. Here they lived and reared large families; Samuel married five times and had more children than money. To this day the Washington estates, "Harewood" and "Mordington," are well-known landmarks. Charles Washington owned the site of and laid out Charles Town, the present county seat of Jefferson County, West Virginia.[8]

Sensing the far-reaching importance to Virginia of this intercolonial and international rivalry for trade and lands, in 1748 Lawrence and Augustine Washington, Thomas Lee, president of the Council of Virginia, John Bradbury, a London merchant, and others organized the Ohio Company. It was promised a grant of two hundred thousand acres of land on the Ohio River, on condition that the company erect and maintain a fort, and within seven years, settle a hundred families thereon. Another grant of three hundred thousand acres awaited the successful fulfillment of the conditions of the first.[9]

In the midst of much opposition, politicians and speculators being increasingly fearful of encroachments upon Virginia's western lands by imperial grants such as those made to Lord Baltimore and to William Penn, the Ohio Company prepared to comply with the conditions of its grant and thus to make it effective. To this end the company imported a large quantity of goods from the mother country to be used in the Indian trade, established a base of operations at Wills Creek, now Cumberland, and engaged Colonel Thomas Cresap to open a wagon road thence to a point on the Youghiogheny River about eighty miles distant. With the aid of Nemacolin, a trusted Delaware Indian, this road was "blazed" in 1750, and, in the same year, some months after Dr. Thomas Walker had set out to explore a similar grant of 100,000 acres for the Greenbrier Land Company in what is now central eastern West Virginia, Christopher Gist was sent by the Ohio Company to locate its lands and to determine the general conditions on the extreme frontier.

Because Gist was Washington's forerunner in the wilderness, he is here given more than passing mention. A native Marylander and a surveyor by profession, at the time he entered the employ of the Ohio Company, he was a farmer living on the Yadkin River in North Carolina near the home of Daniel Boone. Going by way of the "Reystown Path," on October 20, 1750, he reached the Forks where he found the natives in a state of unrest. Disguising his real mission of land prospector for the acquisitive "Long Knives" whose reputation for close bargaining had preceded them, thanks to the Pennsylvanians and the French, Gist concealed his compass and was accepted by the Indians as a friend. Thus he was able to penetrate the country beyond the Ohio to a point on the waters of the Great Miami, encountering as he went many Pennsylvania traders, including George Croghan, and unmistakable evidences of French hostility to Virginians. He returned through Kentucky by way of the Cumberland foothills, and, after a short visit at his home, made a report to his employers.[10]

Although the Ohio Company found Gist's report discouraging, it was not half so much so as was the opposition the Company was then encountering among Virginians. The Governor and Council had refused to allow the company to survey lands, as desired; the faculty of William and Mary College had also refused to commission a surveyor for that purpose; and the Governor and Council had made out "large grants to private persons, landjobbers, to the amount of 1,400,000 acres." As a consequence the members of the Ohio Company feared that they might "be prevented from fulfilling their covenant of settling the lands and completing their Fort in the time specified." Relying upon the royal favor, in November, 1751, they again sent Gist into the interior upon another prospecting expedition and awaited developments. Beset by the opposition of interested but non-participating Virginians, by the intrigues of the Pennsylvanians, and by the growing hostility of the French, they were forced to this action.

At this juncture conditions took a turn favorable to action by Virginians regarding their frontier. Shortly before Lawrence Washington left for Barbadoes in search of health (1751) he became president of the Ohio Company. Although George's early return was primarily to bring his brother's wife, Anne Fairfax Washington, out to Bermuda, whither Lawrence intended to go, it is a fair presumption that George was interested in other phases of his brother's affairs. However that may be, about the same time, the energetic and somewhat impetuous Robert Dinwiddie became governor of Virginia and incidentally a shareholder in the Ohio Company. It may be significant also that George Washington, on his way home from Barbadoes[11] and bearing greetings and good wishes from his brother, called to see the new governor; that, a few months later, following Lawrence's death in July, 1752, George went to Williamsburg to receive from Dinwiddie personally a commission as adjutant for the Southern District of Virginia;[12] and that Lord Fairfax had meanwhile visited Dinwiddie and continued to pay him his respects.

Being interested primarily in permanent settlements rather than in trade, as yet only a few Virginians favored an aggressive policy in the interior. Outstanding among them were Lord Fairfax, the Washingtons, and the Governor. Had Lawrence Washington lived, he, in all probability, would have become their military, as well as their executive, leader, but with his death Dinwiddie himself assumed active direction of the affairs of the Ohio Company, which gave it a semblance of official approval. In this capacity Dinwiddie urged action as necessary to preserve the Protestant religion and human liberty. Little was said of his investments. Instead he vainly implored the assembly for aid and attempted to allay the opposition of the Pennsylvanians to the proposed settlements by offering them the quit rents therefrom until such time as the common boundary line between Pennsylvania and Virginia could be determined.

Equally if not more constructive were Dinwiddie's efforts to allay the suspicions and secure the coöperation of interested Indian tribes. To this end, in 1752, Joshua Fry joined Christopher Gist and Indian chieftains of the upper Ohio for a conference at Logstown, a trading post located on the Ohio River about twenty miles below the Forks on or near the present site of Legionville, Pennsylvania. Probably more with a view to his own colonial interests than to friendly understandings with the Indians, Governor James Hamilton of Pennsylvania attended this conference which resulted in a treaty favorable to the Virginians. It confirmed previous treaties, notably that made at Lancaster, Pennsylvania, in 1744, and approved the proposed settlements. Early the next year, in an effort to keep the northern and the southern Indians friendly, William Fairfax met chiefs of the Iroquois at Winchester, gave them presents, and arranged for another conference the following year.

Thus, so far as the Ohio Company was concerned, the Indian situation was promising, but it was admittedly not all that could be desired. While most Virginians did not yet insist that "The only good Indian is a dead Indian," they were, as of old, willing to extract desired land concessions from signs and grunts made in the process of negotiating "solemn" and "binding" treaties. For such transactions even those receiving no direct benefits found salve for their consciences in the belief that these benighted children of the forest had found salvation, or at least the opportunity to get it. Their ominous protests counted for little, though pointed and unanswerable. For example, a Delaware chieftain at the Logstown conference said: "The French claim all the land on one side of the river, and the English claim all the land on the other side of the river. Just where is the Indian's land?"[13]

Ignoring all such embarrassing inquiries, if indeed they were embarrassing, Dinwiddie directed his attention to the French. Although hostilities between them and the English were then thought to be inevitable, the canny Governor was determined not to be the aggressor. Accordingly in behalf of his Majesty the King of England, Dinwiddie resolved to send to the erring subjects of George's beloved cousin, the most Christian King of France, a solemn warning to cease trespassing upon the preserves of King George. For this mission Captain William Trent, a partner of Benjamin Franklin, was first selected, but Trent advanced no farther than Logstown one hundred fifty miles short of his destination. Here he heard that the French were advancing toward the upper Ohio in large numbers, having previously defeated Indians friendly to the English, and he turned back, winning for himself a possibly undeserved reputation for cowardice.

It was under these conditions that Governor Dinwiddie turned to George Washington, ward of a founder of the Ohio Company, not yet twenty-two years old. Captain Trent having failed, Washington was asked to carry a message of warning to the French, it being understood also that he was to gather all the information possible pertaining to conditions in the frontier. The call was not entirely unexpected, since Washington had previously expressed a desire for it and had been groomed for the opportunity by his friend, Lord Fairfax; but it was a mo-

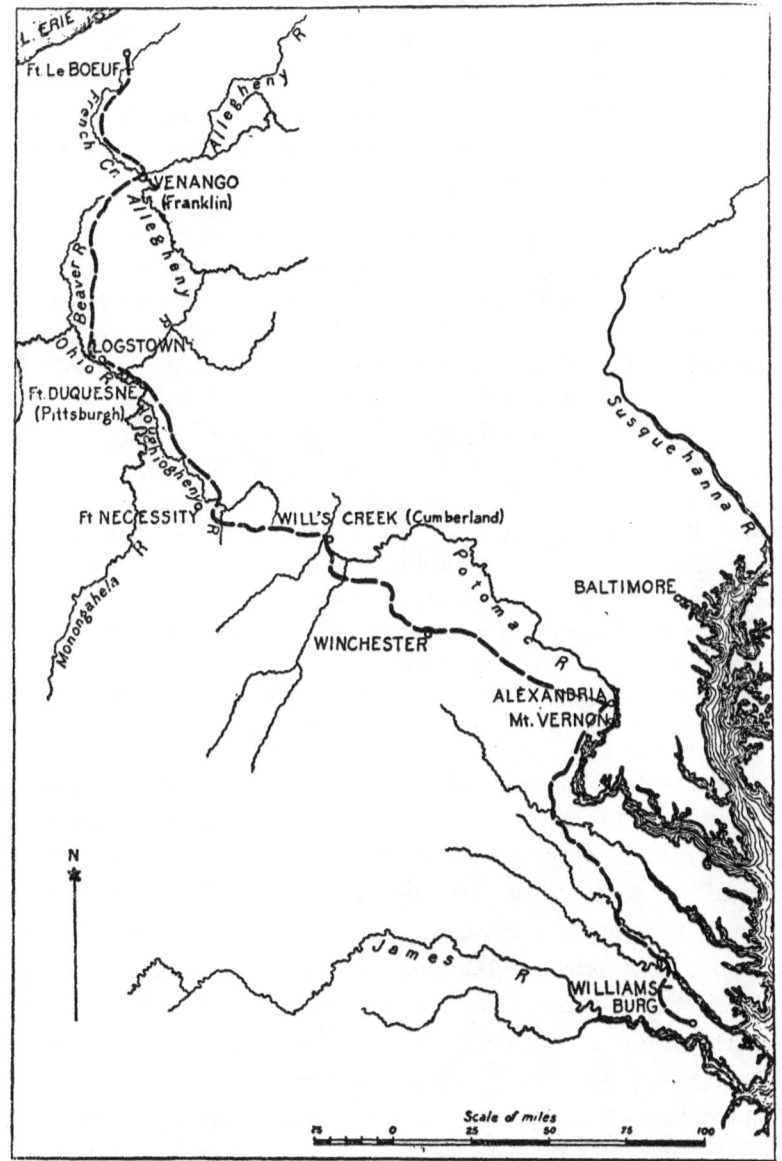

WASHINGTON'S JOURNEY TO FORT LE BOEUF, 1753

mentous undertaking for anyone, regardless of age, experience, or friends. Countless thousands of men had already performed daring feats and have continued to perform them, but rarely did it fall to any to be sent into a veritable hotbed of intercolonial, international, and interracial strife fraught with the bitterness of rival religions, pagan, Catholic, and Protestant, and of rival systems and notions of government. The situation has been aptly described by Professor Alvord:

> The preparations of Virginia to extend her dominion over the rich western territory by actual occupation were watched with increasing jealousy by the men of other colonies, who were far from being satisfied with a policy that would place in the control of any one province the exploitation of such a vast and valuable region. It is therefore not strange that any plans promoted by them should assume the form of a limitation of the territory of Virginia by the erection of independent colonies. The city of Philadelphia in particular was very much interested in the disposition of the West, which was well known there from the accounts of her merchants who at an early date had sent their fur-trading representatives across the mountains. These traders, it was said, were so hostile to Virginia that they were the chief agents in arousing among the Indians fears of the threatened encroachments on their hunting-grounds and were therefore the real instigators of the war, because the French were induced to enter the valley of the Ohio by the clamor of their Indian allies.[14]

Under such conditions the successful performance of a mission such as that entrusted by Dinwiddie to Washington, would have entitled any person to an enviable place in history. Successful performance of this mission required the cunning of a savage, the tact of a diplomat, the patience of a saint, the endurance of a beast of burden. However, it offered a grand opportunity to play a rôle upon a world stage involving the possession of a Golconda and the potentialities of empire. Through experience and natural endowment, as well as through the tutelage of his brother Lawrence and his friend, Lord Fairfax, Washington was prepared for the undertaking; nevertheless it was a grand adventure. Henceforth there were fewer love affairs in his life, and like others of his name, he began to show evidences of having been born old as well as wise.

On the first of his six journeys into the Trans-Allegheny and with no companions of record in the *Diary* which he kept of his adventures,[15] Washington left Williamsburg, October 31, 1753, to deliver a letter of warning to the French Commandant in the Ohio Valley, then supposed to be stationed at the Forks. The next day he stopped at Fredericksburg to take leave of his mother and to engage the services of a jolly Dutch adventurer, Jacob Van Braam, to act as his French interpreter. As Van Braam had been with Lawrence Washington under Admiral Vernon at Carthagenia, had served the Washington family in various capacities, and was supposed to know French, his choice as Washington's companion for this mission was as natural as it was agreeable. Gathering provisions, blankets, and guns at Alexandria, and horses, tents, and other supplies at Winchester, Washington and Van Braam pushed on to Wills Creek, now Cumberland, which they reached November 14 in a rain and snow storm.

The following day with Christopher Gist as guide, "Barnaby Currin and John MacQuire, Indian Traders, Henry Steward, and William Jenkins," servitors, Washington and Van Braam pushed deeper into the wilderness.[16] Going by way of Gist's, now Mount Braddock, Pennsylvania, and Jacob's, a settlement near the present site of Mount Pleasant, Pennsylvania, they did not reach Frazier's on the Monongahela at the mouth of Turtle Creek until the twenty-second of November. Excessive rain and heavy snow prevented their earlier arrival. Here the good news awaited them that the French General, Sieur de Marin, sent to erect a fort at the junction of the Allegheny and the Monongahela rivers, had died, and that the major part of the French army had retired to winter quarters on the waters of the upper Allegheny River.

With the way thus cleared, the Indians also veering to the side of the English because of threatened aggressions of the French, Washington's party pushed forward, the servitors carrying the baggage down the Monongahela to the Forks in a canoe, while Washington and Gist proceeded to the same point on horseback. As he reached his temporary objective before his baggage, Washington had an opportunity to examine that strategic point in some detail. At once he recognized its importance, for, said he, "it has the absolute Command of both Rivers. The Land at the Point is 20 or 25 Feet above the common Surface of the Watter; and a considerable Bottom of flat, well timbered land all around it, very convenient for Building: The Rivers are each a Quarter of a Mile, or more, across, and run here very near at right Angles."[17]

Swimming their horses across the Allegheny River at a point near the present Manchester Bridge, Washington and his companions continued about two miles to a place on the Ohio, where lived Shingiss, king of the Delawares. Here the Ohio Company had planned to build a fort, and for that reason Washington examined the site with care. As compared with "the Situation at the Forks," the proposed site did not appeal to him, either for "Defence or Advantages," especially the latter: "For," said he, "a Fort at the *Forks* would be equally well situated on the *Ohio*, and have the entire Command of the *Monongahela*; which runs up to our Settlements and is extremely well designed for Water Carriage."[18] Later the French, the English, and the American governments put their seals of approval upon the recommendations of this boy engineer.

Accompanied by Shingiss, the following day, the twenty-fifth after he left Williamsburg, Washington reached "*Loggs*-Town." Here lived Tanacharisson, a Seneca chief who, because he owed allegiance to the Six Nations, was called the Half-King. For some reason he was away from his village when Washington arrived. Accordingly Tanacharisson and other sachems were sent for, while Washington acted as host to "the other great Men."

While the sachems were assembling, Washington used his time to advantage. On the day following his arrival a number of Frenchmen, deserters from a company stationed on Big

Beaver Creek, came to Logstown on their way to Philadelphia. "They were," reported Washington, "sent from *New-Orleans* with 100 men, and 8 Canoe-Loads of Provisions to this Place; where they expected to have met the same Number of Men, from the Forts on this Side Lake *Erie,* to convey them and the Stores up, who were not arrived so they ran-off."[19] From them he learned in detail the number, location, and strength of the French forts on the Mississippi and in the Illinois country.

The same day, about three o'clock in the afternoon, the Half-King reached home and upon invitation, went at once to Washington's tent. Shortly before the Half-King, too, had performed a mission of warning and inquiry to the French Commandant, and Washington was anxious to learn from his Indian friend of "the Particulars of his Journey"; of his reception, and of "the Ways and Distance." He reported the roads bad and the temper of the French worse; for in reply to his earnest entreaties, expressed in a formal speech, that the French "Disturbers in this Land" leave it to its rightful owners, "the Indians, as the English had agreed to do [*sic*]," the late French Commandant, in a speech equally formal, had insulted the Half-King by telling him that he owned no land, not even as much as Sieur de Marin could carry under his finger nails.[20]

To all protests and warnings the French were reported to be equally indifferent and insulting. It mattered not that the Half-King called General Marin's attention to a former treaty between his people and the French, in which they "set a silver Bason before us, wherein there was the Leg of a Beaver, and desir'd all the Nations to come and eat of it; to eat in Peace and Plenty, and not to be churlish to one another: and that if any such Person should be found to be a Disturber, I here lay down by the edge of the Dish a Rod, which you must scourge them with."[21] Regardless of this, the general had called the Indians flies and mosquitoes and declared the irrevocable intention of his King to occupy their lands, peacefully if he could, but forcefully if he must. In proof of this resolve the Half-King called attention to the fact that the French had already built forts, one on Lake Erie and another on French Creek, both connected by "a Large Waggon Road."[22]

On the following day Washington and the friendly sachems met "in Council at the *Long-House*," where Washington and the Half-King were the orators of the occasion. As Washington's speech was his first of record, being one of the few informal addresses he ever made that has been preserved, as it betrays latent qualities which might have developed a diplomat, and as Washington was his own reporter, his Logstown address is here reproduced in full.

Brothers, I have called you together in Council by order of your Brother, the Governor of *Virginia*, to acquaint you, that I am sent, with all possible Dispatch, to visit, and deliver a Letter to the *French* Commandant, of very great Importance to your Brothers, the *English*; and I dare say, to you their Friends and Allies.

I was desired, Brothers, by your Brother the Governor, to call upon you, the Sachems of the Nations, to inform you of it, and to ask your Advice and Assistance to proceed to the nearest and best Road to the *French*. You see, Brothers, I have gotten thus far on my Journey.

His Honour likewise desired me to apply to you for some of your young Men, to conduct and provide Provisions for us on our Way; and be a safe-guard against those *French Indians* who have taken up the hatchet against us. I have spoken thus particularly to you Brothers, because his Honour our Governor treats you as good Friends and Allies; and holds you in great Esteem. To confirm what I have said, I give you this String of Wampum.[23]

In an equally formal speech the Half-King accepted this evidence of the friendship of his "Brother the Governor" and promised, with his help, to avenge himself of the insults recently shown the Indians by the French. That his "Brothers may see the Love and Loyalty we bear them," at the same time he promised to send a guard to accompany Washington to the French, asking only that he delay his departure long enough, about three days, to permit the "*French*-Speech-Belt" to be brought from Half-King's hunting cabin and to permit the chieftains whom he had sent for to assemble.

Urging the importance of his mission, and the necessity for dispatch, Washington at first refused to comply with this request, but as the possibility of bringing about a complete breach between the Indians and the French became more evident, even the return of all mementoes of the peaceful relations between them, he tarried from day to day, as requested. Meanwhile he made friends of the sachems, and in so far as it was discreet to do so, informed them of his plans and purposes. These conferences confirmed the decision of the French to retire temporarily, but gave assurances of their intention to return "in the Spring, with a far greater Number," at which time they would surely conquer their enemies, or, in their failure to do so, "they and the *English* would join to cut them [the Indians] all off, and divide the Land between them."[24]

Following a conference with "the great Men," the number in his party having been increased from seven to twelve by the addition of John Davison, an Indian interpreter, and by four Indian guides, "the Half-King, Jeskakake, White Thunder, and the Hunter," on November 30, Washington set out on the road to Venango. As the result of a private conference the Indians had decided not to send more guides, so as not to arouse "the French Suspicions of some bad Design." Descending the Ohio to a point near the present Rochester, the Party cut across country in a northeasterly direction, coming in about fifteen miles to Murdering Town and in about thirty more to a path leading to the Kuskuskies. Thence, almost direct, they reached their destination, an old Indian town on the Allegheny, then called the Ohio, about sixty miles from Logstown. Here they found "the French Colours hoisted on a House from which they had driven Mr. John Frazier, an English Subject."

It was at Venango that Washington first learned directly from the French of their plans and purposes. At first Captain Joncaire, the commander, treated him rather formally, inviting his party to dine and assuming a rather complacent attitude; but soon wine loosened the tongues of the French, and they revealed their sentiments more freely. In this condition they informed the Virginians "That it was their absolute Design to take possession of the *Ohio,* and by G— they would do it."[25] Although admitting the ability of the English to raise two men to their one for service in the interior, they nevertheless chided them with being "too slow and dilatory to prevent any Undertaking" of the French. As a consequence they did not hesitate to reveal the exact location of their forts and the strength of each.

The gasconade in this attitude was soon betrayed by Joncaire's sudden concern for Washington's Indian companions whose presence had been concealed for a whole day. When he learned of the stealth which had thus been perpetrated upon him, Joncaire expressed great concern, but Washington countered his craftiness with a compliment which also concealed a warning. In this Joncaire was reminded of his "great Influence among the Indians" and of Washington's consequent concern for the loyalty of his guides. Undaunted, Joncaire continued to give them presents and to douse them with "Liquor so fast, that they were soon rendered incapable of the Business they came about," the surrender of the "Speech-Belt" and the termination of peaceful relations. It took a whole day to put the Half-King in condition to do this, but Joncaire refused to take him seriously and continued to give him presents and wine. It required all the resources of Washington, Gist, and Davison to separate this child of the forest from his toys and his "spirit" and to induce him to continue the journey.

Although defeated in the practice of a craftiness that approached diplomacy, Joncaire was not thereby bereft of courtesy. Accordingly he sent a French Commissary, La Force, and three soldiers to escort Washington's party to his superior, the new commandant. Four days of hard travel through rain, snow, mire, and swamps brought them, December 11, to their destination, Fort Le Boeuf, on French Creek at the present site of Waterford, Pennsylvania, about twenty miles south of Erie. Here they were introduced to Legardeur de St. Pierre, "an old man with one eye," who only seven days before had succeeded the late General Marin in command. It was to him, a knight of the military Order of St. Louis, that Washington delivered Governor Dinwiddie's letter which said:

The Lands upon the River Ohio in the Western Parts of the Colony of Virginia are so notoriously known to be the Property of the Crown of Great Britain; that it is a Matter of equal Concern and Surprize to me, to hear that a Body of French Forces are erecting Fortresses, and making Settlements upon that River, within his Majesty's Dominions. . . .

It becomes my Duty to require your peaceable Departure; and that you would forbear prosecuting a Purpose so interruptive of the Harmony and good Understanding, which his Majesty is desirous to continue and cultivate with the most Christian King. I persuade myself you will receive and entertain Major Washington with the candour and Politeness natural to your Nation . . . your most obedient Humble Servant, Robert Dinwiddie.[26]

This communication and its bearer St. Pierre received kindly and courteously but his ignorance of English compelled him to send for his relative and interpreter, Captain de Repentigny. Fortunately for Washington, Captain Repentigny knew no more English than Van Braam knew French, and thus it took some time to translate Dinwiddie's letter. Meanwhile Washington took advantage of "an opportunity of taking the Dimensions of the Fort and making what Observations" he could, while his companions, under his direction, made an inventory of the canoes being built and assembled for military use the following spring.[27] Taking time by the forelock they also sent their half-starved and exhausted horses back toward Venango, to save them and to expedite their own return.

After two days deliberation St. Pierre, December 14, sent Washington this formal and positive "Answer to his Honour the Governor's Letter:"

I shall transmit your Letter to the Marquis Duquisne. His Answer will be a Law to me. . . . As to the Summons you send me to retire, I do not think myself obliged to obey it. What-ever may be your Instructions, I am here by Virtue of the Orders of my

General; and I intreat you, Sir, not to doubt one Moment, but that I am determined to conform myself to them with all the Exactness and Resolution which can be expected from the best Officer. . . .

I made it my particular Care to receive Mr. Washington, with a Distinction suitable to your Dignity, as well as to his own Quality and great Merit. I flatter myself that he will do me this Justice before you, Sir; and that he will signify to you in the Manner I do myself, the profound Respect with which I am, Sir, your most humble, and most obedient Servant, Legardeur de St. Pierre.[28]

Thus informed, Washington might have set out for home at once, but for the fact that his Indian attendants were again being tampered with. From the first he had tried to induce the Half-King to break off peaceful relations with the French by formally surrendering the "Speech-Belt" which St. Pierre shrewdly refused to accept. Instead he gave the Half-King presents and liquor, made "many fair Promises of Love and Friendship," and asserted his wish to live in peace and to trade amicably with his Indian brothers.

Attracted more by French fire-water and trinkets than by French oratory, the Indians lingered after St. Pierre delivered his reply to Governor Dinwiddie. Finally Washington went to see St. Pierre about the matter, complaining to him of illtreatment because of the fact that his company, of which the Indians were a part, was being detained. Professing ignorance of the cause, the French continued to dispense presents and wine among the Indians who were unwilling to depart until two days after the formal negotiations ended and then only at the earnest solicitation of Washington himself. His concern over this phase of his negotiations was recorded in his *Diary* in these unmistakable words: "I can't say that ever in my Life I suffered so much Anxiety as I did in this Affair; I saw that every Strategem which the most fruitful Brain could invent, was practised, to win the Half-King to their Interest; and that leaving him here was giving them the Opportunity they aimed at."

In the meantime Washington used his trials to advance his purposes. In the course of his conference with St. Pierre regarding his Indian companions he found an opportunity to ask "by what Authority he [St. Pierre] made Prisoners of several of our *English* Subjects" and was informed that the country belonged to the French; "that no *Englishman* had a Right to trade upon those Waters; and that he had Orders to make every Person Prisoner who attempted it on the *Ohio*, or the Waters of it."[29]

Undeceived, and possibly disillusioned regarding the plans and purposes of the French on the Ohio, and fully informed regarding military and other conditions there, December 16, Washington left Fort Le Boeuf for Venango, traveling by way of French Creek. The passage was tedious and fatiguing, rocks were treacherous, and shoals were passable only by wading through ice-ladened waters. Consequently the party did not reach Venango until the twenty-second. Here they recovered their horses, which were found to be too starved and weak to carry heavy baggage with dispatch. Accordingly it was decided to turn them over to drivers, all others being required to walk, "carrying their Packs to assist along with the Baggage."

Performing packhorse service with others of his party, Washington left Venango December 23. In this fashion he spent Christmas eve and Christmas day, 1753, caring little about the Half-King who had tarried with Joncaire, again to regale himself with wine. Despairing of "getting Home in any reasonable Time" by traveling with his horses and his party, and with the importance of his mission constantly before him, Washington determined to prosecute his journey to the Virginia settlements "the nearest Way through the Woods, on Foot." For this purpose, Van Braam being left behind with the horses and the baggage, he tied himself in a matchcoat and with his gun in his hand and his pack on his back, December 26, he set out with Gist, "fitted in the same Manner."

The days immediately following brought the most thrilling and trying personal experiences of the entire journey. After trying in vain to divert Washington from his course, a French Indian who insisted on accompanying him, suddenly whirled upon his heel and shot at Washington at close range. Gist was for shooting the scoundrel at once, but Washington stayed his hand and gave the Indian the slip. In crossing the Allegheny, Washington was thrown from a raft into deep water, amid floating ice, but he fought his way out, and he and Gist spent the following night on an island with their clothes frozen upon them. As a result "Gist had all his Fingers, and some of his Toes frozen," but the refugees were able to escape their retreat without further mishap. By morning the river had closed with firm and solid ice over which they walked to shore. Thence they went direct to Frazier's.

As the plan was to continue the journey on horseback, while the horses and supplies were being made ready, Washington visited Queen Aliquippa, a wrinkled old squaw who exercised a sort of regal power at or near the mouth of the Youghiogheny River. Rumor had had it that she was displeased because Washington and his party had passed her by on their way to Fort Le Boeuf. In an effort to appease her and to retain her friendship for the English, Washington "made her a present of a Matchcoat and a Bottle of Rum; which latter was thought much the best Present of the Two."

From Frazier's, January 1, 1754, Washington and Gist set out direct to the latter's home which they reached the next day. Here Washington was able to purchase a horse and saddle, with the aid of which he completed his journey without unusual personal incident, but he did encounter unmistakable evidences of the continued westward course of empire. January 6, he met seventeen "Horses loaded with Materials and Stores, for a Fort at the Forks of the Ohio, and the Day after some Families going out to settle."[30] Stopping only one day at Belvoir for "necessary Rest," he reached Williamsburg, January 16, to find himself the hero of the day.

Immediately Washington delivered to the Governor St. Pierre's letter, together with an "Account" of his "Proceeding to and from the French on the Ohio." In his enthusiasm over the confirmation of his worst suspicions, Dinwiddie asked that

GEORGE WASHINGTON CROSSING THE ALLEGHENY RIVER WITH GIST RETURNING FROM FORT LE BOEUF, DECEMBER, 1753

From an engraving by D. Kimberly after a painting by D. Huntington. Courtesy of United States George Washington Bicentennial Commission for the celebration of the Two Hundredth Anniversary of the Birth of George Washington.

the "Account" be phrased in a connected story so as to be readable by his Council. Only one day was allowed for this, and the results were published immediately. Contrary to Washington's expectations, copies were distributed widely both in England and America. As they made most interesting reading, their author's name became known to two continents.[31] More important still they made clear the impossibility of longer averting war between England and France and thus launched a movement which resulted in the practical expulsion of the French from America, and in the birth of the British Empire.

In view of these facts, it is worth while to pause further over this grand adventure to determine from its record something more of the character of its hero. That he did his work well is now the consensus of all, even those of the countries then opposed to him. All now appreciate his cool courage, his infinite patience, his common sense in handling Indians, his immunity to the crafts and wiles of the French, and his rare faculty for dealing with men of all classes and conditions. More significant still, this report was a narrative of wild adventure, wily diplomacy, and personal peril without a word regarding the thoughts and the feelings of the chief participant. There are few more exemplary lessons in the annals of any country.

CHAPTER IV

JUMONVILLE

For a year or more following Washington's return from Fort Le Boeuf, English interests in the Ohio Valley were dominated by the zealous and at times impetuous Governor Dinwiddie. Obsessed with the belief that war between England and France was inevitable, his former selfish interests in the Ohio Company had developed into patriotic zeal. From time to time this was stimulated by additional reports of impending dangers to English interests in America. Even before receiving the French refusal to abandon the Ohio Valley, Dinwiddie had sent Captain William Trent with instructions to build a fort at the Forks.[1] With the aid of his brother-in-law, Colonel George Croghan, an adept at Indian diplomacy, it was expected that Trent would be able to make the most out of the frontier situation for the English.

As Washington's "Account" of his journey of warning to the French[2] confirmed Dinwiddie's course in sending out Captain Trent and otherwise indicated the necessity for immediate action, January 11, 1754, after the Account was made public, Dinwiddie summoned the general assembly to meet at once, but before it convened, upon the advice of his Council, February 14, 1754, he commissioned George Washington Lieutenant Colonel in command of troops then stationed and being trained at Alexandria. With these he was instructed, as soon as possible, to move toward the Ohio River to aid Captain Trent.[3] In an effort to stimulate additional enlistments, Dinwiddie promised two hundred thousand acres of land in the Trans-Allegheny for distribution among such persons as would agree to serve against the French.[4]

Thus without resources other than land, the ownership of

which was then a subject of intercolonial and international controversy, and without the approval of either the colonial or the home taxing powers, a newly arrived and inexperienced governor launched into what has been erroneously called "Dinwiddie's War," "for," according to a reputable historian,[5] "it was begun in his attempt to protect Virginia territory. The first hostile forces sent out were Virginians; the first blood was shed

GEORGE WASHINGTON'S MAP OF HIS
"JOURNEY TO THE OHIO," 1753

by Virginians." But these presumptive deductions place too great a responsibility upon Dinwiddie. Already, as will be shown in this chapter, there were currents and countercurrents in the Ohio Valley which were fraught with the potentialities of empire. Unmindfulness of them would have been a betrayal of one of the most important trusts ever bestowed upon an English colonial governor.

Fortunately for Dinwiddie, as well as for the English, the man for the occasion was at hand. It was true that he was young and only an "adjutant," charged with the duty of "exercising the officers, and inspecting the militia at stated times," and that he was practically without military experience or training. He had played at swords at Belvoir, it is true; but he had never drilled in a company. This was certainly inadequate preparation with which to cope with the soldiers of France, then among the best trained in the world. On the other hand Washington had military traditions, recently enriched by his half-brother Lawrence, and although George was young, he was a person of character and had the courage of his convictions. Tradition has it that his mother continued to discourage his bent for things military, and there is no evidence of Lord Fairfax's enthusiasm over this particular appointment. Washington's own decision, a short time later, to decline the chief command was, however, proof of his becoming modesty, as well as of the fitness of his selection.

While Washington was recruiting and training soldiers at Alexandria, the assembly met in Williamsburg. At once it was addressed by Dinwiddie in a detailed review of conditions on the frontier as reported by Washington, and of more recent happenings there, in which whole families were reported to have been murdered in a fashion shocking even in savage warfare. Dinwiddie climaxed his appeal with a request for supplies to be used "to drive away these cruel and treacherous Invaders of your Properties, and Destroyers of your Families," thus the better to establish "the Security and Prosperity of Virg[ini]a on the most solid and permanent Foundations."[6]

Unselfish as this appeal doubtless was, it was not convincing. Assemblymen did not trust Dinwiddie. They could not forget differences with him over "pistole fees," and some legislators differentiated between the interests of the Ohio Company, of which Dinwiddie was a member, and the interests of the Commonwealth. Some went so far as to deny the rights of either to lands beyond the mountains, so steeped were they in provincialism. In the light of reports of French activities, which were reaching Virginia and other colonial capitals in almost every dispatch, the failure of the Virginia legislators to cope with the situation was not only unpatriotic but stupid.

Among other things these reports affirmed that the French, since the days of the "Grand Monarch" and notwithstanding his "distinguished Delicacy and Politeness," had planned to extend their American possessions "from the Mouth of the Mississippi on the South to Hudson's Bay on the North." This was no "new or partial Scheme of the French, merely for the Sake of Trade, or a Settlement on the Lands, but a Thing long ago concerted, and but Part of a grand Plan for rendering themselves Masters of North America." Already in a dispatch carrying the captions:

> Bella gerant fortes; tu, Pari, semper anna.
> —Ovid
> The Brave shou'd fight; but for the Fops of France,
> 'Tis theirs to cook, to taylorize and dance.

the *Westminster Journal* for September 21, 1753, had announced its protest and warning against the consummation of these plans.

This and like dispatches which went the rounds of the American newspaper press,[7] insisted that the refusal of the French to abandon the Ohio Valley after being formally requested to do so by Washington, demonstrated their disregard for "the Sanction of the most solemn Engagements," and alleged furthermore that the Indians were being rewarded by the French "in Proportion, as they assassinate and make Inroads upon the

English." Moreover, the dispatch alleged that "War, (though not proclaim'd) is actually carried on, and our Blood is spilt and Property invaded on the Sophistry of the most subtile Pretences." In proof of this the "shuffling, evasive, unsatisfactory" answer given by St. Pierre to Dinwiddie's request was quoted and expounded at length with the conclusion that "a good Squadron properly accoutred would soon bring these Violators of the Law of Nations to Reason." In support of this appeal to force it was asked:

>....................Can Britannia see
>Her Foes, oft vanquish'd, thus defy her Pow'r,
>Insult her Standard and enslave her Sons;
>Yet not arise to Justice? Did our Sires
>Unawed by Chains, by Exile, or by Death,
>Preserve inviolate her Guardian Rights,
>And sacred ev'n to Britons, that her Sons
>Shou'd give them up to France?

A dispatch from New York, dated May 13, 1754 and quoted in the *Pensylvania Gazette* for May 16, 1754, contained one of the earliest assertions in American annals of the justifying right of "necessity" as a sufficient cause of hostile action. It traced also the French plans for "making an Establiment on the River Ohio to the Grand Monarch," in support of which plans, Book Twelve of Father Charlevoix's *History of New France* was quoted at length. Indeed, this work fixed the date upon which the French "Scheme" respecting North America "was first laid down in the year 1721, Nov. 8." Continuing, Charlevoix said: "There is not in all Louisiana, a Spot more proper for a Settlement than this on the Ohio, nor where it is of greater Importance to the French to have one. The whole Country that is washed by the Rivers Ouabach and Ohio, is most fertile; there are vast Pastures finely water'd, where the wild Cattle graze by Thousands; besides, the Communication with Canada is, this way, much easier, better, and infinitely shorter, than thro' the River Ilanois: A Fort with a good Garrison here, would be a compleat and sufficient Curb on the Indians in general; but above all, on the Cherokees, at present the most numerous Nation on the Continent."

The feature of this dispatch which concerned New Yorkers most and doubtless caused it to be first published there, was the declaration which it carried, of the intention of the French "to become Masters of Albany, the River Hudson, and New York." According to a plan approved by the French court "There is no other Way . . . for the Preservation of Canada," and "the absolute Necessity of doing this, renders it lawful and justifiable." This course had been decided upon as "the only Measure to compleat and secure the Settlement of Canada, to conquer and secure the Conquest of the Indians, and make them sue for Peace on any Conditions the French shall please to impose on them." As previously stated to Washington when on his mission of 1753 to the French, in the execution of these purposes, they depend upon their ability to cajole and outwit the English, in other words "to use any Disguise or Pretexts, that will be received as probable or plausible."

Meanwhile dispatches from Boston told of grand scale preparations on the part of the French for the consummation of their plans respecting America. To this end 7000 soldiers, together with their wives and children, were reported to have been landed there, 2500 in Canada, 3500 at the mouth of the Mississippi, and 1000 in Santo Domingo. Other reports from the same quarter were to the effect that the French had engaged "three large Tribes of Indians living upon the Lakes to take up the Hatchet against the English; that they were encroaching upon Nova Scotia; and that they were building a Fort near Kennebeck River in Massachusetts province." Thus the French design was clearly revealed, and the Bostonians concluded: "if there is not a vigorous and united opposition effectively to prevent it," they will in a few years, "lay a solid and lasting foundation for making themselves Masters of America."[8]

Under these conditions the Virginia Assembly, the traditional conservatism of which had degenerated to inertia, could hardly refuse a grant, but it was limited to ten thousand pounds which was to be used only for enlisting and maintaining volunteers. Moreover, supervision of its expenditure was placed in the hands of a committee of the house, "thereby making the burgesses the real directors of the war." It mattered not that there was precedent for this course; it was sorely trying to Dinwiddie, who more than once, was on the point of dissolving the assembly.[9] Later he admitted that he had refrained from such a course only in the hope that a timely order from England might accomplish the same end, thus making the rebuke the more severe.

That Washington shared Dinwiddie's sentiments regarding these useless delays and indifferences, there can be little doubt. From time to time he doubtless recalled the reports which he himself had heard upon the frontier of the menacing activities of the French and Indians. Moreover, recruiting was going slowly and his first real experiences as a soldier were proving anything but attractive. By March 9, 1754, he had enlisted twenty-five "loose, Idle Persons, that are quite destitute of House, and Home; and . . . many of them of Cloaths." Continuing, he wrote Dinwiddie, "There is many of them without Shoes, others want Stockings, some are without Shirts, and not a few that have Scarce a Coat, or Waistcoat, to their Backs; in short, they are so illy provided as can well be conceiv'd, but I really believe every Man of them for their own Credits sake, is willing to be Cloathed at their own Expence."[10]

Other factors in the situation must have been as trying to Washington as they were to Dinwiddie. Outstanding among these was the failure of the colonies, even those nearest Virginia, to appreciate the impending danger and to coöperate in meeting it. Among other things tending to make for a lack of coöperation was the fact that the colonies held divergent views regarding the proper uses of western lands.[11] Generally colonies with fixed boundaries insisted upon the alleged right of the home government to hold and use ungranted lands for the common benefit, whereas those claiming extensive unsettled areas under charter grants insisted upon their own rights and prerogatives.

For the most part colonies in the former group favored the formation of new colonies in the West, whereas those in the latter group, in conjunction with certain British financial interests, particularly traders, aimed at a policy of exploitation. All were jealous, the one of the other, but the several suggestions of colonial union made at this time, shed a ray of hope over an otherwise almost hopeless situation.

Closer study throws additional light upon this intercolonial situation, which was probably more responsible than any other one cause for the English military failures in America in 1754. Although sister colonies, South Carolina, North Carolina, and New York, made a better response toward the middle of the year, first reactions to Dinwiddie's appeals were practically negative. Because her "undoubted limits" had not been determined, Pennsylvania would send neither soldiers nor money; Maryland claimed that Virginia had not been attacked; and South Carolina, eager to protect "her Indians" and "her fur trade," at first not only refused to send aid, but also kept the Cherokees from sending it. Of all the colonies first appealed to, North Carolina alone responded. Her contribution was ten thousand pounds, paper currency.[12]

Nor was Dinwiddie more successful in dealing with the Indian situation. Under his directions Virginia did not send delegates to the Albany Congress of 1754, called to consider Indian relations and plans of colonial union.[13] When the Virginians later learned that this congress fell largely under the influence of Benjamin Franklin, Thomas Pownall, and other would-be new colony makers, they did not regret indifference toward it; yet there was no denying Virginia's failures to solve, in her own way, the problems the Albany Congress was authorized to consider.

This was notably true of the Indian situation for the solution of which a conference had been called to meet in Winchester in 1754. The chief purposes of this meeting were further to attach the Cherokees and the Iroquois to the English interests and, if possible, to bring about friendly relations between these two powerful and usually hostile confederations. Although Dinwiddie attended in person, its results were negligible: no Indians of consequence came. In the meantime the French continued to make inroads among the English Indians in the Ohio Valley.

Despite these failures, some of which had not yet materialized, in March, 1754, Dinwiddie resolved upon a policy of aggression. To this end Washington was relieved of chief responsibility for the success of the proposed expedition to the Ohio River, and a Dinwiddie friend and favorite, Joshua Fry, an Oxford-bred Englishman and a professor in William and Mary College, was placed in supreme command of all Virginia troops on the frontier. In conformity with these plans Washington was ordered to lead his poorly clad and discontented volunteers to the Ohio River, "there to aid Captain *Trent* in building Forts, and in defending the possessions of his Majesty against the attempts and hostilities of the *French*."[14] From the outset it was understood that Washington was "to repel force by force,"[15] and that Colonel Fry was to follow him with re-enforcements and instructions to build a fort on the Monongahela at or near the present site of Brownsville, Pennsylvania, then called Red Stone Old Fort.

In these preparations Dinwiddie was motivated no doubt by reports which continued to reach him from the frontier. From "Yaughyaughgany big Bottom," February 19, Trent wrote Washington of his arrival at "the Forks of Monongahela from the mouth of Red Stone Creek," where he had built a strong store house.[16] In two or three days he expected "down all the People," and as soon as they came, he planned "to lay the Foundation of the Fort." The Indians were to join his party "and make them strong" and had asked Washington "to march out to them with all possible Expedition." Trent reported that La Force had made a speech to some of the English Indians, in which he had informed them that "neither they nor the English there, would see the Sun above 20 Days longer; 13 of the Days being then to come." By that time the French expected four hundred Frenchmen would have reached the Forks. Moreover, six hundred French and Indians were reported as then moving against the Shawnee to cut them off from the English. Accordingly the Indians urged Croghan "to hurry the English to come, for that they expected soon to be attack'd."

In a letter to Washington from "Monongahella," dated February 23, Gist told of having learned from a friendly Chickasaw then of the Six Nations, how he, "in his Passage up the Ohio," from a visit to his former tribe, had fallen in with "a Body of near 400 French coming up the River."[17] In quest of a safe-conduct through the Shawnee's country he had accompanied the French to Shawnee Town, where he found the English traders hostile to the French purposes and determined to make prisoners of the French, but they "getting a Hint" of this, had fled. Gist reported also that six hundred French and Indians had gone down "to fall on the Shawneese" to assist their kindred in passing them. All this he thought it "prudent to let the Governor know," as he might wish to send "a Number of Cherokees to join the Shawneese at the lower Town," and defeat the French or "prevent their joining those above." In conclusion he asked to be informed of "the exact Time you [Washington] will be here, that we may speak Truth in all we say to our Friends."

A dispatch from Annapolis, dated March 21 and published with Gist's account as indicated in the last preceding paragraph, confirmed generally its particulars and supplied additional "Intelligence from the Westward." According to the Annapolis dispatch 400 French soldiers had come down from the lakes, 300 of whom had gone to the Lower Shawnee Town to demand the surrender of the English traders "(about 20 in Number)," but the Shawnee had refused to grant their request and had "sent up for the Cataways, to come to their Assistance." According to this same dispatch 22 French then at Logstown and 100 on the Muskingum were to be joined by 400 others "as soon as they can come down from the Lakes." Confirming an item of Gist's letter, this dispatch told of a council of

French and Indians at Logstown, in which the latter were given their choice of dying in twenty days or deserting their "Brothers the English." Upon which "Monocatoocha took his Tommahawk from his Bosom, and said . . . we are ready for you, and will stand by, and join our Brothers against you [the French]."

It was into this maelstrom of international and intertribal rivalry with all its possibilities for misrepresentation and exaggeration, that Washington, accompanied by "two Companies of Foot, commanded by Captain *Peter Hog* and Lieutenant *Jacob Vanbraam*, five subalterns, two Sergeants, six Corporals, one Drummer, and one hundred and twenty soldiers, one Surgeon, one *Swedish* Gentleman, who was a volunteer, two wagons, guarded by one Lieutenant, Sergeant, Corporal and twenty-five Soldiers,"[18] left Alexandria April 2, 1754, beginning actively that "long experience of human stupidity and inefficienty" with which he was to struggle through all his military career, as has been said by the late Senator Henry Cabot Lodge, "suffering from them, and triumphing in spite of them to a degree unequalled by any other great commander." "Dinwiddie, the Scotch governor," Lodge continues, "was eager enough to fight, and full of energy and good intentions, but he was hasty and not overwise, and was filled with an excessive idea of his prerogatives." Getting at the real crux of the situation, he continued: "The assembly, on its side, was sufficiently patriotic, but its members came from a community which for more than half a century had had no fighting, and they knew nothing of war and its necessities."[19]

Equally inexperienced, but little concerned with "impending fate," Washington launched into the wilderness. All went well until April 20, when he reached Cresap's (Old Town) and there learned that the French had forced Captain Trent to abandon fort building at the Forks, and that the Virginians thus engaged were then on their way east. At Wills Creek on April 23, this intelligence was confirmed by Ensign Edward Ward, who had been forced to leave the Forks by a superior force of French and Indians.[20] Ward, an officer in Trent's company, reported to Washington having seen "a Body of more than one thousand French, under the Command of Captain Contrecoeur, who came from Venango with sixty bateaux, and three hundred canoes, and eighteen pieces of artillery." Moreover, Contrecoeur was reported as being in the act of constructing a fort,[21] but Washington was pleased to learn that his former Indian friends remained loyal to the English, in proof whereof Ensign Ward delivered to him a speech and a belt of wampum from the Half-King.

As it had thus become impossible to comply with the letter of his instructions, Washington held a council at Wills Creek to decide upon a course of action. In this deliberation, in which the speech of the Half-King was a factor, it was decided "that it would be proper to advance, as far as Red-Stone Creek on Monongahela, about thirty-seven miles on this side of the fort [Duquesne, then being built by the French], and there to erect a fortification, clearing a road broad enough to pass with our artillery and our baggage, and there to await for fresh Orders." The reasons for this course were stated by Washington to be:

1st. That the mouth of Red-Stone is the first convenient place on the River Monongahela.

2nd. The stores are already built at that place for the provisions of the Company, wherein the Ammunition may be laid up, our great guns may be also sent by water whenever we shall think it convenient to attack the Fort.

3rd. We may easily (having all these conveniences) preserve our men from the ill consequences of inaction, and encourage the Indians our Allies, to remain in our interest.[22]

In a veiled request for reënforcements and haste in sending them, Governor Dinwiddie was notified of this decision by special messenger, as was also the Half-King, the governor of Maryland, and the governor of Pennsylvania.

In the execution of his self-appointed task, Washington encountered almost insuperable difficulties.[23] Bearing assurances of love and affection for their Indian allies and brothers, a speech from him to "the Half-King, and the Chiefs and Warriors of the Shawnese and Loups our Friends and Brethren" paved the way for the advance, but the "jungle" proved "all but impenetrable." As a consequence, at one time he made only twenty miles in fifteen days. In the meantime reports from the Ohio River were increasingly alarming. English traders were retreating; the French were receiving reënforcements and proceeding with the construction of Fort Duquesne; and Monsieur La Force, who only a few months before had escorted Washington from Venango to Fort Le Boeuf, had been seen scouting the country immediately in front of the Virginians with armed men "under the suspicious pretense of hunting Deserters."

Still other factors were equally annoying, the more so because they were largely the result of inefficiency and haste. Probably the most serious of these was Dinwiddie's failure to supply "Spirit," then considered indispensable for satisfactory military service. The whites used it as a preventive for ills incident to such hardships and exposures as "struggling through water up to the arm pits," and it was next to impossible to conduct Indian negotiations without wine. Said Washington, "every Indian that brings a Message or good report; Also the Chiefs who visit and converse in Council look for it."[24] Confusing the situation was the continued absence of Colonel Fry, but, May 17, while at the Great Crossing of the Youghiogheny River, Washington received the gratifying intelligence that Dinwiddie had approved his decision to advance. Equally gratifying was his promise to send reënforcements.

When complaints from the front reached Dinwiddie, he characterized them as "ill-timed" and reminded Washington that a soldier's life, even under the most favorable conditions, was not an easy one. He also informed him that the desired beer and wine were not a part of a soldier's compensation and dwelt at length upon the opportunities of soldiers and officers alike to serve their country and their King.[25] Willing to take second place to no one in such things, Washington offered to serve voluntarily and without pay rather than "upon such ignoble terms."[26] Referring to the alleged inadequate and discriminatory compensation allowed Virginia officers and soldiers, he could not forbear asking Dinwiddie "why the lives of his Majesty's subjects in Virginia should be of less value, than those in other parts of his American dominions?" As most of the Washingtons, including George, were good business men, it is probable that he was not wholly disinterested in the financial side of this situation.

Doubtless relieved somewhat by his frank statements to Dinwiddie on the subject of compensation, while awaiting the arrival of Indian reënforcements being brought to his aid by the Half-King, on May 20 Washington, together with Lieutenant John West, three soldiers, and one Indian, set out from Great Crossing to run down a frontier rumor to the effect that the Youghiogheny River was navigable thence to the Monongahela.[27] Verification of this rumor would have simplified Washington's problems, as it would have enabled him to reach Red Stone and the Forks by a continuous water route. Accompanied by Peter Suver, a trader, who joined the exploring party about one-half mile from its starting place, Washington proceeded as far as the Ohio Pile Falls only to find the stories about the navigation of the Youghiogheny River as baseless as were the numerous other stories which he heard from time to time. Instead of being a clear, deep, navigable stream, as described, the Youghiogheny was found to be "narrow" with "many currents" and "full of rocks and rapid." Although these obstacles were not considered wholly insurmountable, the quest was abandoned as impracticable.

Despite these delays, on May 24 Washington reached Great Meadows with the first wheeled vehicle and artillery to cross the Allegheny Mountains. The latter part of his course thither had been alternately over streambeds and over the famous Nemacolin path. At Great Meadows he received reports of French activities, this time in the immediate vicinity. Accordingly, two days later, May 27, Christopher Gist was sent out with a scouting party to locate the French and Indians, but before

Gist returned a message from the Half-King brought information to the effect that the French were hiding in "a low obscure place" to the westward.

Leaving only a few men to guard his camp, Washington took forty others and in a heavy rain, set out to locate the French. Traveling in "a night as dark as pitch, along a path scarce broad enough for one man," and with his companions "tumbling one over another," the following morning he reached his objective on Laurel Mountain at a point about three miles north of the present Summit House on the National Road,[28] where, after a conference with the Half-King, it was decided to approach the French at once. As he was operating under instructions to meet force with force, Washington was prepared for any emergency. Accordingly the sight which met his eyes must have fired his fighting blood. As reported by the Half-King the French were found in "a low obscure place," the like of which, according to James Veech in a statement confirmed by other historians, "There is not above ground, in Fayette County [Pennsylvania], a place so well calculated for concealment, and for secretly watching and counting Washington's little army.[29]

Accounts of who fired the first shot in the skirmish which followed on Laurel Mountain, May 28, 1754, are conflicting,[30] but under the conditions and the prevailing practices either party would have been justified in firing it. However that may be, this skirmish like the Sarajevo incident one hundred sixty years later, made history. Under the command of the "buckskin-general," as the French sneeringly called Washington, the English subjected their quarry to an effective fire for about fifteen minutes. At the end of this period, further defense being impossible, Monsieur de Jumonville, a lovable young fellow in command of the French, is reported to have fled and to have been surprised and scalped by the Half-King. Nine of Jumonville's companions were killed; another was wounded; one escaped; and twenty-one, including Monsieur La Force, were made prisoners. The English Indians scalped the French

JUMONVILLE'S GRAVE ON THE SITE OF HIS SKIRMISH WITH WASHINGTON, MAY 28, 1754

dead and sent their gruesome trophies to confederates, as a proof of what had happened and as a summons to them to rally to the defense of their country.[81]

For his alleged attack upon the Jumonville party and its alleged consequences Washington was subjected to severe criticism, possibly the severest of his early career. The French, whose account of the affair has been generally accepted, insisted that Jumonville was on a friendly mission, such as Washington had made to the French only a few months before, and that Washington's attack was unnecessary, unprovoked, and unsanctioned by the practices of warfare.[82] Strange as it may seem, in view of the cricumstances and the importance of the accompanying events, the French accounts of this incident have scarcely been questioned, but it is well to recall that they were first published in 1756 on the eve of a world war the echoes of which ceased only with Waterloo.

In part, as set forth in their *Mémoire Contenant le Précis des Faits,* the account was: "That deputy [Jumonville] set out with an escort of thirty men, and the next morning found himself surrounded by a number of English and Indians: The English quickly fired two vollies which killed some soldiers. M. de Jumonville made a sign that he had a letter from his commander; hereupon the fire ceased, and they surrounded the French officer, in order to hear it. He immediately ordered the summons to be read, and as it was reading the second time, the English assassinated him. The rest of the French that escorted him, were, upon the spot made prisoners of war.

"The only one who escaped, and who gave M. de Contrecoeur a circumstantial account of that affair, assured him, that the Indians who were with the English, had not fired a gun; and that at the instant M. de Jumonville was assassinated, they threw themselves in between the French and their enemies."[83]

According to this record Washington was a merciless fellow, capable of outdoing savages in barbarity. That he was then inexperienced, at times hot-headed, and on this occasion without counsel other than that of an Indian chief bent on taking scalps, is true; but there was certainly no truth in the contention that the English and French relations in the Ohio Valley as of May 28, 1754, were the same as, or even similar to, those of the autumn and winter of 1753. From reports reaching Washington almost daily, as Jumonville's party approached his camp and prior thereto, he was justified in concluding that war was a *fait accompli*. These reports told of the marshaling of troops, of their proposed concentration upon a common objective, of the construction of forts, and of the threatening dicta of rulers. As such preparations had in the past meant war, there was no reason why anyone, certainly a person with a bent for war, should have concluded they had another meaning in May, 1754. As already indicated Washington was acting under instructions "to make Prisoners of or kill and destroy" any persons who might interrupt or oppose him in his efforts to reach his objective.[84] Consequently in seeking out the Jumonville party, Washington was within the bounds of his instructions and doubtless thought he was discharging his whole duty.

In the light of subsequent events and Washington's well-known character, the charges of cruelty and assassination made against him by the French savor of propaganda. When did Indians under such conditions fail to fire a gun? Clearly the French, in 1756, like other peoples both before and since, were trying to shift responsibility for precipitating a world war. For this purpose the Jumonville incident was indeed an excellent theme. The facts surrounding it were indefinite and probably never will be determined, but it was an incident fit to arouse patriotic sentiments. M. Thomas, Professor in the University of Paris and in the College of Bouvais, made it the subject of a poem entitled "Jumonville."[85] This poem was sold on the streets of Paris and was later included in a collection of the works of M. Thomas, published by van Harrevelt, Amsterdam 1762, and dedicated to M. Moreau de Sechelles, French Minister of State.

Meanwhile English contemporaneous accounts of the Jumonville incident had ceased to be noticed. Nevertheless, they were published in the American newspaper press, but, in the midst of the stirring events which followed, they were not discussed and were accordingly almost completely forgotten until brought to light by persons interested in the Washington Bicentennial Anniversary.[86] To the satisfaction of his admirers, these accounts shed new and favorable light upon Washington's part in the Jumonville skirmish. To appreciate this one should recall the fact that the English accounts were contemporaneous and comparatively free from propaganda, in the absence of a motive. The narrative which went the rounds of the Virginia, Maryland, Pennsylvania, and South Carolina newspapers as it appeared in the *Pennsylvania Gazette* for June 27, 1754, and the *South Carolina Gazette* for July 25-August 1, 1754, based upon a dispatch from the *Virginia Gazette* for July 19, 1754, was:

We have a certain Account from the Westward, of an Engagement between a Party of English and French, on the 27th of May past, beyond the Allegheny Mountains, in a Place called The Flats, about 80 Miles from our back Settlements, about 240 Miles near N.W. of this Place, and some Miles to the Eastward of the New Fort on the Ohio, which was surrendered to the French by Capt. Trent. Some of the Particulars are as follows: Major Washington had Intelligence, from our Friend the Half King, that a Party of French were encamped on this Side of the Fork, on which he immediately marched at the Head of a Company of about 40 Men, but during their March the Rains fell so heavy that they could scarce keep their Ammunition dry; the French observed them before they came up, and speedily put themselves in Order of Battle, being under the Command of Monsieur Le Force: When the two Parties approached nigh, the French (who were about 36 in Number) gave the first Fire, by which one of Major Washington's Men was killed, and another knock'd down: The English returned the Fire, and killed 7 or 8 of the French, on which the Rest took to their Heels; but the Half King, and his Indians, who lay in Ambush to cut them off in their Retreat, fell upon them, and soon killed and scalped Five of them. Monsieur Le Force finding that they were all likely to lose their Lives under the Hands of the Savages, called to his Men, and advised them to surrender to the English; they immediately, with great Precipitation, ran towards the English, flung down their Arms, and begg'd for Quarter. Major Washington interposed between them and the Half King and it was with great Difficulty that he prevented the Indians from doing them further Mischief, the Half King insisting on Scalping them all, as it was their Way of Fighting, and he alleged that those People had killed, boiled, and eat his Father, and that the Indians would not be satisfied without all their Scalps; however, Major Washington at Length persuaded him to be content with what Scalps he had already got. One of those Five which were killed and scalped by the Indians, was Monsieur Jumonville, an Ensign, whom the Half King himself dispatched with his Tomahawk. Monsieur Le Force, and Twenty more Frenchmen, who were taken Prisoners, are carried down to Williamsburgh. One or Two, it is said, got away before the Rest surrendered, and it is not known what is become of them. Le Force has the Character of an expert Officer, and the Half King reckoned that the English had gained a great Advantage in taking him, telling Major Washington, that That Man (Le Force) was a Thousand.

Whatever may have been Washington's part in the death of Jumonville, there is no doubt of his attitude toward the French at the time. They were the enemies of his country. Had they not made threats against both the English and their Indian allies? Had they not captured and imprisoned English traders who ventured beyond the Ohio River? Had they not taken the Forks of the Ohio by force and driven the English away? Were they not at that very moment planning to defeat and subject the English Indian Allies in the Ohio Valley? From time to time during the preceding weeks Washington had received unmistakable reports of their threatened hostility, to which his letter of May 29 to Governor Dinwiddie is a sufficient testimonial. In part, it said:

These officers pretend they were coming on an Embassy, but the absurdity of this pretext is too glaring, as your Honour will see by the Instructions and Summons inclos'd. These Instructions were to reconnoitre the country, Roads, Creeks, &c., to Potomack, which they were ab't to do. These Enterprising Men were purposely choosen out to get intelligence, which they were to send Back by some brisk dispatches with mention of the Day that they were to serve the Summons, which could be through no other view than to get sufficient Re-inforcements to fall upon us immediately after; this, with several other Reasons, induc'd all the Officers to believe firmly that they were sent as spys rather than any thing else, and has occasion'd my sending them as prisoners, tho' they expected, or at least had some faint hope of being continued as ambassadors.

They finding where we were Incamp'd, instead of coming up in a Publick manner, sought out one of the most secret Retirements, fitter for a Deserter than an Ambassador to incamp in, s[t]ay'd there two or 3 Days, sent Spies to Reconnoitre our Camp, as we are told, tho' they deny it. Their whole Body mov'd back near 2 Miles, sent off two runners to acquaint Contrecoeur with our Strength, and where we were Incamp'd, &c. Now, 36 Men w'd almost have been a Retinue for a Princely Ambassador, instead of Petit, why did they, if their designs were open, stay so long within 5 Miles of us with't delivering his Ambassy, or acquainting me with it. His waiting c'd be with no other design than to get [a] Detachm't to enforce the Summons as soon as it was given; they had no occasion to send out Spy's, for the name of Ambassador is Sacred among all Nations, but it was by the Tract of these Spy's they were discover'd.[87]

Inasmuch as Washington kept rather full accounts of his other activities, it is regrettable that there is so little from him on details of his encounter with Jumonville. When the French account of this skirmish reached him, he was constrained to observe that he had kept no journal "during that expedition" and to note furthermore that his "rough minutes," captured by the French at Fort Necessity, had been "certainly and strangely" altered, some points being omitted entirely, while others had been added. Yet he would not say that a literal translation had not been made. This was true even of that part of the Articles of Capitulation signed at Fort Necessity, in which he twice admitted the "assassination" of Jumonville.[88] Washington recalled something in the Articles about the "death" or "loss" of Jumonville, but admission of more than this he attributed either to the willfullness or to the ignorance of his interpreter, Van Braam. As he had already caused some trouble by confusing "Illinois" with certain "Black Islands," never since located, it is a reasonable presumption that Van Braam's English was as poor as his French and that his approval of Washington's alleged "assassination" of Jumonville was due to ignorance and to the exigencies of the situation under which approval was given.

A letter from Washington to Dinwiddie, written shortly after the departure of the French prisoners from Fort Necessity to Williamsburg, confirmed somewhat English contemporaneous newspaper accounts of the Jumonville skirmish. In part, it said: "I have heard, since they went away, that they should say they call'd to us not to Fire; but that I know to be False, for I was the first Man that approached them, and the first whom they saw, and immediately upon it ran to their Arms, and fir'd briskly till they were defeated."[39] In a letter from Alexandria, Virginia, to a friend in Philadelphia, dated August 1, 1754, Colonel Adam Stephen, who was present when Jumonville was killed, confirmed Washington's account: "let the French term it an *Assassination*" said he, "I am ready to embrace the first Opportunity of being concerned in such another."[40] Furthermore Stephen denied that "Assassination" or "any other Expression objected by Washington" had been used in the Articles of Capitulation at Fort Necessity.

Another contemporaneous account of the Jumonville skirmish, that attributed to Christopher Gist, is, in the details reported, in accord with those given by Washington, Stephen and others.[41] It told of the "total Defeat of a Party of French, that came to attack our People in the Night of the 28th last past." Friendly Indians had informed "the Colonel of their Design, and he, with the Vigilance and Bravery of a good Officer, met them with a Party of about 40 Men, and gave them so proper a Reception, that ten of them fell in the Action, one was wounded, and the remaining 21 were made Prisoners." Of greater importance to Gist than additional details of the skirmish, were the facts that Monsieur La Force, a prisoner, was "a Person of great Influence among the Indians, whose Language he speaks perfectly" and that Washington's "well timed Success had rivetted the Indians to our Interest." As proof of this they had scalped and killed and sent their scalps and "a black Belt to all their Allies, to oblige them to take up the Hatchet (as they express it) and strike the French," whose numbers Gist was assured "from good Intelligence, do not in the whole amount to 600."

Some writers have drawn parallels between the mission of Washington to Saint Pierre and the mission of Jumonville to Washington. It is true that both were on peaceful errands, but the manner of their respective approaches forbids carrying the comparison further. Washington had as his companions a guide, an interpreter, four servants, and four Indians. It is true that he observed and noted signs of military preparations on the part of the French, but it is also true that he proceeded directly to his objective and retired as soon as his mission was ended. On the other hand, Jumonville was accompanied by thirty-four soldiers, and instead of proceeding directly to Washington's camp, he hid in a "low obscure spot" somewhat removed from the customary route of travel but in a position to observe it, while his scouts were spying upon Washington and keeping Contrecoeur at the Forks informed of his movements.

From all available evidence it seems that the French meant to give Washington a peaceful summons to retire, but there is no denying their intention ultimately to use force in the event he refused to go. As determined by the previously announced purposes and large-scale preparations of the French, Washington was to be treated as had been Ensign Ward and those several traders whom they had either driven from their posts in the Ohio Valley or carried to Canada. Contrecoeur's instructions to Jumonville leave no doubt on this point. They were: "we further charge him to dispatch a speedy messenger to us before the summons be read, to acquaint us with all the discoveries he has made, of the day he intends to read them the summons, with all possible diligence after it is read." A reasonable assumption is that hostile demonstrations and preparations on the part of the English were to have been met in kind by the French. Thus the skirmish on Laurel Mountain was only the match which all but ignited the already overstocked tinder box of war.

Because of its betrayal of his immaturity and inexperience, Washington's letter on the same subject to his brother, Augustine, was more informing possibly than was his report to Dinwiddie. While indicating a disposition to consider lightly his first taste of battle, it also leaves no doubt of his belief that it was a beginning of formal hostilities. Said he: "Most of our men were out upon other detachments, so that I had scarcely 40 men remaining under my command, and about 10 or 12 Indians; nevertheless we obtained a most signal victory. . . . We expect every hour to be attacked by superior force, but, if they forbear one day longer, we shall be prepared for them. . . .

"P. S. I fortunately escaped without any wound, for the right wing, where I stood, was exposed to and received all the enemy's fire, and it was the part where the man was killed, and the rest wounded. I heard the bullets whistle, and, believe me, there is something charming in the sound."[42].

A copy of this letter was published in England, where it came to the attention of George II, a former soldier who had heard bullets whistle at the Battle of Dettingen.[43] Commenting upon young Washington's seeming flippancy, George is reported to have said: "He would not say so, if he had been used to hear many." If this comment ever came to Washington's attention, he may have received some satisfaction from the claim that it was among the few pieces of Hanoverian witticism.

CHAPTER V

FORT NECESSITY

EXPECTING to be attacked any time by a superior force of French and Indians bent upon self-interest and revenge, Washington, immediately following his skirmish with Jumonville, fell back from Laurel Mountain to Great Meadows. The possibility of losing his Indian allies by a betrayal of weakness seemed to make imperative a stand at that point which he resolved to hold against all odds. At once he sent a dispatch to Colonel Fry telling of his successful encounter with the French and asking that reënforcements be sent "immediately."[1] Betraying that same fortitude and patience which characterized his later conduct, Washington the same day wrote Governor Dinwiddie: "I will not be surprized let them come what hour they will; and this is as much as I can promise, but my best endeavour's shall not be wanting to deserve more, I doubt not if you hear I am beaten, but you will at the same [time,] hear that we have done our duty in fighting as long [as] there was a possibility of hope."[2] At the same time Washington told Dinwiddie that he had "already begun a Palisado'd Fort [Necessity]."[3]

Despite his determination to have it out as just indicated above, the Jumonville incident concerned Washington. The prisoners taken in the skirmish continued to insist upon their peaceful intentions, but more disconcerting than their claims, were evidences of their truthfulness, disclosed by a search of their effects. Nevertheless, Washington continued to object to the manner of their approach, and Lieutenant West was ordered to take them to Williamsburg at once. At the same time West bore to Dinwiddie a letter confirming Washington's belief that the prisoners were spies, but he bespoke for them that "respect . . . due to all unfortunate Persons in their Condition."

By the same means Dinwiddie was warned against "smooth Stories" about "Privileges due to an Embassy."[4]

So far as Washington was concerned the skirmish on Laurel Mountain was the beginning of hostilities, and he conducted himself accordingly. Work on the proposed fort was pushed, and, June 3, he announced its completion. Although it was primarily for emergency uses, it was considered adequate to withstand five hundred attackers.[5] After all it was only an outpost with Wills Creek as a base of operations.

Next Washington concerned himself with pressing Indian affairs.[6] Despite an inadequate food supply, he found a temporary shelter for Queen Aliquippa and her son, Canachyusay, and the Half-King, together with his party which included twenty-five families with an aggregate of eighty persons. With a view to a possible descent upon the Forks by way of Red Stone and the Monongahela River, when cannon and reënforcements arrived, Washington next summoned a conference of Indians to meet at Red Stone, and in a few days Senecas, Wyandot, Delawares, and other natives were there apprised of his friendly desires. Under more favorable conditions he might have perfected an alliance between the Indians and the English, which would have been a great advantage to the latter.

In the midst of these preparations, June 6 brought disconcerting intelligence. Following an illness which had retarded his efforts to join Washington, Colonel Fry had met his death at Wills Creek, May 31, by falling from his horse.[7] This meant additional responsibilities for Washington who thus became acting commander-in-chief, but any encouragement which he might otherwise have felt because of a deserved recognition, was marred by a letter from Dinwiddie informing him that the chief command had been given to Colonel James Innes, a North Carolinian. As this appointment afforded Washington an opportunity to serve under "an experienced Officer and a man of Sense," he welcomed it,[8] but, like Fry, Innes never reached the military front.

The arrival of Lieutenant Colonel George Muse in Washington's camp, June 10, was timely. He brought nine swivel guns and enough recruits to raise Washington's command to two hundred ninety-three officers and men.[9] Although they were never so welcomed as were Virginians, the simultaneous arrival at Wills Creek of a company of South Carolina regulars under command of Captain James Mackay was also helpful and encouraging. It gave assurance of reënforcements in an emergency and indicated the concern of the colonies in their common fight for possession of the Ohio Valley.

Meanwhile still other problems continued to perplex and plague Washington. First of all was the necessity of keeping his Indian allies happy and contented, so as to prevent them from deserting to the French. To this end Queen Aliquippa was flattered by having her son named "Colonel Fairfax" and by being told this name meant *"the first of the council."* But this displeased the Half-King, who was accordingly named "Dinwiddie" and told that it meant *"the head of all."*[10] By playing upon the ignorance and the credulity of the natives Washington was able to manage them as long as he had bread; but when his supplies were low, it was sometimes embarrassing.[11] On June 12 he had been "six days without flour," and, despite repeated appeals for supplies, no relief was in sight. At another time his embarrassment was relieved, when "Providence . . . sent a trader from the Ohio" with flour which was purchased at twenty-one shillings and eight pence per hundred. The delayed arrival of "suitable stores of ammunition" prevented Washington from moving on to Red Stone and attempting another "advantageous enterprise," but he was resolved to "set off" as soon as possible.

The five days' allowance of flour and the sixty beeves which Captain Mackay brought were duly consumed, and thus his arrival on June 12, only added to Washington's troubles.[12] Mackay, a regular officer, was in command of South Carolina troops which he had organized and drilled for service against the French and Indians. According to a well-established tradition he could not take orders from a subaltern, in this case Lieutenant Colonel Washington, and accordingly Mackay refused either to do so or to coöperate in the execution of Washington's program. Instead he and his South Carolinians camped by themselves and even refused to exchange salutes and countersigns with provincials. Washington's decision, made three days after Mackay's arrival, to resume road building in the direction of Red Stone was doubtless a happy way out of an embarrassing situation. It mattered not that the South Carolinians were thus left free to eat beefsteak, while the Virginians worked and sweltered in the hot sun.

Washington's attitude toward road building, as it affected his own program and Captain Mackay, is another proof of his fortitude and diplomacy. In the same letter in which he informed Dinwiddie of the necessity in the "Publick interest," of his parting with Captain Mackay and resuming road building, Washington continued: "Capt. Mackay says, that it is not in his power to oblige his Men to work upon the Road, unless he will engage them a Shilling Sterling a Day, which I [Washington] would not choose to do; and to suffer them to March at their ease, whilst our faithful Soldiers are laboriously employed, carry's an air of such distinction that it is not to be wondered at if the poor fellows were to declare the hardship of it. He also declares to me that this is not particular to his Company only, but that no Soldiers subject to Martial law can be obliged to do it for less. I, therefore, shall continue to compleat the work we have begun with my poor fellows; we shall have the whole credit, as none others have assisted."[13]

Rather than take issue with Mackay on subjects which neither could determine, Washington decided to appeal to Governor Dinwiddie.[14] Doubtless this course was taken with Mackay's approval, as he and Washington had lived "in the most perfect harmony since his arrival." They had even reasoned the matter together "calmly." Accordingly, in their failure to agree, Washington wrote Dinwiddie that it behooved him, in the interest of the public service, "to lay your absolute commands on one or the other to obey." At the same time Washington let it be known that Mackay questioned Dinwiddie's authority "to give commissions, that will command him." In the event that this were true Washington concluded that Mackay's "absence would tend to the public advantage."

This difference was not adjusted by Dinwiddie until June 25, and it was some days later before Washington received instructions placing Colonel Innes in chief command of all the forces then on the Virginia frontier, while Washington himself was to be second in rank.[15] As Innes continued to absent himself this decision left Washington in practical command, but Mackay continued to act more or less independently even through the crisis that followed.

In the meantime the road to Red Stone was being pushed to completion. As both the wagons and horses used in its construction became increasingly frail and inadequate, that part of the road covering the western slope of Laurel Mountain proved most difficult of construction. But rumors regarding the approach of enemy proved unfounded, and the road was extended. June 18 it reached Gist's [Mount Braddock], where Washington found a number of Indians awaiting him. Among them were parties of Senecas, Delawares, and Shawnee, forty in all, whom he met that evening in a council which lasted three days. In the course of their deliberations the Indians said many harsh things about the French and made many avowals of friendship for the English, but Washington was not deceived thereby. Soon after they departed he made known to friendly Delawares who remained the object of the retiring visitors. They "had been sent by the French to act as spies," but Washington found comfort in the belief that the "treacherous devils" through stories prepared for the French, might be of service to his own designs.[16]

At this juncture Washington decided to do some spying himself. Although his men were short of rations, he was confidently expecting reënforcements, particularly those promised by the colony of New York. With their arrival he hoped to replenish his own supplies and to push on to Red Stone, and, if things went well, perhaps to the Forks. Accordingly, June 21, the day the Indian conference at Gist's broke up, Washington sent two trusted Delawares with instructions to scout the French and report their movements.[17]

It was in the midst of these preparations and counterpreparations, June 28, that Washington received information of the plan of the French and Indians to attack him. At once he called a council of war at which it was decided to make a stand at Gist's, a high point commanding the surrounding country on all sides, and to prepare for an attack. To these ends Captain Andrew Lewis and Ensign John Mercer were ordered to cease road building, and a messenger was sent to Mackay to urge him to come forward with all haste.

Two days later the fortification at Gist's was completed, but that same day, June 30, Washington was informed that the French and Indians were already descending upon him. It has since been determined that there were approximately sixteen hundred of them, of which five hundred were Indians. Convinced of the folly of trying to withstand such a force, Washington called another council which decided that he should withdraw his entire command to Wills Creek, there to await reenforcements and supplies. In this decision the English were motivated by their expectation of immediate reënforcements and by the better-founded conclusion that the French then had no intention to reconnoiter the country to the eastward of the Alleghenies. Thus Washington planned to escape the French and Indians and to avoid a conflict the odds of which were overwhelmingly against him.

However, the retreat from Gist's which began at once, encountered unexpected difficulties. Worn out by hard work and inadequate food, horses proved practically useless in negotiating the return trip across Laurel Mountain. Consequently the fittest among Washington's men were drafted for dray horse service for transporting cannon formerly intended for use in the proposed attack upon Fort Duquesne, while others, officers and men alike, did pack horse service in the transportation of

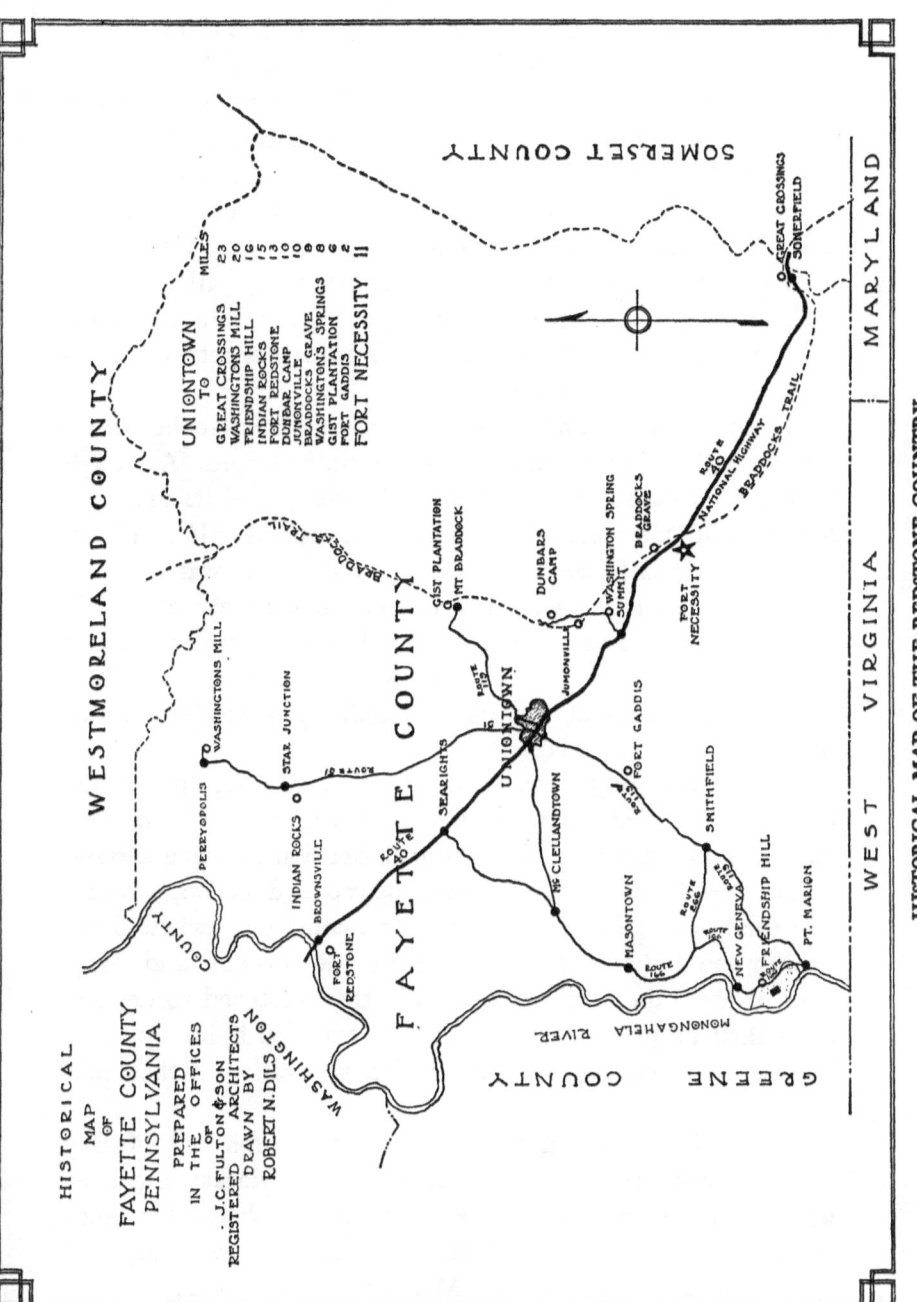

HISTORICAL MAP OF THE REDSTONE COUNTRY

supplies. In this manner Washington returned to Great Meadows after a continuous march of twenty-four hours.[18]

Confronted by the frightful possibility of being overtaken by the oncoming enemy, if the rate of his retreat could not be accelerated, Washington halted at Great Meadows for an inspection. This revealed a deplorable condition: nearly one hundred of his immediate command of approximately three hundred men were found to be sick; for eight days all had been without bread; and there were only two bags of flour and a few sides of bacon at "the Meadows."[19] Thus further retreat was inexpedient. It was in fact impossible.

Under these circumstances the Fort completed at the Meadows a month before became a refuge in time of need. Although inadequate because of its size, necessity compelled its use. Accordingly it was formally occupied and named, "Fort Necessity."[20] The only consolation in its forced use was the possibility of reënforcements which were hourly expected. It should be recalled also that Captain Mackay's command of one hundred men was still at the Meadows, even if it had done little or nothing to provide for its own defense in the emergency with which it was overtaken.

While Washington was preparing his defense, July 2, the French and Indians occupied Gist's. Here they learned from captives and traders of Washington's decision to make a stand at the Meadows and of the half-starved and generally destitute condition of his men. This information only whetted the French and Indian appetites for glory and revenge, and, confident of their ability to achieve both, they hastened to descend upon their prey.[21] In their zeal they traveled light, thus perhaps in a measure defeating the fullest realization of their purposes.

In the face of impending danger Washington and Mackay had meanwhile strengthened their position. Mackay had even learned to coöperate, if he would not always obey. Inasmuch as the fort had been built by the Virginians and was too small to accommodate even them, Mackay decided to dig a ditch along the exposed, or south, side, and to have his men fight from it. After all he was a brave soldier and, when it came to fighting, asked no favors either for himself or his men. While the South Carolinians were engaged in ditch digging, which they continued until it became necessary to exchange their shovels for their guns, Washington's men were making rifle pits and throwing up earthern embankments against outer portions of their palisaded fort. With an aggregate force of four hundred men including sick and other ineffectives, in this way the two commanders made ready to withstand the enemy.

The following day, July 3, the French and Indians under the command of Jumonville's brother, Coulon de Villiers, descended upon Fort Necessity.[22] While they were yet four miles away but steadily advancing over a road which Washington had unwittingly prepared for them, their presence was made known to him by a wounded picket whom enemy skirmishers had shot. By eleven o'clock they reached the edge of the clearing surrounding the fort at varying distances, and soon thereafter a battle was on "which led not only to the expulsion of the French but also to the independence of the American Colonies."[23] In fact, the first important world war had been launched. Before it ended it involved not only England and France but also most of Continental Europe and North America and much of Asia. Of its beginnings Voltaire later said: "A cannon shot fired in the woods of America was the signal that set Europe in a blaze."[24] Of these same beginnings Horace Walpole is reputed to have said: "A volley fired by a young Virginian in the backwoods of America set the world on fire."[25]

Responsibility for this shot has never been definitely determined. According to one account, that attributed to Washington and Mackay, the English fired it,[26] but subsequently Washington denied this in a statement in which he said: "It is well known that we received it at six hundred paces distance."[27] In keeping with their general practice in this war, French accounts generally agreed in fixing responsibility upon the English.[28] If it was indeed "a cannon shot" which was fired, as stated by Voltaire, it was perhaps of English origin, as the French very few heavy cannons at Fort Necessity. Traveling up stream and from Red Stone by a poor road, they were only five days out from the Forks.[29]

Whoever fired the first shot at Fort Necessity, accounts agree that the battle which followed was hotly contested during a period of nine hours, beginning about eleven o'clock A.M., July 3, 1754.[30] At the outset, according to his own account, Washington tried to induce his assailants to fight in the open. For this purpose, while they were about six hundred paces distant, he called all of his men to arms and "drew up in order before our trenches to await their nearer approach." But as they continued to remain under cover, though advancing, Washington retired to his trenches and reserved his fire. Finally convinced that they had no mind to force his position, as he had expected, he ordered his command to fire. From this point the battle settled down to a more or less routine affair, disturbed only by a single feint at an attack on the part of the French and Indians. It rained almost incessantly during the entire time, as a consequence of which Washington's artillery was put out of commission, and the interior of the Fort and the ground immediately surrounding it became a quagmire. (See Appendix A).

As night came on the defenders doubtless considered their doom sealed, so desperate was their situation. Washington's swivel guns had done good execution, and many of the enemy, later and probably erroneously estimated by him at three hundred, were dead and wounded.[31] But one-third of his own total effectives were casualties, thirty of them with their lives; ammunition was all but spent; survivors were starved and exhausted; Indian allies, including the Half-King, had deserted; one hundred sick men out of a total of four hundred, were practical casualties; and the effective assailants outnumbered the defenders five, and probably six, to one.

Knowing that these facts and conditions could not be entirely concealed, an enemy proposal for a parley, made early in the

FORT NECESSITY

evening, was suspected by Washington as a "Deceit" and was declined, care being taken meanwhile to keep them from seeing the inside of the Fort. A second offer of the same kind was declined likewise but with greater coolness and determination. Whereupon the enemy made a third proposal which Washington accepted and sent Captain Van Braam and Ensign William Peyronie to ascertain what was wanted.[32] The resulting "Articles of Capitulation," in the drafting of which Villiers, when not himself participating, was represented by M. de Mercier, were written and signed about midnight,[33] July 3, but they did not become effective until the next morning.

Because of the conditions under which they were drafted but more especially because of the claims and counterclaims to which they give rise, these Articles are of more than passing importance. Prefaced by references to the peaceful relations then existing between France and England and by expressions of a desire to preserve peace, they permitted "the English commander" to "retire into his own country," and to carry with him his remaining supplies, excepting only heavy artillery which, according to a subsequent agreement not a part of the Articles, was destroyed. Since the English had scarcely "any horses or oxen left," they were allowed to keep their supplies and to guard them with troops until such a time as they could return, but they were not to work on any "establishment either in the surrounding country or beyond the Highlands during one year beginning from this day." Although Washington was forbidden to fly the English flag,[34] he was otherwise accorded "honors of war," as an earnest of which he was permitted to withdraw "with beating drums, and with a small piece of cannon." Of greater importance to Villiers was the provision for the immediate return of the prisoners taken, "when they assassinated Sieur de Jumonville." For the faithful execution of this promise hostages were demanded and given. In retreating the English were not to receive hindrance or insult "from us French, and ... as much as shall be in our power from the Savages that are with us."

The Fort Necessity Articles of Capitulation have been accepted as prima facie evidence of Washington's "first and only" decisive military defeat. Confirming this belief were subsequent expressions of Villiers regarding his treatment of the English,[35] as well as Washington's admission of defeat. However, this "defeat" was anything but decisive in itself. On this point one might ask why Villiers, in search of revenge and instructed to pay his Indian allies with scalps, stopped short of his objectives? Prevailing frontier practices would have condoned the complete annihilation of Washington's command as a fitting punishment for the alleged "assassination" of Jumonville, and little was done by the French, certainly on the following day, to restrain their Indian allies. A reasonable inference is that it was not in Villiers's power to have his way at Fort Necessity. In other words, the results of the battle which took place there were not quite so decisive as has been generally conceded.

Whatever may be the facts in this matter, there is no denying that the French at Fort Necessity had limitations. First of all, it was not to their best interest to press the issues of peace and war at that time and place.[36] France was then in the midst of a diplomatic revolution which in a short time, reshaped the map of Europe. As yet her allies in an impending world conflict had not been determined, and until that could be done, she was willing to allow the question of the ownership of the Ohio Valley to rest with the peaceful exclusion of the English, however temporary. Such a course would postpone war, while it, at the same time, seemed to assure the certain and speedy return of the French prisoners taken in the Jumonville skirmish. Doubtless there were among them persons who were very close to Villiers, but he will speak for himself on that point:

We considered that nothing could be more advantageous to the nation than this capitulation, as it was unnatural in the time of peace to make prisoners. We made the English consent to sign that they had *assassinated* my brother in his camp. We took hostages for the French, who were in their power; we caused them to abandon the lands belonging to the King; we obliged them to leave their cannon, which consisted of nine pieces; we had destroyed all their horses and cattle, and made them sign that the favor we granted them was only to prove how much we desired to treat them as friends. That very night the articles were signed, and I received in camp the hostages whom I had demanded.[37]

Despite his use, in the paragraph just quoted above, of such terms as "we made," "we took," "we obliged them," "we granted them," etc., Villiers at Fort Necessity was handicapped otherwise than by the international exigencies of the situation. On their face, the Articles of Capitulation signed there do not reveal this, but it is now known that they were a product of compromise and mutual concession;[38] that they were drafted and signed in the rain and by candlelight; and that the provisions regarding the "assassination" of Jumonville, as already indicated in Chapter IV of this work, was an inadvertence due most likely to the ignorance of Van Braam. If Villiers was actuated by a desire to grant a favor, as he later claimed, it must be said that Washington's confidence in the Frenchman's honesty was equal to any concessions he made.

The truth is that Villiers at Fort Necessity, was himself short of supplies, that he did not have heavy artillery and that his men with their smooth-bore, large-muzzled, short-barreled guns were no match for Virginia sharpshooters with their eight-foot rifles of small bore. On these points respective casualties are significant. Then, too, Villiers is said to have feared for the loyalty of his Indian allies. Besides, and doubtless more importantly still, he expected the English to be strongly reënforced at any time, so effectively had Washington impressed him by his own masterly bearing and by his wise use of Indian agents, both friendly and unfriendly. Under the circumstances the decision of Villiers to hasten his departure[39] from Fort Necessity may have been significant of more than a willingness on his part to carry out a mutual agreement to retire, "they back to their post on the Monongahela, and we to Wills Creek."[40]

Clearly Washington in defeat was the outstanding character at Fort Necessity. By foresight and diplomacy he gained what he could not have won in the wager of battle. If Villiers expected him to be reënforced, he could have himself determined the facts in the situation, inasmuch as he commanded it. If he feared the desertion of his Indian allies,[41] he should have known and possibly did know that Indian warriors rarely desert the winner. As a matter of fact there were few if any desertions among the French Indians, and early July 4, one hundred additional braves joined them and persisted in annoying the retiring English.

It is thus obvious that Washington was already demonstrating those qualities of courage and leadership indicative of his future greatness. Outnumbered four to one, including his ineffectives, his defeat at Fort Necessity was due not so much to the prowess of the enemy as to a needless lack of preparation and coöperation on the part of the American Colonies, to the favoritism and the incompetency with which he was surrounded, and to the absence of enthusiasm on the part of any one, except himself and Dinwiddie. Had the latter ordered all available forces, particularly those from New York, to advance to Washington's aid and had he kept Washington supplied following his skirmish with Jumonville, the story of Fort Necessity would doubtless have been differently told.[42]

To the English the results of Fort Necessity were unmistakably bad. According to Bancroft, the historian, "in the valley of the Mississippi no standard floated but that of France,"[43] but worse still the English Indian allies deserted to the French in large numbers. Speeches, wampum, trinkets, and rum availed nothing to prevent this. The defection extended even to the Six Nations who were reported by the Governor of New York to be "dejected on the defeat of Colo[nel] Washington." The Half-King hid his wife and children and died shortly thereafter believing that the French had bewitched him for his part in the slaying of Jumonville. The effects of Indian desertions were evident during the long hostilities that followed, as may be inferred from an extract of a report of that shrewd and successful Indian agent, Conrad Weiser, in which he said:

SURRENDER OF FORT NECESSITY, JULY 4, 1754
From an engraving by David Shriver Stewart.

FORT NECESSITY AS RECONSTRUCTED AT THE TIME OF THE GEORGE WASHINGTON BICENTENNIAL CELEBRATION

"It was very unfortunate for the English Interest, that, at the same Time the Affections of the Indians were alienated from us by the Abuses committed in Trade, and by our dispossessing them of their Lands, their Opinion of our Military Abilities was very much lessened."[44]

Forgetful of the fact that Washington was practically forced into defending himself at Fort Necessity, critics have condemned him for the selection of such a site. With clumps of elders and briers here and there it was a low open place in the primeval forest, intersected by a small stream. At varying distances from the fort of approximately one hundred yards this spot, then called "the Meadows," was surrounded by gradually rising hills.[45] To the uninformed observer from the National Road which passes to the North at a distance of four or five hundred yards, the site of Fort Necessity, from the military standpoint is today simply impossible, as it was to some persons one hundred eighty years ago. On this point a statement credited to the Half-King and approved by the late Senator Henry Cabot Lodge, as having "a deal of truth," is relevant:

The colonel was a good-natured man, but had no experience; he took upon him to command the Indians as his slaves, and would have them every day upon the scout and to attack the enemy by themselves, but would by no means take advice from the Indians. He lay in one place from one full moon to the other, without making any fortifications, except that little thing on the meadow; whereas, had he taken advice, and built such fortifications as I advised him, he might easily have beat off the French. But the French in the engagement acted like cowards, and the English like fools.[46]

As a precaution against such superficial conclusions as those of the Half-King and the late Senator Lodge, it is well to recall that Washington's first choice of Fort Necessity was deliberate, though not for the engagement which took place there. When he first reached Great Meadows on May 24, 1754, he began to construct there a fort regarding which he wrote Governor Dinwiddie: "We have, with Nature's assistance, made a good Intrenchment, and, by clearing the Bushes out of these Meadows, prepar'd a charming field for an Encounter."[47] And such it seems to have been. First of all, it was an "open place," perhaps the only one there, certainly the largest one available to the youthful commander. As the enemy, particularly the Indians fought from cover which was here removed somewhat beyond the range of the guns then used by the French, a "charming" feature of Fort Necessity is apparent. Bullets discovered in excavations for its reconstruction in replica, have disclosed the fact that from a ballistic standpoint, it was next to perfect for its time and conditions. This conclusion is confirmed by a study of wall angles and possible palisade heights. The Fort had also a water supply from a stream which passed under one of its angular corners. Although 1754 was an unusually "wet" year, other years were exceptionally dry in this region. Therefore a water supply was a matter of prime consideration.

These discoveries and reflections reveal the possibility of still others, all or any of which might throw additional light upon events and conditions in the Trans-Allegheny region on the eve of the French and Indian, or Seven Years, War. However that may be, on July, 4 1754, while Villiers was making ready to hasten back to the Forks, Washington marched away from Fort Necessity at the head of his men on pretty much his own terms and conditions, the Articles of Capitulation under which he retired, in their final form, being a product of compromise and mutual concession. From the beginning of his march to Wills Creek, Washington's chief concern was for the safety of his sick and wounded. Early in the day he was harassed by Indians who interfered with his men; took portions of his baggage; and, most harmful of all, destroyed Dr. Craik's medicine box, thus preventing him from caring properly for the sick and wounded.[48] Consequently on his first day out Washington made only three miles, but after a night of rest, marauding Indians having been driven off, he hastened his march to Wills Creek, where an inspection was made, reports drawn up, and losses determined.

Leaving their men in charge of Colonel Innes and Captain Stephen and seemingly unconcerned with the fact that they had made history, Washington and Mackay set out from Wills Creek direct to Williamsburg to report the details of their defeat. Here, possibly to their surprise, they were received graciously, even honorably. With energy and resourcefulness spurred doubtless by the fact that his own reputation was at stake, Dinwiddie not only stood by Washington in Virginia, but he also wrote letters to Governors in neighboring colonies and to persons in England praising him in the highest terms. As a consequence of these activities and the generally friendly and understanding attitude of the public Washington was promoted from the rank of Lieutenant Colonel to the rank of Colonel, and, excepting only Lieutenant Colonel George Muse, accused of cowardice, and Captain Van Braam, a victim of ignorance and poor candlelight, Washington's officers were all promoted, and each of his men received a bounty of five pistoles, while both officers and men were given land bounties as well.

Shortly after Washington returned to Williamsburg he was again sent to Alexandria to recruit and train soldiers, for, despite the terms of his capitulation at Fort Necessity, Dinwiddie was resolved to strike at the enemy again and at once. For the most part Washington's new job was a round of hopeless routine with ragged idlers and insolent adventurers. Mutinies were frequent, and some of his immediate command deserted. On August 20, twenty-five slipped away while he was at church, and he reported others as ragged and without credit, "even for a Hatt." To prevent the complete disruption of his command he finally asked Dinwiddie, "how far the Martial Law may be extended," for it had become "absolutely necessary that an Example be made of some for warning to others."[49]

Trying as these experiences must have been, they were not half so disturbing to Washington as was Dinwiddie's nonchalant refusal to abide by the conditions of Washington's capitulation at Fort Necessity, particularly his promise to return the French prisoners. In this matter Dinwiddie maintained that Washington had no authority to make binding promises regarding prisoners not in his possession, but Washington regarded Dinwiddie's refusal to return the French prisoners as involving his own personal honor and integrity. Besides, he had given his friends, Van Braam and Robert Stobo, as hostages for the fulfillment of his pledge.[50] Although the indifference to Van Braam could have been justified on the ground of fit punishment for troublesome pretentions, Captain Stobo was a capable and patriotic engineer, who perhaps more than any other person was responsible for Fort Necessity, and the French prisoners were helpless. Meanwhile the ethics and justice involved in their capture and detention had become a subject of international interest and comment. Nevertheless, Dinwiddie remained adamant.

The comparative quiet in the recruiting and training of soldiers at Alexandria gave Washington an opportunity to ponder and assimilate the lessons of his most recent experiences. Fortunately for him, for his country at large, and possibly for the world, he had this time to think. Already in the international limelight, he had scarcely settled himself, when varying reports of his experiences, most of them uncomplimentary, began to reach him. In France he was an "assassin," in England a "braggart," and among his recent Indian allies a plain fool.[51] These and similar criticisms pricked him to the heart and caused him sleepless night hours.

There were still other phases of this situation. It was first of all an acid test of Washington's friends who, without notable exception, remained loyal. Among them was Dr. Craik who was with Washington at Fort Necessity and who formed an attachment for him that lasted as long as they lived.[52] Washington, the true soldier, probably found great satisfaction in the fact that no one, not even the fickle Half-King, spoke of him as a coward, but more consoling and sustaining was a consciousness of work reasonably well done, and that against great odds, with practically no intelligent coöperation on the part of superiors. Atoning somewhat for this indifference was the satisfaction, rare to subalterns, of having been able to point out, at various times, some of the mistakes and shortcomings of the ruling Virginia hierarchy.

Presumptuous as Washington's criticisms of his superiors may have been, they were in the main wholesome, as such things are when motivated by character and patriotic purpose. In the face of the criticism Washington himself was receiving, his criticisms of others and his friends' intercessions for him were a part of the give and take of life out of which come moderation, self-restraint, knowledge, and progress. Suffice it to say that Washington never again rushed unprepared into any important undertaking for which he was responsible; never again did he yield quite so completely to his passions and prejudices in dealing with men; and never again did he build a defense so vulnerable as was Fort Necessity. In fact, he was already in a fair way to become the American Fabius, a distinction which he later merited and received.

CHAPTER VI

BATTLE OF THE MONONGAHELA[1]

CHAFING UNDER the sting of defeat at Fort Necessity and laboring under the impression that the French were temporarily off guard at Fort Duquesne, Governor Dinwiddie, in the summer of 1754, set about to retrieve the English losses in the Ohio Valley and to vindicate their claims to ownership of that region. It was for this purpose that George Washington was again stationed at Alexandria to enlist and train volunteers, but the assignment was only a small part of the enlarged and aggressive program then in process of formation. In behalf of civil and religious liberty,[2] Dinwiddie again appealed to the Virginia Assembly for funds; governors of neighboring colonies were entreated in the same strain to the same end; and because of alleged supineness and malicious designs of colonial assemblies, the home government was asked for immediate succor.[3]

Equally significant of a new mind and purpose were the comparatively generous responses to these requests. Colonies most directly concerned showed a disposition to coöperate in the common defense; and, as the result of a conference between the governors of Virginia, North Carolina, and Maryland, a plan of military operation was agreed upon. This contemplated the immediate capture of Fort Duquesne and the planting of the English flag on Lake Erie.[4] To this end Governor Horatio Sharpe of Maryland displaced Dinwiddie as commander-in-chief of the forces raised in the central and southern colonies; colonial assemblies seriously considered the situation; Virginia, appropriated twenty thousand pounds, "a handsome Supply"; to which the home government added ten thousand pounds and two thousand stands of arms. It mattered not that the former grant carried a rider appropriating two thousand five hundred pounds to pay the expenses of Peyton Randolph, Esq., on a mission to England to prefer charges against the impetuous Dinwiddie.[5] In comparison with anything yet given him, the Virginia grant was unprecedented and was for that reason, encouraging and acceptable.

As Governor Sharpe was now in command, thus placating somewhat the differences between Virginia and Maryland, it was decided to build a fortified outpost at Wills Creek, now Cumberland, Maryland.[6] For this purpose Colonel James Innes, left behind following the capitulation of Fort Necessity, was selected and subsequently recruits were drawn from Washington's "ragmuffins" at Alexandria for the defense of the fort. Ignoring the strategy of the situation, which would have indicated an attack at some point on the Lakes, Washington's previous defeat at Fort Necessity, together with the influence of land jobbers, particularly those of the Ohio Company, determined this location. The new post was named Fort Cumberland in honor of the Duke of Cumberland, victor of Culloden and Captain General of the English Army. At the time of its construction it was the most advanced fortified English outpost in the West, which, together with Dinwiddie's enthusiasm, was the magnet which led General Braddock to his death on the Monongahela.[7]

Although honeycombed with inefficiency, these military preparations were doubtless pleasing to Washington who admittedly liked to "hear the bullets whistle." It must therefore have been with great reluctance and a real desire to vindicate principles that, in October, 1754, he resigned his military commission and retired to Mount Vernon. While seemingly trivial, these principles involved more than the immediate points at issue. They were fraught with a rising tide of resentment of discriminations of the home government against things colonial and explained in part why Washington later became a "patriot." They also throw light upon Washington's character, revealing a person of courage, force, and independence.

Although other things, such as Dinwiddie's alleged incompetence, must have been involved, the assigned reason for Washington's retirement was his dissatisfaction with certain rules and regulations controlling the rank and authority of officers in the regular and provincial armies. To avoid such differences as had arisen between him and Colonel Mackay at Fort Necessity, Dinwiddie hit upon the plan of dividing all the armed forces under his command into ten independent companies, with no officer higher than a captain. While automatically demoting Washington, this ruling was not nearly so objectionable to him as was an order from the home government that regular officers of whatever rank should outrank provincials whenever and wherever a question of jurisdiction was involved. This placed Washington under officers whom he formerly commanded, and rather than accept such a status, he resigned. As has been truthfully said: "The degradation of being ranked by every whippersnapper who might hold a royal commission by virtue, perhaps, of being the bastard son of some nobleman's cast-off mistress was more than the temper of George Washington could bear."[8]

In an effort to dissuade Washington from this decision, Governor Sharpe offered him a commission with the rank of colonel and the duties of captain. Whether or not Sharpe's previous criticisms of Washington's alleged failure at Fort Necessity and his subsequent inability to explain these criticisms influenced Washington in declining this offer, would be difficult to determine, but the fact remains that he declined it in what amounted to a rebuke to "his Excellency."

The opportunity thus afforded a private citizen to condemn the senseless dicta of official bureaucracy, while giving expression to his own convictions and sentiments, was just too good to let pass, and Washington accepted it in these words: "I think the disparity between the present offer of a company and my former rank too great to expect any real satisfaction or enjoyment in a corps, where I once did, or thought I had a right to, command. . . . If you think me capable of holding a commission that has neither rank nor emolument annexed to it, you must entertain a very contemptible opinion of my weakness, and believe me to be more empty than the commission itself."[9]

A commendable feature of Washington's retirement from military life was its sincerity. Without a suggestion of the bluffer or the temporizer, he simply burned his bridges behind him. Unlike the small man, he said nothing about prerogatives or his plans for the future, doubtless conscious of the fact that they would take care of themselves. He carried into retirement, however, the consolation that he had helped to open a way to the interior, and that, too, against great odds; that he had "stood the heat and brunt of the day, and escaped untouched in time of extreme danger"; and that he had the thanks of his country for services rendered.[10] To some, this self-consolation was doubtless only the vain babblings of a conceited braggart; but as now seen, it flowed from a fountain of conscious power and patriotic fervor.

While Washington, at the age of twenty-two, was indulging himself in the language and the thought of a retired veteran, the home government announced its purpose to send Major General Edward Braddock to command his Majesty's troops in America.[11] This generalissimo, the first of a long list, was almost three times Washington's age; he had seen forty-three years' service, most of it in the famous Coldstream Guards; and he had heard bullets whistle in the bloody battles of Dettingen, Culloden, Fontenoy, and Bergen-op-Zoom. Although born in Ireland, he was neither Irish nor Roman Catholic; although obsessed with a zeal for discipline, he is said to have been unable to control his own appetites and passions; although a veteran, on the American frontier he was a raw recruit.

In the absence of knowledge of military conditions in America at the time of his arrival, Braddock's virtues and weaknesses cannot be fully appreciated. In command of the famous 44th and 48th regiments of five hundred soldiers each, he landed at Hampton Roads, February 20, 1755, whence he proceeded directly to Williamsburg.[12] Here he reported his entire command "all in Health, not one Sick," but he was disgusted to find the assembly and Dinwiddie wrangling over taxes and prerogatives.[18] Pennsylvania and Virginia were also sparring for advantages, the bone of contention being the route of Braddock's proposed march into the interior, involving as it did control of the first important intercommunication between the East and the West. He was literally besieged by horse traders trying to dispose of their sickliest nags. In their greed for profits, South Carolina, Pennsylvania, and New York were trading with the enemy, thus helping to keep them in supplies; the defense of the Virginia frontier was being left entirely to militiamen and indifferent rangers; recruits for his own expedition were being drawn from volunteers, vagrants only being drafted; and the only experienced local leader was reported as sulking in retirement.

Nor was the Indian situation any better. Despite the fact that an attack upon Fort Duquesne was contemplated and that such an undertaking was next to impossible without the aid of Indian allies, the Indians had all but vanished. In departing they had not even concealed their disgust with Washington's defeat at Fort Necessity and with Dinwiddie's subsequent failures in Indian relations. It is true that George Croghan had succeeded in salvaging about a hundred warriors and squaws, but these were wholly inadequate for the execution of the proposed undertaking. Moreover, the Winchester conference of 1754, called with a view to bringing about friendly relations between the Cherokees and the Iroquois and enlisting their united coöperation with the British, had failed. As a consequence the Indians, other than the Cherokees and the Iroquois, were almost completely in the control of the French.[14]

Indeed, Braddock seems to have been foredoomed from the beginning, but the Americans and America were not alone responsible for the workings of fate. On this point it should be recalled that the "famous 44th and 48th regiments of two thousand regulars" actually contained an aggregate of less than one thousand men; that they had recently mutinied in Ireland; and that their selection for the American expedition was rather a punishment than a reward, as was also the selection of their commander. Horace Walpole characterized the former as "the worst type, who, had they not been in the army, would probably have been in Bridewell [prison]."[15]

In the face of admitted difficulties, Braddock, after the manner of one accustomed to obeying and being obeyed, set about the task before him. February 26, 1755, he took up temporary headquarters at Alexandria, a short distance from Mount Vernon, where George Washington was then residing as a private citizen with possibly greater interest in the British regulars than in his estate. However that may be, he found a way, probably through the forgiving and appreciative Dinwiddie or through Colonel John L. Peyton and others who appreciated the merits of Washington's services at Fort Necessity, to let "the General" know that he would be willing "to make this Campaigne," provided it could be arranged without embarrassment in the matter of his previous commitments.[16] The presence of British regulars, with the rare opportunity thus afforded to learn military discipline from a reputed disciplinarian, had fanned Washington's increasing fondness for things military and made imperative some response to duty's call. He was probably already regretting his civilian status and had expressed a desire to join the Braddock expedition as a volunteer.

Fortunately its leader was not devoid of appreciation of character and worth in others, a good sign of their presence in himself. He was in desperate need of counsel, and, contrary to general impressions regarding him, he had sense enough to seek it. Thus knowledge of Washington's accomplishments sufficed to convince Braddock of his possible helpfulness to him. It mattered not that the young ex-colonel had only a few months before suffered defeat at the hands of the French and Indians; that he was still the laughingstock of certain social and military circles in Europe; and that former Indian allies continued to speak of him as a fool. Braddock considered him entirely competent and desirable for a place in his official family. Accordingly, seven days after Braddock's arrival in Alexandria, he asked the young Virginia civilian to join his command in the capacity of aide-de-camp.

The day following the receipt of this invitation, March 15, 1755, Washington accepted it in his usual dignified and straightforward manner.[17] It offered a rare and agreeable position in which to serve his country and his King, while attaining an intimate "knowledge in the military profession." Subsequently the details of his services were arranged through Robert Orme, an associate staff officer; and, having put his personal affairs in shape and arranged to carry on a clandestine correspondence with Sally Fairfax and possibly one or two other women friends, Washington was off again to war. The entreaties of his mother against such a course were met by the gracious assurance that the God to whom she had commended him on a previous occasion would care for him on this. In a parting shot at Virginia's incompetent officialdom, Washington doubtless took pride in informing it of his opportunity to serve his country in a position of honor and trust, where questions of rank and pay did not enter.

Rejoicing in his freedom from all commands, except those of his immediate superior, Washington joined Braddock's army May 1, 1755, at Frederick, Maryland. Here he first met Braddock, and May 10, Washington's appointment to be "Aid-de-Camp to His Excellency General Braddock" was announced.[18] Although they detested provincials, his fellow staff officers, together with the British regular officers, greeted Washington cordially, a recognition of his accomplishments. This was notably true of Braddock, who admired him at first sight, a fact as complimentary to the General as it was to the young student of military tactics.

Washington's ability to throw himself whole-heartedly into his new duties was doubtless as gratifying to himself as it was to his associates. Instead of the brutal, obstinate, and incapable commander that he has since been pictured to have been, Braddock was a counselor and a friend, who, in Washington's words to his brother, "Jack," "uses, and requires less ceremony than you can well conceive."[19] Had it occurred to the sturdy Britisher, however, that his young staff officer in "observing everything and forgetting nothing" was learning lessons to be used later in breaking the British power in America, he probably would have been less kind and indulgent, since Braddock loved his country supremely.

In the meantime other plans for the proposed expedition were being rapidly formulated. The governors of Massachusetts, New York, Maryland, Pennsylvania, and Virginia had met Braddock in conference at Alexandria and agreed upon a plan of campaign. This contemplated the immediate capture of forts Duquesne, Niagara, and Crown Point, and the erection of a British fortress upon Lake Erie. More important still, the interested governors promised to raise a common fund to make these undertakings possible, and to be responsible for the erection of the proposed fortress.[20]

The General was, however, far from sanguine. It is true that his crack regiments were being recruited to their full strength by provincials, mostly Virginians, "but their languid, spiritless and unsoldierlike appearance considered with the lowness and ignorance of most of their officers gave little hopes of their good behaviour." More discouraging still, Braddock found it next to impossible to keep his soldiers, of whatever origin, sober by any amount of whipping. In desperation he was preparing to leave Alexandria; sutlers were forbidden to sell any soldier more than one gill of spirit a day; and drunks were to receive two hundred lashes for each offense.[21]

Nor was the situation from the viewpoint of necessary supplies more encouraging. Pennsylvania and Maryland had refused to pay anything toward them, and the twenty thousand pounds voted by Virginia had "been expended tho not yet collected." Predicting that the home government would have to be largely responsible for financing his expedition, despite many promises to the contrary, Braddock hoped, nevertheless, "to be upon the mountains early in May," and sometime in June to be able "to dispatch an Express with some Account of the Event of our operations upon the Ohio."

Alternating between hopes and fears, Braddock, April 9, ordered a detachment of his army to leave Alexandria for Fort Cumberland. It consisted of companies of the 44th Regiment, commanded by Sir Peter Halkett, and marched by way of Winchester, Virginia. Nine days later, Colonel Thomas Dunbar followed, leading the main body of the 48th Regiment by way of Frederick, Maryland, while Braddock and Colonel Gage, later of Revolutionary fame, in command of heavy artillery, brought up the rear, by way of Winchester. With each command, in addition to the regulars, were detachments of "pioneers," carpenters, and rangers, most of whom were Virginians.

The names of the minor officials in these commands suggest an official roster of Virginians in the American Revolutionary Army. John Rutherford, William Polson and Hugh Mercer commanded "independents" and pioneers, while Thomas Waggener, Adam Stephen, Peter Hogg, and Thomas Cocke were in command of Virginia rangers. Joining the command later were Andrew Lewis and Captain Robert Stewart, each in command of Virginians. Christopher Gist and his son, Nathaniel, acted as guides, and George Croghan, temporarily a Virginian, and Andrew Montour were interpreters.[22] For the Virginians the French and Indian War was indeed a training school for the Revolution.

Practically all of Braddock's command, which included many officers in addition to those indicated, assembled at Fort Cumberland between May 10 and May 20, but success in reaching this outpost had not disillusioned its capable and vigilant commander. Promised funds and supplies had not arrived, nor were they in sight. In desperation Washington was sent east for money which he borrowed to the amount of four thousand pounds. Dinwiddie was unable to supply a penny. To transport his loan to the interior, Washington conscripted eight militiamen, the only persons whom he actually commanded on this expedition. They were two days in getting ready for the trip, and Washington expressed the belief that "they wou'd not have been more than as many seconds dispersing" in the event of danger.[23]

At this juncture, horses, cattle, and wagons were more important to Braddock than was cash, but as he had no reason to expect the former from promised sources, he appealed to Benjamin Franklin, then "postmaster of Pennsylvania, and a Man of great Influence in that Province." By placating certain selfish interests of the Pennsylvania Germans, Franklin was able to provide quickly "150 Waggons and a Number of Horses," as a result of which Braddock saw in him "almost the only Instance of Ability and Honesty" he had found "in these provinces." For a rather extravagant use of profanity in expressing his condemnation of these things, he has long since been forgiven, for said he to a superior: "It would be endless, Sir, to particularize the numberless Instances of the want of public and private Faith, and of the most absolute Disregard of all Truth, which I have met with in carrying on of His Majesty's Service on this continent."[24]

Under such conditions Braddock's force again became demoralized.[25] When "not fed with Bread, and paid with Money," officials joined privates in talking about the rights of "Englishmen and Protestants." To pangs of hunger were added snake bites and the annoyance of wood ticks, and tried and trusted officers were forced to the conclusion that the day upon which they bought their commissions was the most unfortunate of their lives. Either of Braddock's two cooks could have made "an excellent Ragout out of a Pair of Boots," but that was impossible because of a lack of materials. The customary thousand lashes amounted to sheer cruelty, but they were used, nevertheless, for Braddock had resolved to be as free with his punishment as his soldiers were with their offenses.

This deplorable situation was intensified when Croghan's Indian recruits reached Fort Cumberland.[26] Probably a fortunate circumstance for everyone, the promised Cherokees and Catawbas did not come, for the crude war dance, demoniacal yells, and shameless indecency of those who did come shocked and discouraged the "brutal" Braddock who was forced to use drastic measures to prevent scandalous indecencies of his officers with the Indian maidens. Even the Princess Bright Lightning was so completely captivated by the gorgeous uniforms of the British, as to give herself to reckless abandon. These disciplinary measures offended "Jack the Black Hunter" who deserted, losing to Braddock's force a man who, under the circumstances, was worth a whole company of regulars. Practically all the natives followed their leader, leaving only eight to remain with Braddock to the end.

Refusing to trace the causes of their undoing to America rather than to individuals, Washington, with a flash of patriotism that bespoke his later Revolutionary fervor, resented Braddock's wholesale and profane impeachments of things American. With "his two thumbs up into the armpits of his vest" he even went so far as to advise the General and to argue matters with him.[27] That Braddock did not throw something more than oaths at Washington, was a tribute to both, which has not been duly appreciated. After all, each was being tested in the crucible of trials and tribulations, which often makes friendships at the same time that it tests and tempers them.

Fully warned by Franklin and others of impending dangers, particularly those besetting a long line of march into an inaccessible wilderness infested by a savage foe, on May 29, Braddock ordered his vanguard to advance. The route followed was that later known as Braddock's Road, then only a narrow and abysmal opening through a dense forest. In the course of the next two weeks his entire force, aggregating more than two thousand men, more than half of whom were provincials, was pushed into this death trap. Washington urged action. When the route was not a stream of mud, it was too frequently a veritable cloud of dust. Descriptions of this famous highway approach the classical.[28]

Hampered by inadequate transportation, Braddock made slow progress through the wilderness. Supplies were insuffi-

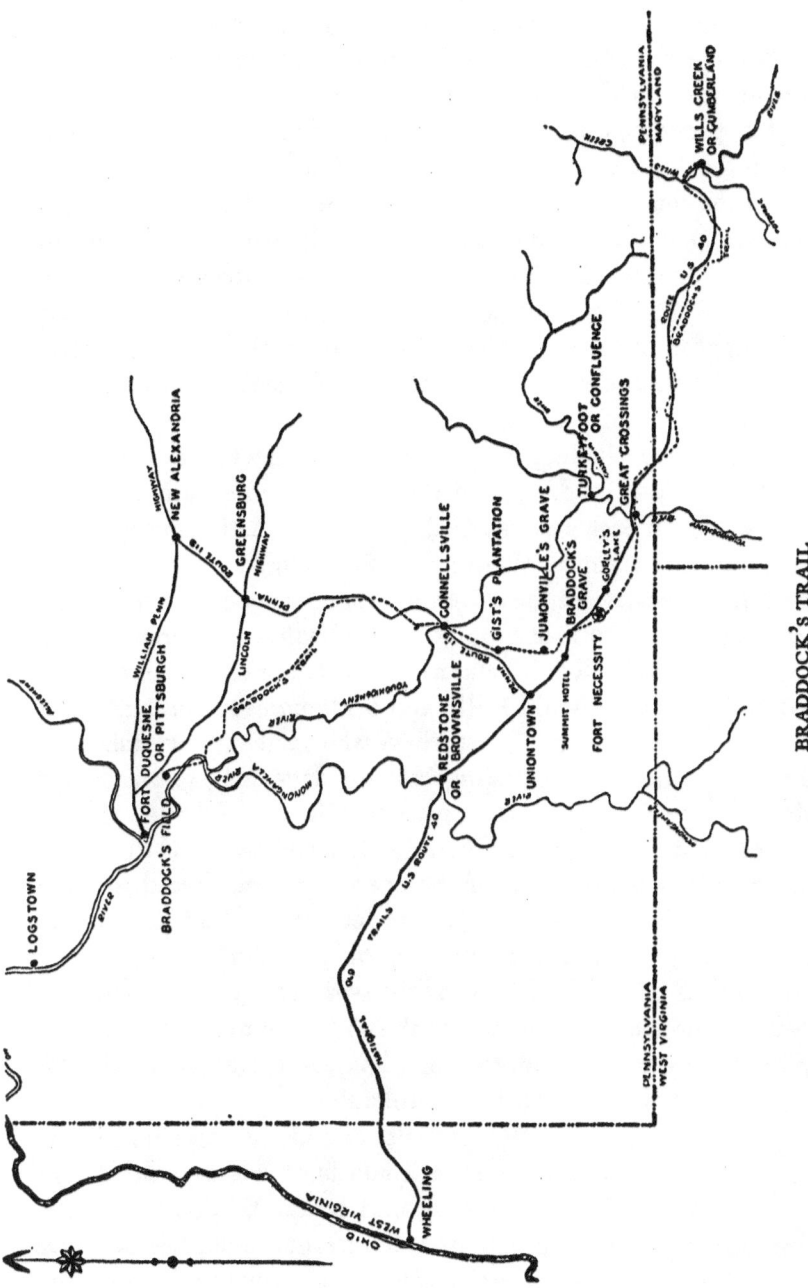

cient, and from too frequent contacts with stumps and boulders his wagons were literally jolted to pieces. However delay meant defeat, even in the absence of the enemy. Accordingly Washington proposed that the command be divided so as to permit sending a lightly armed advance guard to reconnoiter the way, while the main body carried forward the artillery and supplies. Strange as it may seem in the light of all that has been said of the "intractable" Braddock, this advice was accepted (see Appendix B).[29] Thus by sheer force of character and ability, Washington became a determining factor in this historic expedition. Who can doubt that under more favorable conditions, he would have been a saving factor?

Thus emancipated, Washington and the brave Braddock, "ever greedy to lead," joined the vanguard in a dash for a victory of which each felt reasonably certain. Although the General wavered at times, Washington was delighted with the prospect, his chief discomfiture coming from his superior's proneness to discipline "instead of pushing on with vigour, without regarding a little rough Road," and after the European fashion "halting to level every Mold Hill" and bridging every brook.[30] But for the fact that at this juncture Washington was overtaken by a serious illness, incapacitating him for days, his experience and driving power might have saved the day.[31] Instead, chafing for action and dispatch as the only effective means of thwarting the reported preparations of the enemy, he was forced to tarry by the roadside under absolute orders from Braddock not to move except with the permission of Dr. Craik who was instructed to dose his patient freely with Dr. James's powders. But for the General's assurance that Washington would be permitted to join him before Fort Duquesne was attacked, this punishment would have been intolerable.

The foregoing incident presents one of the most interesting and possibly significant personal contacts of this expedition. In it there is the allegedly austere and brutal Braddock, "a very Iroquois," playing the part of a tender and sympathetic nurse for a sick youngster. That he did not care for provincials other than Washington and Benjamin Franklin, was, considering particularly the slothful and dissipated soldiers with whom he came in daily contact, possibly a sign of wise selection rather than of a depraved and unappreciative character. While lamenting the loss of his own best mount, and complaining of the inattention of unnamed friends, Washington showed himself amenable to discipline, while not forgetting or even losing interest in his mission. Throughout, his chief desire was to rejoin his command, which he wrote Orme he "wou'd not fail in doing ere you reach Duquisne, for 500£."[32]

Although emaciated and suffering from excessive weakness, Washington was able to realize his wish. Following Braddock in a covered wagon from Dunbar's camp by way of Gist's and Stewart's Crossing, on July 8 he joined the General in his camp just below the mouth of the Youghiogheny and about two miles east of the Monongahela.

The next morning, to avoid the defile of Turtle Creek, Braddock's troops, with bayonets fixed and presenting one of the most brilliant spectacles Washington had ever seen,[33] marched to the Monongahela which they forded to the southwest shore. Moving thence along the left bank for about three miles they recrossed the River at Frazier's, just below the mouth of Turtle Creek. Thence they proceeded along the north bank of this stream to a small tributary flowing into it from the north, and later known as "Fall Hollow," now "Ardmore Road Hollow." Following this stream for about a quarter of a mile to comparatively open land Braddock's army of approximately thirteen hundred men, including five hundred regulars, came upon approximately six hundred French and Indians under the leadership of Captains de Beaujeu and Dumas.

The story of the "Battle of the Monongahela" or "Braddock's Field" has been too frequently and too well told to need repetition here.[34] Enough of its strategic setting will be indicated to make clear its possibilities for surprise and slaughter. A few miles ahead stood Fort Duquesne, the surrender of which had already been decided upon by its commander, Contrecoeur.

But for the insistence of young Captain Beaujeu, this course would have been followed without resistance. With the aid of his Indian allies, Beaujeu begged to be permitted to annoy and harass the attackers. As there was nothing to lose and everything to gain, his request was granted, and he and his followers promptly advanced into the pathway of the enemy. Here the French and Indians were surprised and fired upon, their first impulse being to flee. In fact one hundred French Canadians did seek refuge in their fort, and their Indian allies, terrified at the death of Beaujeu, would have followed, but for the masterly control of Dumas, second in command, who as if guided by the gods, rallied his followers and completely enveloped the British on both sides of the pathway over which they were proceeding with the possible purpose of intercepting the French at Washington's crossing on the Allegheny River.

The remaining part of this battle was one of the most spectacular scenes in American annals. Fighting at short range from behind trees, logs, and stones, the French and Indians, with unerring accuracy, poured volleys of lead into the British. By the use of his sword and oaths Braddock compelled his men to remain in formation. Although these tactics afforded his only means of advance or retreat, they exposed his men to frightful execution. Unable to see the French, the English milled like panic-stricken animals, killing more of their companions than of the enemy. It was only after five horses had been shot from under him and he had fallen mortally wounded that Braddock ordered a retreat which instantly became a rout. But for the forceful intervention of attendants, he would have been run down and trampled into the earth by his own men, who could no more be restrained than "a gang of wild bears from the mountains." (See Appendix B).

Throughout this scene of carnage, Washington conducted himself with characteristic coolness and valor, a greater hero in defeat than in victory. On horseback for the first time since his illness, he wore a buckskin shirt instead of a regulation uniform, and sat upon a pillow to protect his bony and emaciated body from the rigidness of the saddle. It was only after committing him to the care of his own bodyservant, Bishop, with instructions to "Keep an eye on him," that Braddock had consented to his taking the field that day. In keeping with his position and his own ideas of discipline, he remained close to the General; but at a crucial point in the contest, when it had become a problem of extricating themselves with the least possible loss, he asked to be allowed to join the Virginians in the vanguard where they had borne the brunt of the fighting, as well as the losses. Braddock's reluctance in granting this request was as stupid as was the act of his own men in shooting down the rallied Virginians, when, under Washington's leadership, they were attempting to flank the enemy and save the day. That Washington escaped the shots of the enemy and of his companions is nothing short of marvelous. As his is as correct as any of the numerous and varied accounts of this important encounter, he will give it in his own words to Governor Dinwiddie:

We were attack'd (very unexpectedly I must own) by abt. 300 French and Ind'ns; Our members consisted of abt. 1300 well arm'd Men, chiefly Regular's, who were immediately struck with such a deadly Panick, that nothing but confusion and disobedience of order's prevail'd amongst them: The Officer's in gen'l behav'd with incomparable bravery, for which they greatly suffer'd, there being near 60 kill'd and wound'd. A large proportion, out of the number we had! The Virginian Companies behav'd like Men and died like Soldiers; for I believe out of the 3 Companys that were there that day, scarce 30 were left alive: Captn. Peyrouny and all his Officer's, down to a Corporal, were kill'd; Captn. Polson shar'd almost as hard a Fate, for only one of his Escap'd: In short the dastardly behaviour of the English Soldier's expos'd all those who were inclin'd to do their duty to almost certain Death; and at length, in despight of every effort to the contrary, broke and run as Sheep before the Hounds, leav'g the Artillery, Ammunition, Provisions, and, every individual thing we had with us a prey to the Enemy; and when we endeavour'd to rally them in hopes of regaining our invaluable loss, it was with as much success as if we had attempted to have stop'd the wild Bears of the Mountains. The Genl. was wounded behind in the shoulder, and into the Breast, of w'ch he died three days after; his two Aids de Camp were both wounded, but are in a fair way of Recovery; Colo. Burton and Sir Jno. St. Clair are also wounded, and I hope will get over it; Sir Peter Halket, with many other brave Officers were kill'd in the Field. I luckily escap'd with't a wound tho' I had four Bullets through my Coat and two Horses shot under me. It is suppose that we left 300 or more dead in the Field; . . .[35]

A leader in action, Washington was a hero in retreat.[36] Leaving eight hundred and seventy-seven dead and wounded upon the battle field, he and the famous Indian scout and trader, George Croghan, rushed to the aid of the wounded Braddock in an effort to save him from scalp hunters and the feet of panic-stricken men and horses. Ignoring Braddock's request to be permitted to die upon the battle field and thwarting his attempts at suicide, Washington and Croghan used his wide silk sash as a stretcher from which he was transferred to a horse, thence to a wagon. In this he was carried to the rear over "the worst road in the world," jolting his life away. The fact that the road was his own handiwork did not mitigate the severity of its punishment. Four days later Braddock died near the present site of his monument on the National Road near Fort Necessity and his remains were buried nearby in the center of the highway which later bore his name. Washington read the burial rites of the Anglican Church over his body.

Meanwhile, Washington, at Braddock's request, had performed heroic service in extricating the wounded and starving from the scene of carnage on the Monongahela, into which Braddock and his aides with varying degrees of responsibility had led them. The dead were left upon the battle field, a prey for vultures and wild beasts. After regaling themselves in an excess of scalping, the French and Indians appropriated the enemy artillery and supplies, including a wagon load of presents for the natives. It was not until years later that the bones of the fallen were buried.

Unlike the Jumonville skirmish and the Battle of Fort

ORIGINAL GRAVE OF GENERAL BRADDOCK BY A SMALL STREAM NEAR HIS PRESENT GRAVE

BRADDOCK'S GRAVE AND MONUMENT ON U. S. HIGHWAY 40 NEAR FORT NECESSITY. HIS REMAINS WERE REMOVED TO THIS SITE IN 1804

Necessity, the Battle of the Monongahela placed Washington in a favorable light before the world. Virginians loved him for his heroic and partly successful efforts to save their provincials; the French respected him for his bravery; the English praised him for his loyalty to his fallen chieftain and his subordinate officials; and Indians described him as having a charmed life. In the history of the world rarely has any person so young received such universal recognition. It is worth recalling that this was Washington's third appearance on the world stage in less than two years.

In the light of subsequent events the disillusioning effects of the Braddock Expedition were of more consequence to Washington and his country than was the publicity he himself received. For the first time in his life he found it necessary to deny a much exaggerated report of his death and his dying speech. Meanwhile he was learning that endurance is largely a matter of will and courage, a fact which served him well at Valley Forge and elsewhere, but his greatest discovery was that British regulars were not invincible and that it never pays to underrate the enemy. Nor could he attribute Braddock's undoing wholly to rashness and to unwillingness to follow new methods, for back of it was a long story of jealousies and inefficiencies, together with general mismanagement. There is much truth in a statement since made, to the effect that Braddock was defeated before he landed in America. All told it was a bitter experience of which Washington made the most in the service of his country both at the time and later.

CHAPTER VII

DEFENDER OF THE FRONTIER

IF THE Jumonville and the Fort Necessity incidents did not arouse the French and Indians to their maximum enthusiasm and resourcefulness, the Battle of the Monongahela did. To an already long drawn out effort to right alleged grievances, it added zest of triumph, for at once "The West rose like a nest of hornets, and swarmed in fury against the English Frontier." In all seriousness Captain Dumas, the French hero of the Battle of the Monongahela, reported Pennsylvania, Maryland, and Virginia ruined and their settlements over "a tract of country thirty leagues wide, reckoning from the line of Fort Cumberland," devastated, while "six or seven different war-parties" were in the field completing the work of destruction. He boasted that these successes had cost the French only "two officers and a few soldiers," that the Indian villages of the Ohio Valley were full of English prisoners "of every age and sex," and that the enemy had lost far more since "than on the day of his defeat" on the Monongahela.[1] The French gasconade in these matters moved Captain Robert Stobo, a prisoner in their possession, to say "I would Die ten thousand Deaths to have the pleasure of possessing this fort [Duquesne] but one day, they are so vain of their success at the Meadows, it's worse than death to hear them."[2]

Although Washington, like others, may not have realized the seriousness of this situation, he was keenly alive to it. It has been said that he was then sick of war and desirous of devoting his whole time to his estate and his friends, but it is hard to conceive of such an attitude in a soldier by inclination and by choice. Instead he was as willing and as ready as ever to serve his country in any way possible, provided only his services were compensated and recognized. In justification of this position on August 2, 1755, he wrote his half-brother Augustine, then a member of the Virginia Assembly, reciting his past services and his inadequate compensation. His conclusion was that he could not be blamed in the event he left his family again, for trying to do so "upon such terms as to prevent my [his] suffer[in]g."[3]

Two weeks later these reasons were repeated in a letter to his cousin Warner Lewis,[4] but another letter of about the same time to his mother betrayed an unmistakable hankering for war. Already apprised through private sources of a movement to make him commander-in-chief of the Virginia forces, he informed her that it would reflect dishonor upon him not to accept the call, "if the Command is press'd upon me by the gen[era]l voice of the Country, and offer'd upon such terms as can't be objected against." Although she had protested against his going to war again in any event, he could assure her only of his resolve not to go, except in "an honourable Com'd." and provided also it came unsought.[5]

The following day, August 14, 1755, Governor Dinwiddie commissioned Washington to be Colonel of the Virginia Regiment and Commander-in-chief of all the forces now raised or to be raised for the "defence of His Majesty's Colony." At the same time he was given full power to act either offensively or defensively as he might determine "for the good and Welfare of the Service."[6] Previously the assembly had voted him three hundred pounds as a reward for his "gallant behavior and losses," and in response to the earnest pleas of Dinwiddie to the effect that something be done to preserve "the most dear and most desirable of all human Treasures—RELIGIOUS AND CIVIL LIBERTY,"[7] it voted forty thousand pounds in paper for the support of an army of twelve hundred men to be raised by voluntary enlistments. At the same time the militia law was strengthened and a bounty of ten pounds was placed upon the scalps of all hostile male Indians above the age of ten years.[8]

These preparations and manifestations of serious purpose, although ridiculed as the ill-advised and ineffective efforts of an allegedly incompetent governor, were timely. As the "whole of" Colonel Dunbar's artillery had been lost and his troops were "extremealy weakened by Deaths, Wounds and Sickness," it was judged "impossible to make any farther Attempt," and in August, 1755, he led his troops from the frontier into winter quarters near Philadelphia.[9] Meanwhile the demoralized militia had been disbanded.

Thus by the use of guns and supplies recently captured from the English and by way of the road they had recently built, hundreds of gleeful, triumphant savages under direction of the French, occupied themselves in wholesale slaughter and destruction. Their belief that the British power in America was broken forever added zest to their lust for vengeance. Says an historian, "The situation was almost as though the dykes of Holland had been cut and the ocean had begun its inundation.... The people of the frontier, in panic, rolled back in waves over the mountains into the Shenandoah Valley, the savages upon their heels.... For a time it looked as if the British would be swept from the American continent."[10] Contributing to this dreaded possibility were rumors and fears of Negro slave insurrections.

By spring, 1756, reflection upon the possibilities of this situation, together with the admitted inevitableness of war between France and England, aroused Virginia gentry to the seriousness of the situation. Accordingly "a great Number of the principal Gentlemen ... voluntarily associated themselves under the command of the Honourable Peyton Randolph, Esq., at their own Expense," to serve on the frontier, thus the more effectively and readily to relieve the suffering of their fellow subjects and to chastise and revenge the insolence and cruelties of "the French and their barbarous Allies."[11] For this purpose, following a preliminary meeting at Fredericksburg in May, 1756, they repaired to Winchester, where early the following June, they were visited by Washington who reported thence "all well" and ready to move to Fort Cumberland. Randolph and William Byrd having meanwhile paved the way for understandings with the Catawbas and the Cherokees, one month later Washington was back in Winchester at the head of two hundred Fairfax militia.[12]

When, in August, 1756, official knowledge of the formal declaration of war between France and England reached Washington in Winchester,[13] he at once "in the most solemn Manner," ordered "a grand Parade" which he staged "at Fort Loudon, where the Soldiery being properly drawn up, the Declaration was read aloud" and "Healths were drank" to the success of his Majesty's arms and "a total Extirpation of the French out of America." This was followed by "a triple Discharge of the Artillery" accompanied by three rounds of "Musquetry" and "loud Acclamations of the People." Then, proclaiming the declaration at street crossings, the army made the rounds of the town, after which, returning to "the grand Parade," the declaration was read again, and messengers having been dispatched to Fort Cumberland and other frontier outposts with orders to proclaim the war declaration "at the Head of the Troops," Washington dismissed his immediate command with the following "Exhortation" of loyalty and devotion to King George:

"You see, Gentlemen Soldiers, that it hath pleased our most gracious Sovereign to declare War in Form against the French King, and (for divers good Causes, but more particularly for their ambitious Usurpations and Encroachments on his American Dominions) to pronounce all the said French King's Subjects and Vassals, to be Enemies to his Crown and Dignity, and hath willed and required all his Subjects and People, and in a more especial Manner commanded his Captain General of his Forces, his Governors, and all other his Commanders and Officers, to do and execute all Acts of Hostility in the Prosecution of this just and honorable War; and though our utmost Endeavours can contribute but little to the Advancement of his Majesty's Honor, and the Interest of his Governments, yet, let us shew our willing Obedience to the best of Kings, and by a strict Attachment to his royal Commands, demonstrate the Love and Loyalty we bear to his sacred Person; let us by Rules of unerring Bravery strive to merit his royal Favor, and a better Establishment, as a Reward for our Services."[14]

Shortly thereafter Washington was at Fort Cumberland, where he established the uniform of the officers of the Virginia regiment. This was a blue coat, cuffed and faced with scarlet and trimmed in silver; blue breeches and a silver faced hat. But his chief concern was for an adequate defense. Together with Governor Dinwiddie, he hoped to find it in offensive action, his objective during the next three years being to remove "the cause," the French occupation of Fort Duquesne. A tour of inspection from Fort Cumberland to Fort Dinwiddie in Augusta County had already revealed something of the hazards to be encountered along the frontier; but to meet these he found only inefficiency, lack of equipment, selfishness, drunkenness, and insubordination, a situation making any sort of military action next to impossible.

Dinwiddie tried to remedy the situation by sending "rangers" to replace the "dastardly cowardly" militia, but his reënforcements deserted, and were defended in this course by the judges who tried them. Washington would have dealt with them by force, but he was told that "it was impossible to get above 20 or 25 Men; they having absolutely refused to stir; choosing as they say to die, with their Wives and Familys." Believing that they were more encompassed by fear than by the enemy, Washington sent recruits to relieve rangers reported "blocked up by the Indians in small Fortresses," but in this, as in other things, he met with opposition. Except when accompanied by force, his orders were unheeded and met by threats against his life.[15]

In desperation Washington was on the point of resigning his commission. With this in view, October 11, 1755, he wrote Dinwiddie that "unless the Assembly will Enact a Law, to enforce the Military Law in all its Parts," he would be compelled to "decline the Honour that has been so generously intended me; and for this only Reason" that he could see nothing but failure ahead. He witnessed with alarm "the growing Insolence of the Soldiers, the Indolence and Inactivity of the Officers" and the possibility of his army becoming "a Nusance, an insupportable charge to our Country." "If these Practices are allowed off," he concluded "we may as well quit altogether, for no duty can ever be carried on, if there is not ye greatest punctuality observed, one thing always depending so immediately upon another."[16]

Thinking that they controlled the balance of power in the situation and that success was impossible without their aid, Washington had attempted to enlist the natives in the British interest. Andrew Montour, a guide on the ill-fated Braddock expedition, was known to have detached a number of Indians from the French, and Washington in turn tried to enlist them as active allies of the British. To this end he wrote Montour a letter savoring a little of flattery. Attention was called to our "Glorious Cause," and a wish was expressed that Montour, through his personal contacts with the Indians, would "animate their just Indignation to do something Noble, something worthy themselves, and honourable to you [Montour]."[17]

Reminding the natives of his position as commander-in-chief of the Virginia forces and of his consequent power to entreat them "as Brethren and Allies," Washington asked to be remembered to particular Indians who were to be told "how happy it wou'd make Conotocarious [Washington's Indian name] to have opportunity of taking them by the hand at Fort Cumberland, and how glad he wou'd be to treat them as Brothers of our great King beyond the waters."[18] But still mindful of Braddock's defeat, the Indians proved as intractable as did the militia.

An altercation with Captain John Dagworthy in command of Maryland troops at Fort Cumberland, complicated the situation.[19] A royal commissioned officer under Braddock and commander of a fort beyond the jurisdiction of Virginia, Dagworthy refused to obey Washington, or to give him supplies. As Washington could not subsist his forces without such aid, the situation placed him in a quandary, which Dinwiddie would not, possibly could not, solve. He ordered Washington to arrest Dagworthy, but this Washington refused to do, offering to resign instead. In an effort to prevent this, his officers drew up a memorial referring the whole matter to Governor Shirley of Massachusetts, then commander-in-chief of the British forces in America. This memorial Washington was asked to present to Shirley in person.

Taking advantage of the winter season, during which the frontier was comparatively quiet, the natives having retired to their villages north of the Ohio River, Washington, February 4, 1756, set out on a five hundred mile trip to Boston. In characteristic Southern style, accompanied by his aides, Captain George Mercer and two servants, he made this journey a tour of state. Adding to its glamour were the facts that he traveled on horseback and that he was then probably the most graceful rider in America. Moreover it afforded his first opportunity to see American city life, and he consequently made a sort of vacation of the trip.[20] Forgetful of Indians and recalcitrant troops, he celebrated his twenty-fourth birthday in Philadelphia and tarried long enough in New York City to attend a theater party or two in company with the beautiful and wealthy Mary Philipse of Yonkers, sister-in-law of Beverley Robinson, son of Speaker John Robinson of the Virginia House of Burgesses. Shopping and gambling on the way, he finally reached the New England metropolis where Shirley was eagerly awaiting him, knowing that he would be able to recite incidents in the last days of Shirley's son, William, who had fallen on Braddock's field. It was possibly through such narratives that Washington found a way to the old gentleman's heart. Sufficeth it to say, he brought back to Fort Cumberland orders to the effect that Captain Dagworthy would be subordinate to him, whenever their respective jurisdictions clashed.[21]

In Washington's absence but with his approval, Major Andrew Lewis, later of Point Pleasant fame, undertook to defend the frontier by offensive action. To this end he led an expedition to the Ohio River by way of the Big Sandy. Aside from being the first body of British troops to reach the former stream south of the Forks, the Lewis expedition came to naught. Indeed it sustained losses of men and supplies, but its worst effect was an additional blow to British prestige among the natives.[22]

Upon his return to the frontier, April 6, 1756, Washington found the situation there nothing short of appalling. A savage inundation was again sweeping Hampshire, Frederick, and Augusta counties and at places threatened to pass the Blue Ridge Mountains. Throughout a vast region to the westward, extending at some points eastward beyond the Blue Ridge, settlers had either been driven out or forced to take refuge in fortifications, which were then being assailed almost daily by the ever vigilant savage. Men who tarried behind or were caught by surprise were killed without quarter; their women folk were assaulted and carried into captivity; and their children were dashed to death against trees and boulders, sometimes in the presence of their parents. To withstand this scene of carnage and bloodshed, possibly without parallel in American border warfare, Captain John Fenton Mercer led a scouting party of about one hundred men into Hampshire County, but he, together with some of his men, was surprised and killed. As a result of these and similar events, in May, 1756, Washington reported the roads over the Alleghenies as much used by the Indians and French as they had been by Braddock's men a year before.[23]

Despite his ever-present interest in property and material things, Washington was capable of the deepest sentiments and emotions. Of this fact his reports of the incidents and conditions upon the frontier contain unmistakable evidence. In a note of April 22, 1756, he was willing to make of himself an "offering to savage fury, and die by inches to save a people!" His greatest regret was his ability to see their situation, to know their danger, and to participate in their suffering without having it in his power "to give them further relief, than uncertain promises." If the danger had not been so imminent, he would have resigned a command from which he had never expected to reap either honor or benefit. Despite the fact that he was almost certain to incur the displeasure of Virginia officialdom, he hesitated to leave his post "while the murder of poor innocent babes and helpless families may be laid to my account here!"[24]

During the next ensuing months the burden of Washington's communications was similar to that just quoted, but they told of other than French and Indian atrocities. Conscientious objectors were being arrested, detained, and threatened, and in April, 1756, he sent Monsieur Douville's scalp to Dinwiddie with the request that those who had taken it be rewarded according to their "merit." Realizing the legal difficulties in the way, no bounties being offered for white scalps, he hoped that the matter could be adjusted, "as the monsieur's [scalp] is of much more consequence." It mattered not that Douville carried on his person orders from Captain Dumas, directing him to "employ all his talents, . . . to prevent the savages from committing any cruelties upon those, who may fall into their hands," and adding that "Honor and humanity ought, in this respect, to serve as our guide."[25] At this time Washington was not overscrupulous in dealing with Indian enemies, who, as previously indicated, were considered good only when dead. Their instigators, the French, were, if possible, held in even less esteem.

Complicating the situation to the point of moving Washington again to suggest his resignation, were charges of "the greatest Immoralities and drunkenness" among his troops and officers, and of a neglect of "proper Discipline." Although he was not in charge when these indictments were made, the fact that they had "inflam'd" the Assembly[26] produced a similar effect upon Washington. Accordingly he answered them in no unmistakable language. While not attempting to speak for individuals, he called his commission and his orders to witness how much he had "both by threats and persuasive means, endeavoured to discountenance gaming, drinking, swearing, and irregularities of every other kind." He had also "practised every artifice to inspire a laudable emulation in the officers for the service of their country, and to encourage the soldiers in the unerring exercise of their duty." How far he had failed in

DEFENDER OF THE FRONTIER 119

these ends, he could not say, but he insisted that his efforts to attain them merited some consideration. He was, however, resolved to "act with a little more rigor, than has hitherto been practised, since I find it so absolutely necessary."[27]

This promise, together with the criticisms provoking it,

THE VIRGINIA FRONTIER, 1756-1758

doubtless influenced Washington's subsequent efforts at discipline. On May 8, 1756, Dinwiddie sent him "a death Warrant for shooting Sergeant Lewis,"[28] accused of cowardice. Washington also asked permission from the Assembly to inflict more than corporal punishment on deserters. If he could have laid his hands on two alleged horse thieves, he would have meted out to one a thousand lashes, and would have induced a general court-martial to condemn the other to "a life eternal."[29] In this manner Washington contended with idleness, drunkenness, and desertion as long as he remained on the frontier.

To those of maudlin sentiments the results of these practices were as surprising as the practices themselves were disgusting. By 1760 "the best judges" pronounced Washington-trained soldiers superior to "all other provincial troops." Something of the effectiveness of Washington's methods as well as the qualities of his soldiers may be judged also from the fact that "Virginia had less than half the number of people killed by Indian raids than the other provinces had suffered during the same period."[30] When it is recalled that these soldiers came largely from the individualistic Scotch-Irish and clannish Germans of western Virginia, their record was not only a tribute to their young commander but also to themselves.

Moved by enemy attacks, the Virginia Assembly, in the spring of 1756, again came to the rescue of the frontier.[31] Among other things it authorized an increase in the army and appropriated twenty-five thousand pounds additional paper for its uses, two thousand pounds of which were to be used for the construction of fortifications throughout a frontier three hundred fifty miles long and from twenty-five to one hundred miles wide. Other acts provided for conscripting soldiers, for provisioning militia, and for constructing a fort in the Cherokee country in what is now Tennessee.

Encouraging as these measures were, their effectiveness was nullified somewhat, as far as Washington was concerned, by the appointment of the Earl of Loudoun to be Governor of Virginia and Commander-in-chief of the British forces in America. In

May, 1756, England had formally declared war against France, which was to be prosecuted in earnest but with new objectives and policies.[32] Among other things was a plan for conducting Indian political relations. Heretofore such matters had been left to local governors, but they were now placed in the control of two Indian agents, one, Sir William Johnson, for the district north of the southern boundary of Pennsylvania, and the other, Edmund Atkins, for the district south thereof. The announcement of further plans and policies had to await Loudoun's arrival in America, late in July of that year.

For Washington, as for Virginians in general, this announcement was even more revolutionary. Profiting by Braddock's mistakes, Loudoun declined to come to Virginia, going directly to Philadelphia, which henceforth became the chief base of military operations for Pennsylvania and the southern colonies. Virginia was ordered to send troops thither to coöperate in proposed military operations to the westward, and Washington was ordered to prepare the Virginia frontier to withstand attacks. This order had the effect of withdrawing him from the scene of operations and making him responsible for a task to which he could lend only half-hearted interest.

Nevertheless, Washington addressed himself to the work assigned him.[33] A fort inspection trip carried him from Cumberland to within a few miles of the North Carolina line, but whatever enthusiasm he might have developed for his service was alloyed by another difference with the irascible Dinwiddie. He objected to Washington's proposal to withdraw the Virginia troops from Fort Cumberland, to his request for a Chaplain for his regiment, and to the brevity of the report of his tours of inspection. In support of his desire to retain Fort Cumberland Dinwiddie insisted that "to give up any Place of Strength" would "raise the Spirits of the Enemy." Moreover, he urged its retention because "It is a King's fort."[34] In any event he asked Washington not to abandon it until after the arrival of Loudoun. As was to be expected, Loudoun decided for its retention, but Dinwiddie left the ultimate decision to Washington and his "other Gentlemen Officers," who, in the face of Washington's objections and possibly out of deference to the new commander, voted for retention.[35]

Relegated to a quiet sector of the war area and ordered to maintain a strict defensive position, Washington became somewhat restless, even irritable, possibly suspicious. His superiors were charged with neglect and with a desire to supersede him; he frequently asked for leave; and more than once he was on the point of resigning his commission. But for the intercession of friends, Landon Carter, Colonel Fairfax, and others, he probably would have given up in disgust after the publication, over the signature "Centinel X," of a scurrilous attack upon his officers and men which first appeared in the *Virginia Gazette* in the autumn of 1756.[36]

More discouraging still was Loudoun's written criticism of Washington's conduct, which the latter correctly attributed to Dinwiddie's influence. This opened the way for a direct appeal which Washington made in a long and convincing letter to Loudoun. Against Dinwiddie's advice but with his permission, Washington later visited him in Philadelphia, where the young colonel's ability and earnestness again impressed a superior officer but fell short of their immediate purposes. It is doubtful whether Washington accomplished this partial victory by revealing his innermost thoughts. These were probably more freely stated in a letter to his friend, John Robinson, which reveals the extreme difficulties, even embarrassments, of Washington's position. In part, he said: "my strongest representations of matters relative to the peace of the frontiers are disregarded as idle and frivolous; my propositions and measures, as partial and selfish; and all my sincerest endeavours for the service of my country perverted to the worst purposes. My orders are dark, doubtful, and uncertain; *to-day approved, to-morrow condemned.* Left to act and proceed at hazard, accountable for the consequence, and blamed without the benefit of defence! If you can think my situation capable to excite the smallest degree of envy, or afford the least satisfaction, the truth is yet hid from you, and you entertain notions very different from the *reality* of the case. However, I am determined to bear up under all the embarrassments some time longer, . . . The severity of the season, and nakedness of the soldiers, are matters of much compassion, and give rise to infinite complaints."[37]

In face of this determination, Washington a few days later sent to Speaker Robinson a formal proffer of his resignation. Meanwhile rumors seem to have come to him of dissatisfaction with his conduct and of plans to supersede him. These did not disturb him on his own account; for he freely admitted that his inexperience might have led him into "innumerable errors," and he expressed a desire to do anything for the good of his country, love of which had ever been "the first principle" of his actions. Furthermore, he let it be known that he had "diligently sought the public welfare." In such reflections he found a cordial which he was sure would abide as long as he was able "to distinguish between Good & Evil."[38] In this mood he was willing to give up his command. In the same strain he reviewed his futile record to his friend Richard Washington, a London merchant, in these words: "I have been posted then for twenty Months past upon our cold and Barren Frontiers, to perform I think I may say impossibilitys that is, to protect from the cruel Incursions of a Crafty Savage Enemy a line of Inhabitants of more than 350 Miles in extent with a force inadequate to the taske, by this means I am become an exile and Seldom inform'd of those opportunitys, which I might otherwise embrace, of corrisponding with my friends."[39]

These conditions tended to strain the usual friendly relations between Washington and Dinwiddie, but the seriousness of the threatened breach was greatly overestimated.[40] It is true that Dinwiddie denied Washington's requests for leaves, and scolded him for asking for them, but to the end of his administration he regarded him as an officer of "great Merit and Resolution." On the other hand, Washington did not entertain so favorable an opinion of Dinwiddie, who, more than any other one person, discovered and advanced him. Taking advantage of a temperament that made such a thing easy, insinuating persons made much out of Dinwiddie's official contacts with Loudoun. Nevertheless, Washington continued to respect his paralytic chief, now suffering from a new attack, and to obey him implicitly. However, Dinwiddie could not refrain from accusing him of ingratitude, and in one of the last letters ever written by him to Washington, that of September 24, 1757, Dinwiddie expressed the wish that his successor would show Washington "as much Friendship as I've done."[41]

The French and Indians having been diverted thence to the region of the Great Lakes, the Virginia military frontier was comparatively quiet in the summer of 1757, and Washington took a turn at politics. After frequent and futile intercessions with Dinwiddie and certain justices of the peace in an effort to prevent Winchester grog dealers from demoralizing his little army, Washington sought to represent Frederick County in the House of Burgesses as a reformer. Being both a tithable and a landowner in that county, he was eligible for the position to which he aspired, but he had to oppose Hugh West, Jr., an Alexandria lawyer, whose father was a man of influence and desired his son's reëlection. As with one accord, the "booze" dealers and their friends, the horse traders and moralists, also opposed Washington's candidacy. As a consequence he was defeated, receiving only forty-one votes to two hundred seventy-one for his opponent.[42]

Under the strain of these disappointments and the accompanying accusations, the severest of which was that of padding his payrolls, Washington's health began to break. As a result the charges of graft against him were more than he could bear complacently, and he accused his best friends of malicious designs upon his character. He reiterated also his old charges against deserters, tippling houses, horse traders, and his superiors, begging at the same time for another leave, which, as usual, was denied. Finally a fellow officer revealed to Dinwiddie that "For upwards of three Months" Colonel Washington had "labour'd under a Bloody Flux" which had developed into a "bad Fever, . . . Stitches & violent Pleuretick Pains upon which the Doct'r Bled him and yesterday he twice repeated the same operation." As this treatment did not give relief, the doctor had recommended a change of climate, which Washington, because of his debilitated condition, respectfully asked through the intercession of a fellow officer.[43]

This appeal was more than Dinwiddie could bear, and Washington was granted leave, together with a wish for his speedy recovery. But it was not until well into the next year that he was able to leave camp and proceed to Williamsburg. Thence he went to Mount Vernon, where, at the age of twenty-six he settled down to await "an approaching decay"[44] and to consider relinquishing his command to "some other person more capable of the task."

As in the history of the English people, the year 1758 marked a turning point in the life of George Washington. In that year the plans of William Pitt, the Elder, for crushing the French power throughout the world took definite form, turning English fortunes from defeat to victory. While Pitt was formulating these plans, Virginia physicians were restoring Washington to health. As a result, in mid-summer 1758, he resumed his command on the frontier.

In the meantime other events had cast a silver lining over the clouds that had threatened Washington's plans for the future. Among other things, the frontier in his absence had been visited by repeated attacks, thus reminding all of the need of a continuous and vigorous defense. More important still, he had met the beautiful and wealthy widow of John Parke Custis, who had promised to become his wife, and soon thereafter, by one of those foibles peculiar to politics, the constituency which repudiated him the year before, elected him to membership in the House of Burgesses. In this contest he prevailed over Thomas Swearingen, a former favorite of "the meaner class," by a majority of three hundred ten to forty-five. It is probably significant that Washington absented himself from this poll; that liquor was used freely to influence voters in his behalf; and that his "friends" refrained from attacking tippling houses and horse traders.[45]

The immediate future seemed to offer new opportunities for Washington's military ambitions. In pursuance of Pitt's plans, announcement was made of a proposed attack upon Fort Duquesne. Rumor had it also that the attacking party would be sufficiently strong to insure success. Inspired by these new objectives, the Virginia Assembly authorized the enlistment of additional troops, increased its appropriation for war purposes, and raised the bounty on Indian scalps.[46] The natural inference was that Washington would play a prominent part in the proposed activities.

As usual Washington's joys were not without alloys. Among the latter was the announcement that General John Forbes had landed in Philadelphia and that he planned to construct a military road from a point in Pennsylvania to Fort Duquesne. In 1755 Colonel James Burd had cut a road from Carlisle to the top of Allegheny Ridge, leaving the Raystown Path, later Forbes's Road, a little beyond Bedford and running southwest. The possible use of this road was enough to arouse any Virginian, certainly one interested in the Ohio Company. Accordingly Forbes was accused of being under "Pennsylvania influence" and the superior advantages of "a good road already made," were insistently urged by the Virginians.

It mattered not that the road proposed by Forbes was forty miles shorter than that built by Braddock and that the eastern base of the former was to be in a rich farming country in the "bread basket" of the colonies. Virginians accused Forbes of entertaining superstitions but with him the conditions favoring the new road were decisive. He was doubtless influenced also by his poor opinion of Virginia soldiers, who, with the exception of "a few of their principal officers," were described by him as "a bad Collection of broken Inn-keepers, Horse Jockeys, & Indian traders," while the men under them were "a direct copy of their Officers."[47] As Washington was not in Forbes's confidence, he

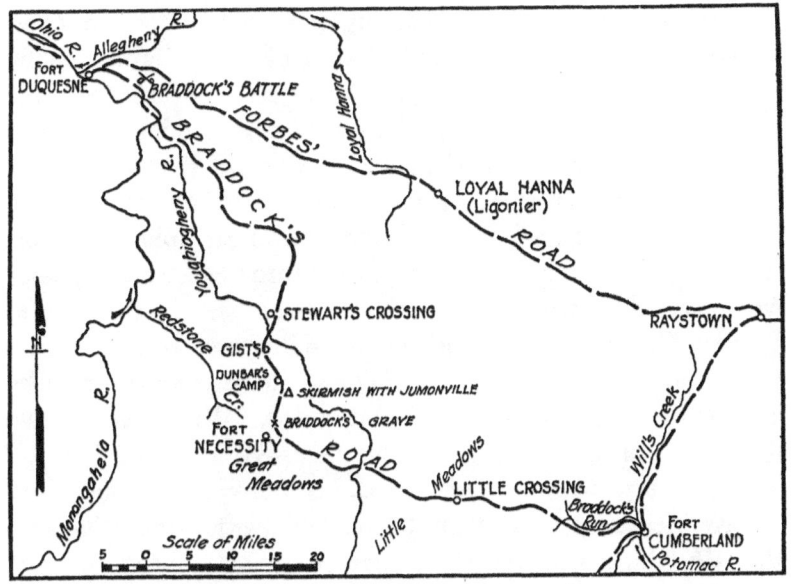

ROADS TO FORT DUQUESNE, 1758

could not understand his "suicidal delays," which were later revealed to be a part of the plan of campaign, involving the exhaustion of the enemy and coöperation with major movements to the northward.

Laboring thus in the dark Washington continued to hold out for the Virginia route. In the event the proposed road through Pennsylvania were used, he saw only "the luckless Fate of Poor Virginians to fall a Victim to the views of her crafty Neighbours; and yield her honest efforts to promote their common Interest, at the expense of much Blood and Treasure." Worse still, he was certain that use of the proposed road would entail ultimate defeat. "Our Enterprise Ruin'd," said he, "and we stop'd at the Laurel Hill this Winter; not to gather Laurels."[48] Rather than face such an eventuality, he threatened to make "a full representation of the matter to His Majesty." However, if it could be shown that he was wrong, he was, as usual, willing to acknowledge his error "as becomes a Gentleman, led astray by judgment and not by prejudice."

Although convinced of Washington's sincerity, Forbes questioned his wisdom and suspected him of being influenced by provincial rivalries. To Forbes the rejection of the Virginia route involved the impossibility of two wrongs making one right, and, unlike Braddock, and under wholly different conditions, Forbes had the courage of his convictions. When informed by his engineers, Colonel Henry Bouquet and Sir John St. Clair, that the road by way of Raystown (Bedford) and Fort Ligonier was practicable, suggestions looking to the use of other routes angered Forbes. At this crisis of the controversy Bouquet wrote him regarding the Virginians: "They believe everything to be easy which flatters their ideas," and added, "What I shall have to tell you on this point cannot be discussed in a letter."[49]

His every suggestion unheeded, his motives questioned, and his experience ignored, it must have been with some reluctance that Washington obeyed the orders of General Forbes to leave Fort Cumberland and join the main army in Pennsylvania. He reached Raystown September 13 and at once took charge of a construction party, with orders to push the Virginia-hated route to completion as rapidly as possible. The severity of this assignment was doubtless mitigated somewhat by the fact that "the new road" had already reached a base for the proposed attack. Here drawing upon his experience with Braddock, he submitted to General Forbes two plans of approach and made enthusiastic by the possibility of action, he was soon as eager to reach Fort Duquesne by way of the new road as he had formerly been by the Virginia route. His interest and approval were reflected in acts of the Virginia Assembly repealing recently enacted laws conditionally withdrawing Virginia's support from the Forbes expedition.[50]

However irksome Washington's services as a road engineer in Pennsylvania may have been, his experiences in the Battle of the Monongahela were available to oppose precipitate action, even if they would not restrain the impatient Major James Grant who, with the approval of Colonel Henry Bouquet, led a command of Scotch Highlanders and provincials, including

Virginians, in a premature attack on Fort Duquesne. At the head of a force aggregating more than eight hundred men, Grant attempted this hazardous undertaking, September 14, 1758, being accompanied by Major Andrew Lewis, Captain Thomas Bullett, and other officers experienced in Indian warfare. Every indication pointed to the success of an attack, which because of "Grant's thirst for fame," was bungled. As a result Grant, together with Major Lewis and other officers, was captured, and twenty-two officers and two hundred seventy-eight men were killed. Others were wounded or made prisoners.[51] Except for the fact that this defeat was only an incident in a campaign, it might have put the entire force to rout, but unlike Dunbar at the Battle of the Monongahela, Forbes held his ground and pressed forward.

While taking delight in reporting that Virginians had again conducted themselves creditably under fire, Washington could not refrain from strictures upon the hated "new road." Meanwhile fellow Virginians were making observations upon the alleged grasping and designing qualities of the Pennsylvania Dutch, and Washington was calling attention to the fact that nature was changing the face of the Pennsylvania mountains so that it would soon be impossible for "men half-naked" to live in tents. With Colonel Stephen and others, he feared lest the road upon which they were working would never be completed. At any rate, a rumor to that effect reached General Forbes, who wrote Bouquet that: "Col. Washington and my friend, Col. [William] Byrd, would rather be glad this was true than otherways, seeing the other road (their favorite scheme) was not followed out. I told them plainly that, whatever they thought, yet I did aver that, in our prosecuting the present road, we had proceeded from the best intelligence that could be got for the good and convenience of the army, without any views to oblige any one province or another; and added that those two gentlemen were the only people that I had met with who had shewed their weakness in their attachment to the province they belong to, by declaring so publickly in favour of one road without their knowing anything of the other, having never heard from any Pennsylvania person one word about the road."[52]

In the meantime the French and Indian power in the Ohio Valley, as elsewhere in North America, was crumbling. The treaty of Easton, concluded October 26, 1758, broke the French spell over the Pennsylvania Indians and natives residing to the westward; Fort Frontenac on Lake Ontario, and Louisbourg had fallen; and despite almost incessant rains, impossible roads, and his own illness, General Forbes concentrated his forces near Fort Ligonier. Not realizing that a bloodless victory was within his grasp, he hesitated for a time, and even talked of going into winter quarters, but his soldiers and officers were impatient for action. At this juncture word came of further Indian defections from the French and of starving and helpless conditions at Fort Duquesne. When Washington and others, fully equipped for any contingency, went to investigate these reports, they found them more than true. Fort Duquesne was a smouldering ruin, and three days later Washington informed Governor Fauquier that the coveted fort "or the ground rather on which it stood, was possessed by his Majesty's troops on the 25th instant."[53] About a year thereafter it was replaced by Fort Pitt.

For Washington, as for others, there was substance for profound thought in the events culminating at the Forks of the Ohio in November, 1758. For the first time in his life, he had had an opportunity to experience the differences between a party and an army, between a battle and a campaign. His failure to appreciate these differences was perhaps largely responsible for his inability to see anything good in Pennsylvania or Pennsylvanians or to appreciate the fine qualities of General Forbes and William Pitt, and for his proneness to overemphasize the importance of the Indian as a factor in international war on a grand scale. His experiences did, however, advance his thinking to a world plane, on which basis they were more thoroughly assimilated during the years immediately following. As an initial step thereto they doubtless inspired new confidence in

British regulars and must have been a cause of renewed devotion to the mother country.

Despite the world aspect of the events in which he participated in the autumn of 1758, Washington's mind reverted to other and immediate consequences. Like other realists of his day in America, he was concerned with plans for the capture of Fort Duquesne by the British; with the control and use of lands in the Ohio Valley; and with the fur trade, "not only of the Ohio Indians, but, in time, of the numerous nations possessing the back countries westward of it." To prevent these benefits from going to any one colony, even to Virginia, and certainly to Pennsylvania, he recommended a joint colonial commission, a forerunner of federal union, with power to regulate trade and other intercolonial matters. Although he was unwilling to see Fort Pitt abandoned, he objected seriously to having the sole responsibility for its maintenance and defense fall upon Virginia, and for the last time before he became commander-in-chief of the armies of the Continental Congress, his pleas again went forth in behalf of his naked and starved soldiers. Disillusioned by the results of a campaign that had defied all his predictions and expectations and added nothing to his own military reputation, and ignoring the numerous pleas of his officers and soldiers, he resolved to leave the army forever, to marry, and to settle down at Mount Vernon to enjoy domestic felicity.

CHAPTER VIII

THE FRONTIER ADVANCE

SIX WEEKS after his service with Forbes at the former site of Fort Duquesne, George Washington (January 6, 1759) married Martha Custis, the widow of Daniel Parke Custis, and after a brief honeymoon, came to Mount Vernon to live the life of a Virginia planter. As such his chief interest was in the cultivation of tobacco, in which his initial efforts, his land being unexploited, were successful. His total production for 1760 was 65,000 pounds, approximately double that for any previous year, and it increased to 89,000 pounds in 1763, after which it declined perceptibly.[1]

Although Washington's main dependence was upon tobacco, he had other economic interests. Among other things he owned, bred, and sold Negro slaves, and he grew corn, wheat, oats, rye, and barley in large quantities but mostly for domestic uses, for which he had his own mill and his own still. At one time he owned one hundred thirty horses and more than one hundred cows. He engaged in fishing for commercial purposes, a seasonal catch of shad in 1772, netting £40. He was interested in efforts to drain the Dismal Swamp; he marketed lumber and timber from his own forests; his mother's affairs received his constant and affectionate attention; and the estate of his ward, John Parke Custis, was so well administered that Custis was among the richest men in Virginia at the time he came of age.[2] By 1772 Washington's lands east of the Alleghenies aggregated more than twelve thousand acres,[3] and Martha's efforts to supplement the family income and keep down expenses by supervising the weaving, the sewing, and the dairying for the home plantation met with George's approval.

However self-sufficing the Washington establishment, a product of the domestic age of economy, may have been, it was not at times a paying proposition.[4] This was certainly true of years immediately preceding the American Revolution, when its owner was compelled to ask the indulgence of creditors. Not only had tobacco production declined, but prices had fallen. Possibly because of the poor soil upon which it was produced, Washington's tobacco rarely, if ever, brought the best price, a fact he could not understand. Other enterprises were equally unremunerative: he bought butter for domestic uses; the Dismal Swamp improvement was a veritable rat hole for surplus earnings; and Washington's salary as a legislator did not pay his expenses while in Williamsburg.[5] The plight of the Virginia farmer of this period was indeed desperate.[6]

But for political and social diversions, these conditions might have been intolerable. Washington continued, however, to speak of himself as a successful planter and to praise farm life. Although revenues from his estate were not always adequate to his needs, his was indeed a full life.[7] Missing many roll calls, sometimes for whole sessions, he represented Frederick County as a Burgess from 1757 to 1766, when he was elected from Fairfax, his home county, which he represented continuously, when present, during the next ten years.[8] As a Burgess, Washington was as much interested in society as in legislative duties which served to keep him in touch with political currents both at home and abroad. From the standpoint of regularity his church and lodge (Masonic) attendance was upon a parity with his assembly record,[9] but there is every evidence that he enjoyed all with a sincere fervor and devotion.

In Washington's affections there was no place to compare with Mount Vernon.[10] With the greatest freedom guests came and went; there worries incident to crop failures, low prices, frauds and disappointments, were lost in the chase and the convivial cup; and no end of attention was given his stepson "Jacky," and Jacky's sister "Patcy," an epileptic, who died at the age of sixteen.

Preoccupied with these cares and pleasures, Washington soon

lost interest in the army. By mid-summer, 1761, the "dispossession of the French in most parts of North America" had become "too stale to relate,"[11] and that too, despite the fact that Gorée, Guadelupe, Ticonderoga, and Niagara had fallen; that both Wolfe and Montcalm had died upon the Heights of Abraham; that the French fleet had been decisively defeated in Quiberon Bay; and that the English were in possession of Pondicherry in far-off India.

Temporarily lost in efforts to become a successful planter on lands poorly favored by nature, Washington could not have been wholly indifferent to the results of the war between the French and the English. Permeated with the traditional Washington land-hunger, he still saw in the West a land of opportunity. The fall of Fort Duquesne had practically cleared the Ohio Valley of enemy, even the ubiquitous Shawnee, and as the heir of his half-brother Lawrence and a beneficiary in his own right under the Dinwiddie Proclamation of 1754, promising two hundred thousand acres of "his Majesty the King of England's land on the Ohio River," to persons who would volunteer to fight the French and Indians, Washington was eager to claim his own. He was therefore in sympathy with an effort made in 1760 to revive the Ohio Company of 1748, and, in 1763, he joined his half-brother, John Augustine Washington, Richard Henry Lee, Arthur Lee, William Fitzhugh, and others as incorporators of a Mississippi Company, which petitioned the king for two and a half million acres west of the mountains.[12]

Similar interests and traditions were meanwhile keeping Washington in touch with his lands and friends in the valley of Virginia. Until 1766, the annual hustings brought him into Frederick County and afforded an opportunity to visit his Bullskin estate and Lord Fairfax at Greenway Court. Other visits to Bullskin and Greenway Court were less regular but could be expected any time in the harvest and planting seasons. In August, 1761, he was at Warm Springs, now Berkeley Springs, Morgan County, West Virginia, where he found "about 200 people . . . full of all manner of diseases and complaints."

This outing sufficed to abate his own fever "a good deal"; but his pains grew "rather worse," and his sleep was "equally disturbed."[13] Six years later he was back at "The Springs" with Patcy, his afflicted stepdaughter.

In his plans to possess himself of lands in the Ohio Valley, Washington, together with others with similar purposes, encountered many difficulties. Under charter claims of 1609, Virginia was making grants west of the mountains and was tending otherwise to ignore the Dinwiddie promise of 1754. Moreover, the French and Indian War was no sooner ended than plans began to be hatched for the formation of new colonies west of the Alleghenies.[14] More discouraging still, along the entire Appalachian frontier Indians under the leadership of Pontiac, were making a last stand against the British, particularly the "Long Knives," or Virginians, in a so-called conspiracy; and to prevent similar outbursts, in 1763, the King issued a proclamation forbidding colonial governors to issue land patents to would-be settlers beyond the Alleghenies and entrusting the administration of Indian affairs there to agents created for that purpose seven years before. Although intended primarily to control the Indian situation, the Proclamation of 1763 was motivated also by schemes of land jobbers and would-be commonwealth builders, as well as by plans for the fur trade. To this latter end it was proposed to make Fort Pitt an emporium of trade, surpassing in importance either Quebec or New Orleans,[15] and land jobbers temporarily took cover.

The years immediately following 1763 were momentous in determining the future of the American frontier beyond the Alleghenies. Like Washington, most persons regarded the Proclamation of 1763 as "a temporary expedient to quiet the Minds of the Indians," and were willing for the traders to have their way. Accordingly, under direction of Baynton, Wharton, and Morgan (1765-1766) the fur trade along the Ohio River gave employment to more than three hundred men and to a sixth as many batteaux; but it was practically ended by 1768, and Fort Pitt was on the point of being abandoned and destroyed.[16] Ignoring paper manifestoes and the plans of embryo capitalists, traders and settlers had meanwhile pushed beyond the Alleghenies in such numbers as to call for their removal by force. As this was impossible, there was nothing left but to let the settlers have their way.

Meanwhile Washington's interest in western lands grew apace. Anticipating Horace Greeley by more than a hundred years, he was advising his impecunious friends to go west before land-grabbing immigrants appropriated the best lands. In reply to a letter from his friend and neighbor, Captain John Posey, asking for an additional loan and the use of Washington's name as an endorser, he, June 24, 1767, urged Posey to sell all his belongings "raising to Negroes, and even Land if requisite." His advice to Posey shows such a comprehensive grasp of the West and its possibilities that it is here quoted at length:

For if the whole shoud go, there is a large Field before you, an opening prospect in the back Country for Adventures, where numbers resort to, and where an enterprising Man with very little Money may lay the foundation of a Noble Estate in the New Settlemts. Upon Monongahela for himself and posterity. The Surplus money wch you might save after dischargg. your Debts, would possibly secure you as much Land as in the course of 20 yrs woud sell for 5 times yr prest Estate. For proof of which only look to Frederick [County], and see what Fortunes were made by the Hite's . . . Nay how the greatest Estates we have in this Colony were made; was it not by taking up and purchasing at very low rates the rich back Lands which were thought nothing of in those days, but are now the most valuable Lands we possess? Undoubtedly it was, and to pursue this plan is the advice I w'd offer my Br. were he in yr. Situation, but to you I only drop it as a hint for your serious reflectn; because I do not expect, nor woud by any means wish to see you adopt any Scheme of mine without duly attending to it weighing, and well considering of it in all points and advising with your friends. I woud only ask whether it would be better to labr. undr. a load of debt, where you are, wch. must inevitably keep you in continual Anxiety, and dread of yr. Creditors; by selling the produce of yr. labour at under value, (the never failg. consequence of necessitous Circumstances) with other evils too obvious to need Inumeration, and which must forever lend a helping hand to keep you low and distressed or to Pluck up resolution at once and disengage yourself of these Incumbrances and Vexations Abiding where you are if you can save your Land and have a prospect of reaping future advantages from it, or to remove back, where there is a moral certainty of laying the foundation of good Estates to yr. Childn.[17]

Washington was meanwhile losing no opportunity to lay the foundation of good estates to himself. In 1766 his boyhood friend, William Crawford, made a permanent residence at Stewart's Crossing on the Youghiogheny River in what is now Fayette County, Pennsylvania, where he, together with many other pioneers, secured land grants. At this vantage point Crawford received a letter from Washington dated September 21, 1767, directing him to "look me out a Tract of about 1500, 2000, or more Acres . . . as contiguous to your own Settlemt. as such a body of good Land coud be found." This he had been informed could be done "about Jacobs Cabbins." Already experienced with the results of cultivating comparatively poor lands, Washington let it be known that the desired tract "must be rich . . . and if possible . . . good and level." "As nothing is more certain than that the Lands cannot remain long ungranted," he advised haste in their location, and as "a good deal of Land" and in large tracts was desired, he was willing to associate himself with Crawford to advance their common interests.[18]

At this juncture the purchase of lands was not so important to Washington as was the necessity of preëmpting them for purchase. The Proclamation of 1763 was still binding, and large grants such as he desired, were made as a rule, only to groups of individuals. He was certain, however, that the Pennsylvania practice of making grants in tracts of only three hundred acres each, could be circumvented by making several contiguous entries, provided "the expence of doing which is not too heavy." Although it was then illegal to acquire lands "in the King's [Virginia's] part," Washington instructed Crawford, "under the guise of hunting other Game," to spy out suitable tracts for future entry, requesting that his, Washington's, interest in the matter be kept secret, as he did not wish his opinion regarding the King's Proclamation to become known. Nor did he wish to "give the alarm to others."[19]

September 29, 1767, Crawford informed Washington that "the chief parts of the good land" between the Youghiogheny and the Monongahela Rivers had already been taken. He had, however, located "a fine piece" on Chartier's Creek about twenty-five miles from Fort Pitt, which he asked Washington to join him in acquiring. Regarding the lands "in the King's part," he was not so encouraging. Indians still claimed them and opposed their entry without pay, and the ownership of these lands was a subject of controversy between Pennsylvania and Virginia. A rumor was current also to the effect that Sir Wm. Johnson had ordered the Indians to vacate these lands and that "the great men of Philadelphia" wished them for themselves, and rival prospectors were reported active in many sections of Trans-Allegheny Virginia.[20] Nevertheless, Crawford was willing to become Washington's partner and to undertake the somewhat hazardous work of locating tracts of land suitable for future purchase.

The rumored interest of "the great men of Philadelphia" was well founded. Although they had lost heavily in the fur trade, they too had caught "the vision of the inexorable march of the white man across the American continent." More important still they had sold their viewpoint to Lord Shelburne, English Secretary of State, who was then characterizing as "nonsense" contentions to the effect that American colonial boundary lines extended from "sea to sea," which was another way of saying that the newly acquired lands beyond the Allegheny Mountains belonged to the King of England to dispose of as he pleased. This pronouncement was a death-blow to individual claimants, to the pretentions of the Ohio Company, and to Virginia's claim under her charter of 1609, by which she would have extended her boundary from "sea to sea, west and northwest,"[21] but it revived the possibility of new colonies west of the Alleghenies.

Under these conditions the Pennsylvanians again became the aggressors. Through their influence in 1768, Sir William Johnson concluded at Fort Stanwix a treaty whereby interested Indians ceded to the King of England their claims to all the lands in what is now Trans-Allegheny West Virginia and a large part of Kentucky. At the same time and place Samuel Wharton, William Trent, William Franklin and others secured a private grant later known as Indiana. This comprised about five thousand square miles and, although made in the King's name, it was for the "sole benefit and behoof of the despoiled traders," who had failed to make a success of the fur trade following the French and Indian War and who, together with others, in the same year began a movement looking to the formation of a new colony west of the Alleghenies to be called Vandalia. For this purpose the King was petitioned for a land grant, sometimes referred to as the Walpole Grant because of Thomas Walpole, a London banker, interested in the proposed new colony.[22]

Confident that "the lines of the colonies would be extended soon" and that officers would receive promised lands "agreeable to his Majesty's Proclamation," Washington had meanwhile taken time by the forelock. Already Crawford acting "as if for himself," had surveyed a tract in southwestern Pennsylvania, "taking all the good lands and leaving out the sorry, only some joining the mill seat."[23] Other surveys made for Washington in 1770 and 1771 included the site of Fort Necessity, which he wished for sentimental reasons, and the "Washington Lands," on Miller's Run near what is now Canonsburg, Pennsylvania, previously described by Crawford as being on Chartier's Creek.

For various reasons, some of which have already been indicated in this chapter, Crawford was not so successful in locating lands in Virginia. Further complicating the situation was the prolonged controversy between Virginia and Pennsylvania regarding their common boundary. Moreover, the "Indian traders' lands" were said to have priority, and numerous prospectors were abroad in the land with tomahawks, chains, and compasses. But this situation only stimulated Washington to activity on his own behalf. Consequently in the later part of 1769 he petitioned the Virginia Executive Council for permission to make the desired surveys. Meanwhile, "as a Lottery only," he bought up the claims of fellow officers, when they could be had "for little or nothing," as usual taking care not to make purchases in his own name. In this manner he acquired claims to thousands of acres, many of which were never surveyed and patented.

Stimulated by the activities of the Pennsylvanians, the Virginia Executive Council, December 1769, permitted Washington to locate two hundred thousand acres allotted claimants under the Dinwiddie Proclamation of 1754, provided the surveys did not encroach upon prior settlements. In pursuance of this action in August, 1770, these claimants met in Fredericksburg, Virginia, where it was resolved to locate the desired grants in the region of the Great Kanawha, beyond "the traders' lands" and the new settlements in the Trans-Allegheny. For this purpose, Washington, an experienced frontiersman, now anxious to visit the West again, was chosen to represent such persons as filed their claims with him and bore their part of his expenses.[24]

On his fifth journey to the Trans-Allegheny, October 5, 1770, Washington left Mount Vernon in company with Doctor James Craik and servants. Traveling horseback the first day out he reached Leesburg, forty-five miles distant, where Washington's "Portmanteau horse faild in his Stomach." Twelve days later after an uneventful journey by way of Fort Necessity and Braddock's Field, the party reached Fort Pitt, approximately three hundred miles inland. On the way out the party had found suitable stopping places at Washington's brother Samuel's, Jolliff's, Pritchard's, Cox's, Rumney, Wise's, Killam's, Fort Cumberland, Great Crossings, Gist's, Crawford's (where Captain William Crawford joined him), and Stephenson's. At

Old Town Washington had learned from Colonel Cresap, just returned from England, additional "particulars of the Grant said to be lately sold to Walpole and others."[25] Throughout the entire journey Washington had an eye out for good lands, and at Captain Crawford's, he "Went to see a Coal Mine," the content of which "seemed to be of the very best kind, burning freely and abundance of it."

Instead of a smoldering ruin such as he had witnessed twelve years before, Washington found Fort Pitt a pentagonal structure, two sides of which were brick, "the others Stockade." A moat encompassed it, and it was garrisoned by two companies of Royal Irish commanded by Captain Charles Edmonstone. About three hundred yards "distant" was "the Town [Pittsburgh]," which consisted of about twenty log houses inhabited by Indian traders and arranged in streets along the Monongahela. Here Washington lodged in "a very good House of Publick Entertainment" kept by Samuel Sample.[26]

Through the intercession of officers at Fort Pitt, Washington met and was reconciled to George Croghan with whom he had quarreled in 1754 over horses which Washington had seized, thus entailing a considerable loss to Croghan. As he was now a landed potentate claiming between two hundred thousand and two hundred fifty thousand of the choicest acres in the vicinity of Pittsburgh, some of which Washington wished to purchase, he could well afford to cultivate Croghan's acquaintance. Accordingly Washington accepted his invitation to dine at Croghan Hall on the Allegheny about five miles from Fort Pitt, where doubtless possible land purchases were discussed and a meeting between Washington and "the White Mingo and other Chiefs of the 6 Nations" took place. In the course of this interview, Washington received "a String of Wampum" and "a Speech" which summarized the Indian situation and again welcomed him to the interior.[27] In response he assured the Indians "that all the Injuries and affronts" that had passed between them and the Virginians had been forgotten. Continuing, he made the timely and diplomatic observation "that the Virginians were a People not so much engaged in Trade as the Pensylvanians, etca. w[hi]ch was the Reason of their not being so frequently among them; but that it was possible they might for the time to come have stricter connections with them."[28]

The same day, October 19, Washington returned to Pittsburgh and made ready to descend the Ohio. "The boys" in charge of the horses having been ordered back to Crawford's with instructions to meet Washington there later, the following day he set out on the last lap of his journey. Colonel Croghan, Alexander McKee, and Lieutenant Robert Hamilton accompanied him as far as Logstown. Thence Washington's party traveled in two canoes, one for the exclusive use of attending Indians, among them the "Pheasant," and the other for Washington and his white companions, Dr. James Craik, William Crawford, Joseph Nicholson, Robert Bell, William Harrison, and Charles Morgan.

Eleven days later the party reached the mouth of the Great Kanawha. Meanwhile Washington had committed to the pages of his *Diary* either names or descriptions, sometimes both, of the numerous intervening islands and tributary streams between that point and the source of the Ohio River. Accompanying these were general descriptions of the lands passed, together with the patent observation that "the Hills on one side" were "opposite to the bottoms on the other." Although hundreds of white men had previously descended the Ohio, the lands bordering upon its banks were still the domain of the forest primeval, with only here and there an intervening savannah. The Mingo Town of about sixty warriors, located on or near the present site of Steubenville, Ohio, was the only native village of consequence passed in their course. Here they received the disconcerting intelligence of the murder of white men farther down stream, but they pressed forward and found that this report had its origin in the accidental death of a white trader. Otherwise their experiences were most pleasant. The intermittent call of wild turkey and the sight of grazing deer verified their notions regarding the fatness of the land. Near the mouth of the Great

Kanawha they saw many buffalo and "a Couple Birds in size between a Swan and a Goose,"[29] the like of which Washington had never seen. They were probably either blue heron or American bittern.

In his descent of the Ohio, Washington recorded meeting only one important Indian hunting party, that of Kiashuta who was sojourning on the east side of the Ohio about thirty-five miles below the mouth of the Little Kanawha. For "necessity,"

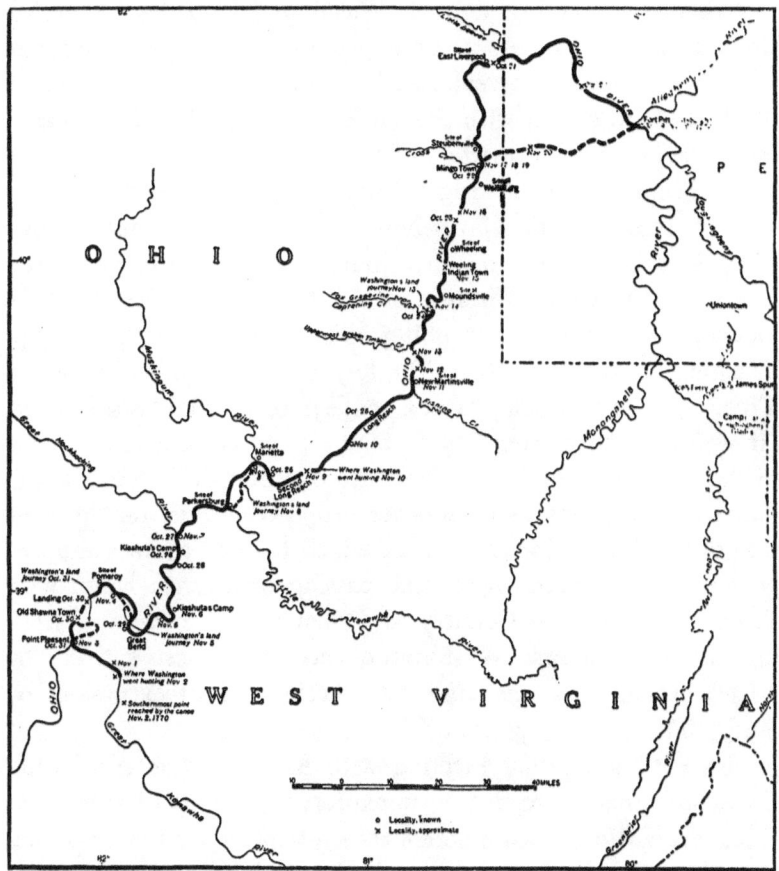

WASHINGTON'S JOURNEY ON AND ALONG THE OHIO RIVER, 1770. THE ROUTE FOLLOWED BETWEEN FORT PITT AND WILLS CREEK WAS PRACTICALLY COTERMINOUS WITH BRADDOCK'S TRAIL.
SEE PAGE 103.

as well as for friendship's sake, Washington, having met him before, thought it advisable to pay his respects in person, for which he was agreeably rewarded with "great kindness" and "a Quarter of very fine Buffalo."

At the earnest invitation of the Indians the two parties spent the night near each other. "After much Councelling the overnight" the next morning the Indians came to "my fire," and with extreme formality Kiashuta rehearsed the incidents and accords of the meeting between Washington and the Indians at Colonel Croghan's. As a result promises of mutual peace and friendship were again reaffirmed, as was also the intention of the Indians to get on with the Virginians, provided they treated them with fairness in matters of trade.[30]

In keeping with his original intentions, but contrary to subsequent understandings, neither Washington nor any of his party surveyed lands on this journey. After exploring the Great Kanawha for a distance of about fourteen miles above its mouth, some of his party going four or five miles higher up, Washington marked "two Maples, an Elm, and Hoopwood Tree," on the east side, "as a Corn[e]r of the Soldiers L[an]d (if we can get it) intending to take all the bottom from hence to the Rapids in the Great Bent into one Survey." He also indicated the beginnings of another proposed survey on the west side of the Great Kanawha, after which he took courses and distances of that stream, noted the passing of a canoe laden with sheep for the Illinois Country, and then set out for home. Both up and down stream Washington traveled almost entirely by water, but the accompanying map discloses short excursions by land. These side trips were for inspection purposes.[31]

Except for another meeting with Kiashuta who gave additional information regarding unexplored portions of the Great Kanawha Valley, Washington's return trip up the Ohio was uneventful. Among other things he learned from Kiashuta that the length of the Great Kanawha River between its mouth and its falls was greater than the distance between the two Kanawhas; that the bottom land on the south side of the Great Kanawha was almost continuous throughout its length; that the bottoms on the north side were rich; and that canoes could not be used upon the Great Kanawha above "the Falls." As Washington placed dependence in his informant, he was thus able, in a measure, to master his new environment by a minimum of effort.[32]

November 17, 1770, Washington summarized observations of his journey in a general description of the Ohio, of the lands through which it flowed, and of the life and conditions along its banks. Thence from a point about ten miles north of the present site of Wellsburg, West Virginia, and opposite "Mingo Town" he journeyed overland to Fort Pitt. In preparation for this journey he sent his canoe and baggage ahead by "two Delaware Indians" who performed the service for six dollars and "a Quart Tinn Can." As his horses had not yet arrived, his own departure overland was delayed somewhat, but he used the time to complete his description of the Ohio and its environs. One of the most significant of the observations then recorded, was that "the People from Virginia and elsewhere, are exploring and Marking all the Lands that are valuable not only on Redstone and other waters of Monongahela but along down the Ohio as low as the little Kanawha; and by next Summer I suppose will get to the great Kanawha, at least." October 21, he reached Pittsburgh.

Washington's second Pittsburgh sojourn of this journey was not so eventful as was his first, but it was important. There he met a relative of Colonel Croghan, Dr. John Connolly, who had traveled over "a good deal of this Western Country both by Land and Water." From him Washington learned much about the Illinois Country and the lands along the "Shawana" or Cumberland River.[33] He also met parties from whom he gathered additional data regarding the proposed Vandalia colony.

After settling with Indian and other attendants and paying sundry bills, among them one to Samuel Samples for a dinner given by Washington to officers and other gentlemen at Fort Pitt, November 23, he departed thence for home. Crossing swollen streams by swimming his horses, and renewing acquaintances at the several stopping places passed on his way out, he reached Mount Vernon, December 1 after an absence of nine weeks and one day. None the worse for wear he at once resumed the rounds of his mill and enjoyment of the chase.

One of the chief results of Washington's visit of 1770 to the Ohio Valley was his heightened concern regarding the proposed Vandalia colony. On April 15, 1770, he had written Governor Botetourt setting forth in some detail its proposed bounds. At the same time he had expressed the belief that its authorization "will give a fatal blow ... to the interests of this country." He closed with a plea for consideration of the land claimants under the Dinwiddie Proclamation of 1754 and with a request that his "Lordship" use his "kind interposition, and favorable representation" to have his Majesty "confirm this land to *us*."[34] Information gathered in the interior confirmed Washington's conviction regarding the menacing influence of the proposed colony to rival claims and heightened his determination to thwart it.

This decision was confirmed by information which had reached eastern Virginia in Washington's absence. Upon his return he learned that George Croghan, William Trent, William Franklin, and others had merged their land claims into the Grand Ohio Company and had renewed the movement looking to the formation of a new colony west of the Alleghenies. It mattered not that they had provided for claimants under the Dinwiddie Proclamation and the Old Ohio Company. Rumor had it that the proposed colony would be closely attached to the King and that the rights and interests of individuals would not be safe-guarded as in the older colonies, certainly not in those accustomed to a large degree of self-government.[35] As an agent and attorney for officers and soldiers of Virginia, as well as in his own right, Washington appreciated the situation and felt his responsibilities. As usual he was for action, but he was unwilling to move without the approval of his clients. Accordingly they were asked to meet him in March, 1771, in Winchester, Virginia.

At this, the second meeting of the Virginia officers of the French and Indian war interested in western lands, Washington made a detailed report of his trip of the previous year, and it was resolved to have the lands which he had located on the Ohio surveyed at once. It mattered not that the hazards of this undertaking were great, that the costs would have to be borne by those interested, and that the Virginia Executive Council, December 15, 1769, had temporarily forbidden such surveys. The fact remained that the choice lands along the Ohio were being taken. Accordingly the surveys were authorized, and soon thereafter William Crawford was employed for that purpose.

As a result of Crawford's activities, Washington, November 7, 1771, reported to George Mercer, agent of the Ohio Company of 1748, that[36] "we have Surveyed Ten of the largest Tracts we can find in the district allowed us, and have been able to get 61,796 Acres, and for this we have been obliged to go between 2 and 300 Miles below Fort Pitt, as the Lands thereabouts are thought to be within the Pennsylvania Government; at least, are Survey'd under those Rights, and held by such a number of Individuals, that it was thought to be Impolitick to engage in private disputes, whilst there appeared but a gloomy prospect of getting any Land at all."

Early in 1772 Lord Dunmore arrived in Virginia to succeed Governor Botetourt who died in October, 1770, and temporarily conditions became more favorable for Washington and his clients wishing to validate their western land claims. Like Dinwiddie twenty years before, Dunmore caught the western land fever and secretly and possibly effectively joined those opposed to the Vandalia, or Walpole, colony. Soon Dunmore and Washington were fast friends and planned to visit the Ohio Valley together. Because of his inability to make "absolute and bona fide" grants, Dunmore declined, however, to approve Washington's request to be permitted to continue his surveys.

This refusal brought from Washington an historical review of the questions involved and a warning to the effect that longer delays in perfecting land titles would result in losses to "the Officers and Soldiers who have suffered in the cause of your Country." Inasmuch as "Emigrants" were "daily and hourly settling on the choice spots waiting a favourable opportunity to solicit legal Titles, on the ground of preoccupancy when the Office shall be open'd," Washington thought it wrong to deny prior claimants the right to make legal preëmptions.[37]

As a result of these representations and a formal petition Dunmore permitted the desired surveys but restricted them to twenty tracts. With the aid of his council he also determined the proportions of land allowed each claimant, which ranged from fifteen thousand acres for field officers to four hundred acres for privates. Although encouraging, these concessions left obstacles in the way of individual claimants anxious to survey and patent lands of their own choosing and at once. Inasmuch as others were then acquiring lands through patent, settlement, and even tomahawk rights, Washington resented this discrimination, alleging that it put "the soldiers upon a worse footing, than the meanest individual in the community." He added furthermore this philosophic observation "that no country ever was or ever would be settled without some indulgence." He further analyzed the situation in these questions and their terse answers: "What inducements have men to explore uninhabited wilds, but the prospect of getting good lands? Would any man waste his time, expose his fortune, nay, life, in such a search, if he was to share the good and the bad with those that come after him? Surely not."[38]

Meantime a homestead war was in progress in the vicinity of Fort Pitt.[39] A victim of financial reverses, the result of excessive borrowing and plunging, and obsessed with enthusiasm for the Vandalia enterprise, in which he was personally interested, Croghan was selling his holdings in wholesale fashion and as recklessly promising valid titles. At the same time he questioned the legality of Washington's holdings and tried to prevent him from using them to advantage. The interposition of Dunmore in an effort to oust Pennsylvanians from the Monongahela Valley and to overthrow the governments established there, at the same time disallowing their land grants, did not help the situation. In fact, it came near precipitating war between Pennsylvania and Virginia. In the course of ensuing events the Washington-Crawford interests were outstanding participants. In some instances rival claimants were ejected by force, and they vied with others in the use of log cabins and other devices to establish coveted land claims.[40]

Ever awake to his own interests and never averse to a fight when they were involved, in 1773 Washington planned another visit to the Trans-Allegheny, which he probably would have made but for the death of his stepdaughter in August of that year. As in the past, western lands doubtless occupied much of his attention, and communications from his partner, Crawford, regarding them were awaited with concern. Of incidents thus revealed in the homestead war these are typical: "The man that is strong and able to make Others Afraid of him Seems to have the Best Chance as tims go now. . . . I do not find I can get you the Quantity of Land . . . without I cold stay all Summer and be on the spot as People Crowd out in such numbers the Like never was seen," and "they took your Land and say the[y] will keep it. I could Drive them away but they will com back Emedetly as soon as my back is turned. They man I put on the Land they have drove away and Built a house so Close to his dore he cannot get into the house at the dore . . . there is no getting them of[f] without Force of Arms."[41]

Out of this bonanza condition, fraught with intercolonial rivalries and plans for new commonwealths, Washington emerged the owner of several potential estates. They were scattered here and there in southwestern Pennsylvania and along the Ohio and the Great Kanawha rivers and varied in size from approximately two hundred fifty to eleven thousand acres. The aggregate of his tracts in southwestern Pennsylvania was almost five thousand acres, while his lands on the Ohio and Great Kanawha rivers then actually surveyed and patented, reached more than twenty thousand acres.[42]

Although the titles to his western lands were somewhat clouded, as were also the uses to be made of them, Washington was not satisfied with the amount of his holdings and wished to acquire still others. In 1772 Governor Dunmore was willing to grant patents to lands lying below the Scioto River in what is now Ohio, to officers and soldiers under a proclamation of 1763. As Washington was a claimant in his own right under this proclamation and by purchase from others and was contemplating the possibility of "some new revolution . . . in our political System," he wished to have his lands aggregating ten thousand acres, surveyed at once. Moreover, he desired to have his survey in one tract and as near the mouth of the Scioto as possible, "but for the sake of better land" he was willing to go "down to the Falls, or even below." Nor was he averse to joining the initial rush to Kentucky and acquiring a tract embracing a salt spring upon Kentucky River, a grant which he then planned to turn "to an extensive public benefit, as well as private advantage."[43]

Washington's land-grabbing activities of the pre-Revolutionary days extended to the lower Mississippi and to West Florida. In the latter country he acquired the claims of Captain John Posey and the Reverend Dr. Thurston, each connected with "Lyman's Military Adventure." In the location of these claims Washington enlisted the services of his friend, James Wood, then sojourning in Florida, who was instructed to look out for "good Lands easy to be obtained, and not difficult to keep under the established Rules of Government." Washington directed also that lands chosen for him on the Mississippi should be as far up stream "as the Navigation is good."[44]

Although the Boston Tea Party, December, 1773, was a godsend to Washington in many ways, certainly in the matter of western lands, this patriotic and somewhat selfish demonstration of the New Englanders gave new momentum to the ball of revolution, then growing ever larger in America. Henceforth land interests, certainly those on the frontier, became more and more involved in matters affecting the mother country and will be treated accordingly. In other words, what Washington hoped for from Westminster, the rejection of the Vandalia petition, was accomplished in Boston. One of the results was the validation of additional land claims in the Trans-Allegheny, thus augmenting his private fortune and his public influence.

CHAPTER IX

IN THE REVOLUTION

ON THE EVE of the American Revolution Washington was trying to establish a permanent settlement on his lands near the mouth of the Great Kanawha River and the proposed capitol site of the Vandalia colony. Although his title to these lands was not questioned, he doubtless thought that possession amounted to the proverbial nine points of the law. Virginia had not yet opened a land office west of the Alleghenies; surveys there were still a matter of individual initiative and expense; and, in the midst of an ever-increasing number of claimants, settlement rights were necessary to clinch other preëpmtions. In this move Washington was doubtless motivated also by the example of his half-brother Lawrence, who, ignoring the dicta of an Established Church and other conventions of a somewhat aristocratic society, had planned to colonize the lands of the Ohio Company, of which he was president, with Palatine Germans. Already Washington was as liberal in practice as Thomas Jefferson later became in theory.

In this movement Washington was to all intents and purposes a modern real estate promoter, promising everything to everybody. Irish, Scotch, English, and German immigrants alike were to have religious and civil liberty, and that too within the bounds of Virginia which maintained an Established Church and a local government not renowned for liberalism. Referring to reported suspicions of certain interested Palatines to the contrary, Washington saw "no prospect of these People being restrained in the smallest degree either in their Civil, or Religious Principles."[1] His reason for this statement, namely: "these are Privileges, which Mankind are solicitous to enjoy, and Emigrants must be Anxious to know,"[2] would have done credit to either Thomas Jefferson or to Thomas Paine.

In this mood Washington appealed to his old friend and fellow officer, John David Woelper, or as Washington spelled his name, "Wilper," for aid in inducing Germans to emigrate to America. Although Woelper's chief concern seems to have been to sell his own land claims to Washington, he was not averse to helping him, stating his decision and understanding of the situation in these words: "Sir, as you have Some Intainsion, to Impord Some of my Countery man, To Sattlen your Land, and to Resolve your Quistion, which you has macke, to your Servant, To which I will give you, my Humble answer, to the best of my knowledge, and Informaision," adding, in equally good Pennsylvania Dutch, the following directions for lodging, or rather "packing" the desired colonists for shipment to America: "They are Logged in Bed Stals, macke of boards, 6-feet Long and 2 feet waith, This Bed Stals, are so Regulatted, acorting, to the vessel, Some Bed Stals are made for 2.3.4.5.6. Fraight, to hold, and Lay in it, and To keep Theries Nessisary by them, The other paggach, muss be but Down, in the hold,—."[3]

For some reason, possibly aversion to the method of lodging the desired immigrants, Washington did not follow Woelper's suggestion. In 1773 and 1774 his agents were active in Ireland and England, in the latter of which his press advertisement attracted so much attention as to cause Lord Hillsborough to predict the consequent depopulation of that country.[4] Already both England and Ireland had supplied thousands of persons who indentured themselves for short periods to those willing to pay their passage to America. As their exodus had not produced appreciable results in the population of either country, certainly not in the number of indigent poor, Hillsborough's fears were as baseless as they were perhaps insincere. Nevertheless Washington was able to purchase "four men convicts, four indented servants for three years and a man and his wife for four years." Their total cost, one hundred ten pounds, was not considered excessive, as they were "country convicts" and "likely people."[5] In an advertisement of 1774, announcing plans to send carpenters and pioneers to his western lands, he offered "leases for lives, renewable forever."[6] Thus it seems he was not averse to building up in the heart of the New World a society not unlike that of Medieval Europe, and that too despite his avowed leanings toward civil and religious liberty.

In this novel enterprise on March, 1774, "more than twenty servants and hirelings" left Mount Vernon for the Great Kanawha River.[7] They were under the direction of Valentine Crawford and were provided with "a great number of tools, nails, and necessaries"; but because of threatened Indian hostilities in the interior, they were unable to proceed beyond Redstone on the Monongahela. Here they were detained temporarily, but in time Crawford found it necessary to dispose of them. The entire "parcel" was offered to Gilbert Simpson, then engaged in building a mill for Washington on his lands near the present site of Perryopolis in Fayette County, Pennsylvania, but Simpson refused to purchase "for fear they would run away." Later he took some of them, and Crawford found it necessary to use others in the construction of a blockhouse, so threatening had the Indian situation become, even on the Monongahela. About May 1, 1774, one thousand refugees crossed that stream in a single day, and Crawford was able to find employment for the "hierlings" as militiamen. The remaining "servants" he sold like cattle to the highest bidder, one "parcel," Peter Miller and John Wood, for forty-five pounds; and another, consisting of Thomas McPherson and his wife, James Lowe and Jones Ennis, for sixty-five pounds. Agreeable to Washington's instructions, Crawford would have sold all the servants, had not "the confusion of the times put it out of" his power.[8]

This "confusion" was brought on by a new rush of settlers into the Trans-Allegheny, even into the "Dark and Bloody land." Both Harrodsburg and Louisville were founded in 1774, and about the same time new settlements were made along

WASHINGTON'S MILL, BUILT 1774-1776, NEAR PRESENT PERRYOPOLIS, PENNSYLVANIA

the upper Great Kanawha and the upper Ohio Rivers. These aggressions brought protests from the Grand Ohio Company,[9] from British officialdom, and as usual from the natives. Because of the treaties at Fort Stanwix and Lochaber, the Iroquois and Cherokees were restrained, but the Shawnees, former inhabitants of the Cumberland Valley and transient residents in the Great Kanawha Valley then living north of the Ohio River in the present state of Ohio, proved intractable.[10] Following Dunmore's meddling in the affairs of western Pennsylvania, and the murder of Logan's family at Yellow Creek, the clash, long feared by the mother country, was on, and plans for planting new settlements along the Ohio and the Great Kanawha rivers were temporarily abandoned. Soon thereafter the vicinity of Washington's would-be settlement became the scene of one of the bloodiest Indian battles in American annals. This, the Battle of Point Pleasant, was the major engagement of Dunmore's War.[11]

Washington's attitude toward this war was not clearly revealed. Already preoccupied with the effects of the "Intolerable Acts," he was persuaded that Americans were no longer governed by principles of justice and that redress could not be had through formal petitions. Accordingly while the American frontiersmen were marshaling their forces for war, Washington was helping to formulate the famous "Fairfax Resolves"[12] and getting ready to attend the first Continental Congress. When the Battle of Point Pleasant took place, he was in Philadelphia hobnobbing with "Boston gentlemen." When those disappointed with Dunmore's alleged precipitous course in concluding peace with the Indians were formulating the "Fort Gower Address," Washington was helping to draft the equally threatening "Declaration and Resolves" and the "Association" of the First Continental Congress. That he was in complete accord with the leading Virginians of his day in their resentment of British aggressiveness is attested by the fact that the Virginia delegation to the First Continental Congress, finding it necessary to retire before its sessions were ended, deputized Washington to sign their names "to any of the proceedings."

Intense interest in these and similar things easily explains Washington's seeming indifference to Dunmore's War, but further explanation might be found in the facts that Dunmore commanded his own army and that the frontier militia, of which his army was composed, was commanded by its own officers, among them being Major Andrew Lewis. In speaking of this war one of these commanders, Colonel William Preston, a western landowner, doubtless expressed the sentiments of many, possibly those of Washington, in these words: "The Oppertunty we hav[e] So long wished for, is now before us."[13] Immediately upon the termination of hostilities, Washington's agent, William Crawford, expressed the general sentiment of all those interested in the West in these words: "we may with propriety say we have had great success; as we have made them [Indians] sensible of their villany and weakness, and, I hope, made peace with them on such a footing as will be lasting."[14]

That this expressed Washington's sentiments is evidenced by the fact that he at once resumed his efforts to plant a permanent settlement on his lands at the mouth of the Great Kanawha River. For this purpose, January 10, 1775, he found an "overseer" in James Cleveland, formerly employed on the Mount Vernon estate. For the necessary manual labor Washington bought another "parcel of servants" who were temporarily lodged at Mount Vernon for safe-keeping.[15] Cleveland becoming ill, the enterprise was temporarily entrusted to William Stevens who was instructed to proceed to Simpson's on the Youghiogheny, there to complete arrangements for the proposed journey down the Ohio.

Other instructions to Stevens testify to Washington's infinite capacity for essential details and to the practical character of his experiences. Diligence was to be used in the construction of necessary living quarters; as much land as possible was to be made ready for corn; Major Crawford was to be consulted about a "Hunter" and "a good one"; "Peach Stone Kernals" were to be planted, two thousand of them; without arousing his servants suspicions, precautions were to be taken against their running away; a list of everything carried down the river, "though never so trifling," was to be left at Simpson's; and frequent reports were requested.[16] One cannot restrain the observation that Washington would have been as successful in founding commonwealths as he was in building and defending them.

With instructions already at hand Cleveland, in April, 1775, again took charge of the settlement project, and was soon thereafter at his post on the Great Kanawha. His reports, in the form of letters, are typical of those of others who have founded and attempted to found pioneer settlements. They told of the loss of needed supplies in a long and hazardous water journey, and of the building of log houses and the clearing and planting of new lands, of efforts to stock these lands with cattle and other domestic animals, of shortages of food supplies, and of the utter uselessness of indentured laborers. Many of these sought refuge in neighboring Indian villages, so that Cleveland, to avoid loss to his employer, was compelled to spend a large part of his time hunting them and compelling their return. As a result he concluded that "the time lost and the expense" was more than the enterprise could bear, and Cleveland resolved to permit the more untractable to go their way. Others were sent to Colonel Crawford with instructions "to sell them on the best terms."[17]

With the help of hirelings and a few Negroes, Cleveland was able to make a good showing in the way of improvements. April 2, 1776, he appeared before the County Court of Fincastle to have his effects recorded, according to law. A previous appraisement had fixed their value at £1100.15-7½. This represented fourteen buildings, three of which were designated as dwelling houses of four to five rooms each, whereas the others, except a barn, were just plain houses, or cabins. Twenty-eight acres had been cleared and were producing "large crops of corn, potatoes, & turnips." Near two thousand "peach stone cornols" had been planted.[18]

Thus, long after the beginning of hostilities between the colonies and the mother country, the Washington "settlement" on the Great Kanawha River was a going concern. What it might have become, had not the Indians again turned against the Virginians, can only be a matter of conjecture. "As it was, nothing came of the attempt." At least seventy-five miles from the settlements upon the upper Great Kanawha River and with small protection from Fort Blair at its mouth, which was soon deserted, there was nothing to do but to abandon the project. The houses were later burned, presumably by Indians.[19]

Meanwhile Washington had made an important decision. While he was planning another trip to the Ohio River, this time to look after his settlement, the Second Continental Congress offered him the chief command of the forces raised or to be raised for the defense of American liberties. On the same day, June 15, 1775, the Virginia Burgesses named him a member of a commission authorized to conclude a final treaty with Indians interested in the results of Dunmore's War.[20] The proposed treaty was to clinch the effects of the Battle of Point Pleasant and otherwise to complete the unfinished work of Dunmore on the frontier and was for that reason important, but Washington's choice in the matter is well known.

Although not generally appreciated, this decision marked a turning point in American political thought and practice. Had Washington accepted the Virginia appointment, he would probably have continued his fight for particularism as in 1758, when he preferred Braddock's Road to Forbes's Road and could see little good in Pennsylvania and Pennsylvanians.[21] Thanks to the benign influence of more constructive forces, his vision and patriotism had meanwhile risen to a higher plane. He was now able to speak of the "American Empire," and his friend Patrick Henry had become an "American."

Negotiations for the final termination of Dunmore's War took place at Pittsburgh in the autumn of 1775 and resulted in a treaty, concluded jointly by representatives of Virginia and of the Continental Congress.[22] Thus in a very real way the latter body had superseded the mother country. As Washington had opposed its plans for the government and control of the West, he could not, in the light of his personal interests, have been ignorant of or indifferent to the possibilities of this change of jurisdiction. There is, however, no evidence that he opposed it. He too had become an American.

On this point, Washington's relations to the Continental Congress during the period that he served it as commander-in-chief of its armed forces is something that inspires thought and admiration. It is perhaps the most beautiful and wholesome thing in his career. This was certainly true of the time during which he was a practical dictator. Instead of adorning himself with the conventional trappings of regal power, as a Napoleon or an Hohenzollern would have done, Washington continued to advise with that discredited body, and, at the earliest possible opportunity, he turned back to it the powers temporarily entrusted to him.[23] His ability to do this, without any apparent thought of another course, was the measure of his Americanism, of his faith in a new order, of his greatness. That it influenced his outlook toward western lands, few will question.

The scope and character of the grievances leading Washington into rebellion must not be overlooked. His approval of and participation in drafting the "Fairfax Resolves" of his home county, and the "Declaration and Resolves" and the "Association" of the First Continental Congress, leave no doubt of the fact that his grievances embraced taxation, trade, and commerce, but he was also concerned with matters affecting the American frontier, on the future of which he had staked his fortune. Despite his liberality in matters of creed, he opposed the Quebec Act, not primarily because it extended the bounds of Catholicism to the Ohio River, but because it intercepted an incipient westward extension of English possessions and English institutions. A casual reading of his correspondence covering the two decades immediately preceding the American Revolution leaves no doubt of Washington's answers to such questions as: Whenever possible in their common efforts, did not British regulars cast the brunt of war upon American provincials? Were not these provincials denied promised land grants because of efforts to please jobbers and court favorites? In Dunmore's premature peace negotiations following the Battle of Point Pleasant, did he not forfeit an opportunity of a generation?

If the cumulative effects of these grievances did not make a rebel out of Washington, other events of the last days of the Dunmore regime in Virginia were equal to that consummation. About the time that Washington was named commander-in-chief of the Continental Army, it was currently reported there that Dunmore had declared null and void patents granted by him for lands surveyed in 1772 and 1773. As these were the dates of some of Washington's patents, he was much concerned, expressing his inability to believe in the "reality" of the report. Fortunately it was unfounded, but as much could not be said of reports regarding Dunmore's efforts to use Indians and Negroes against the Virginians.

Undoubtedly Washington sympathized with the sentiments of the "Fort Gower Address," anticipating by months the more famous "Mecklenberg Declaration." This "Address" was issued November 5, 1774, as a protest against the unsatisfactory condition of things in Virginia both in the older settlements and upon the frontier. It was issued by active participants in Dunmore's War and upon the soil of what is now the state of Ohio. While expressing confidence in Dunmore, it committed its authors to the use of arms "for no other purpose than the honor of America and Virginia."[24]

From the beginning to the end of the Revolution, Washington placed much, possibly chief, dependence upon the Continental soldiers and militia of the American backwoods, particularly those from Virginia. With his approval and possibly at his suggestion, Congress, in one of its first acts following the opening of hostilities, voted to send him ten companies of riflemen to be drawn from Pennsylvania, Maryland, and Virginia, and about the same time, through an address to the captains of the "several independent companies" in Virginia, Washington entreated them not to relax their "discipline."[25] August 6, 1775, accompanied by Captain William Hendricks at the head of a company of Pennsylvania riflemen, Captain Hugh Stephenson and Colonel Daniel Morgan joined Washington in Cambridge with the first recruits from beyond the Potomac.[26] As Stephenson's command was largely from present Berkeley County, West Virginia, while Morgan's came from and near Winchester, Virginia, it is probably true, as reported, that Washington greeted each of them personally, calling them by name.

Because of his reputed prowess in a series of Indian wars, the fame of the American frontier soldier was already abroad in America, even in Europe. Their arrival at Cambridge must therefore have encouraged Washington, who knew their qualities better than anyone else. It was stimulating also to the country at large. In contemplation of their arrival, John Adams wrote his wife: "These are an excellent species of light infantry. They use a peculiar kind of musket, called a rifle. It has circular or—groves within the barrel, and carries a ball with great exactness to great distances. They are the most accurate marksmen in the world."[27] Possibly a better characterization of the strength and methods of the Virginia frontier riflemen was given by Richard Henry Lee:

"This one County of Fincastle can furnish 1000 Rifle Men that for their number make most formidable light Infantry in the world. The six frontier Counties can produce 6000 of these Men who from their amazing hardihood, their method of living so long in the woods without carrying provisions with them, the exceeding quickness with which they can march to distant parts, and above all, the dexterity to which they have arrived in the use of the Rifle Gun. Their is not one of these Men who wish a distance less than 200 yards or a larger object than an Orange —Every shot is fatal."[28]

That Washington made good use of these soldiers goes almost without saying. Wherever light infantry was needed, they, under his orders, were generally present. Scarcely had Morgan arrived in Cambridge before he was sent off with

Arnold on an invasion of Canada. There were few important battles of the Revolution in which frontiersmen did not function more or less effectively. This was certainly true of Saratoga, where Morgan and his Virginia neighbor, Horatio Gates, each commanding Virginia riflemen, played important, yes, decisive rôles. This was true also of Cowpens, of King's Mountain, and of still other engagements.

Washington's appreciation of these soldiers was evidenced by the numerous trusts reposed in them, but he had a sentimental attachment, as well as a feeling of security, for the mountains and valleys whence they came. These sentiments manifested themselves in various ways and on various occasions but never more strikingly than in 1776, following his retreat beyond the Delaware. He was then said to have been in despair and to have contemplated the necessity of finding a temporary retreat beyond the reach of his pursuers. In reply to a discouraging remark from Colonel Joseph Reed regarding the possibility of such a course, Washington said: "We must retire to Augusta County in Virginia. Numbers will be obliged to repair to us for safety; and we must try what we can do in carrying on a predatory war; and if overpowered we must cross the Alleghany Mountains."[29]

Another manifestation of the same sentiment came near the close of the war. In reply to a call for volunteers, Mrs. William Lewis of Augusta County, Virginia, had permitted her remaining sons of seventeen, fifteen, and thirteen years, respectively, to join the Continental army with the injunction, "Go, my children. I spare not my youngest, my fair haired boy, the comfort of my declining years." When this incident was related to Washington he is reported to have exclaimed: "Leave me but a banner to place upon the mountains of Augusta, and I will rally around me the men who will lift our bleeding country from the dust, and set her free!"[30]

Throughout the Revolution Washington's time was "so constantly taken up and engrossed by public matters" that he scarcely bestowed a thought on his private affairs and his "business . . . West of the Alleghanies." It will be recalled that his efforts to perfect titles to western lands had resulted in abortive failures. Plans for new commonwealths west of the Alleghenies followed, and there was always the possibility that "some new revolution . . . in our political system" would put to naught plans for recouping his declining resources by selling or removing to his western lands. In September, 1775, he asked Thomas Everard of Virginia to take charge of his interests on the Great Kanawha River.[31] Nothing coming of this, they were mentioned from time to time in letters to others, and October, 1778, General Andrew Lewis was asked regarding the possibility of perfecting new land titles. But more significant still was a statement of the same date to the effect that Washington had not had time to think about his western holdings.[32]

Despite this indifference and neglect, in 1779 certain Britishers looked upon Washington as being primarily a western land speculator. He was accused of having tricked Dunmore into granting land titles to which Washington's claims were still questionable. As proof of his large holdings in the West, his land advertisements of 1773 were called into evidence. In these matters he was pictured by the Reverend Bennett Allen, M.A., in the *London Morning Post* for June 7, 1779, as being: "Ambitious, with the fairest professions of moderation, and avaritious under the most specious appearance of disinterestedness—particularly eager in engrossing large tracts of land, though he has no family, but by a widow lady of fortune he married, who bore children by a former husband." His holdings on the Ohio were placed at two hundred thousand acres which, it was claimed, he purchased from army and militia officers "for a trifle," and then procured "an order of the council of Virginia to extend the proclamation of 1763 to the Provincials employed in the last war."[33]

Although this characterization was wide of the truth, leisure alone was all that was needed to arouse Washington's latent interest in western lands. This leisure came while he was stationed at Newburg pending the final peace negotiations leading to American independence. While thus detained he made a horseback trip of three weeks through the present state of New York. On this journey he traversed practically the entire length of the Mohawk River, incidentally seeing Lakes Champlain, George, and Oneida. As a result of observations made on this trip he pointed out the commercial advantages of the Mohawk Valley and located choice lands which he and George Clinton later acquired to the amount of six thousand acres.[34]

Whatever may be said of Washington's interest in western lands, his chief concern during the period of actual fighting for independence was in their defense. On his way to Cambridge he took steps looking to the protection of New York and New England against back door attacks. Expressing in a formal address the expectation that Canadians were "capable of distinguishing between the blessings of liberty, and the wretchedness of slavery," he invited them to rally to the "cause of America" and informed them that "the grand American congress have sent an army into your province, . . . not to plunder but to protect you."[35]

In these appeals and assurances Washington shows little knowledge of the Canadians. Unlike him they did not care about the Quebec Act, and their comparative inexperience with democratic institutions rendered them impervious to appeals involving academic questions of taxation and representation. Later a great number of loyalists sought refuge in Canada, and through their influence the Canadians remained loyal to the British Empire. Consequently their country became a base of rear attacks upon the revolting colonies.

While giving every possible aid in concentrating frontier militia about Saratoga, thus making possible the successes that followed there under the leadership of his fellow Virginians, Gates and Morgan, Washington was somewhat chagrined because of the comparisons which followed, particularly those involving himself and the hero, Gates. Simultaneously Washington had been losing important engagements to General Howe, as a consequence of which his critics would have superseded him by the new hero. To this movement Washington paid little attention, but, confidentially, he brought to the attention of his friend, Landon Carter, some pertinent observations. Among these was the fact that "The northern army, ... was reinforced by upwards of twelve hundred militia, who shut the only door by which Burgoyne could retreat, and cut off all his supplies." Nor did Washington hesitate to call Carter's attention to his own "case," saying[36] "The disaffection of a great part of the inhabitants of this State [Pennsylvania], the languor of others, and the internal distractions of the whole, have been among the great and insuperable difficulties, which I have met with, and have contributed not a little to my embarrassments this campaign." He was willing, however, to trust the outcome to a "superintending Providence."

From the beginning of hostilities one of the most trying frontier problems was that of the Iroquois. They occupied a strategic area in western New York, the control of which, through their loyalty to the English, had been an important, possibly a determining, factor in century-old encounters with the French. True to their traditions most Iroquois remained loyal to the British and persisted in fighting their enemies. The consequences were menacing, and there was a possibility of their proving fatal. Accordingly, in 1779, Washington sent General John Sullivan with instructions to remedy the situation at all costs. With the coöperation of Colonel Daniel Brodhead stationed at Fort Pitt, Sullivan marched against the Iroquois by way of the Susquehanna River and effected a destruction wellnigh complete. Iroquois warriors were killed, their wives and children were dispatched in a ruthless manner, and their crops and villages were destroyed. Of the success of this expedition and its consequences Washington on October 20, 1779, wrote General Lafayette predicting that Sullivan's victory over the Iroquois, together with the simultaneous defeat of Mingo and Muncey tribes on the Allegheny River, would be "productive of great good; as they are undeniable proofs to them, that Great Britain can not protect them and that it is in our power to chastise them, whenever their hostile conduct deserves it."[37]

Sullivan's success against the Iroquois not only furthered the cause of independence but also enhanced Washington's prestige among them. Formerly the "destroyer of villages," he now became the destroyer of peoples. Eleven years later he was addressed in the Federal capital by Iroquois chieftains as "the Great Counsellor in whose heart and wise mind all of the *thirteen fires* have placed their wisdom." At the same time he was told that "to this day, when your name is heard, our women look behind them and turn pale, and our children cling close to the necks of their mothers."[38] The defeat of the Iroquois was a retaliation in kind for their atrocities in the Wyoming and Cherry valleys.

During the Revolution, Fort Pitt was the key to the Ohio Valley, but during the first three years of hostilities while the Indians continued to keep their peace treaties,[39] Washington paid little or no attention to the frontier defense. In May, 1778, he confessed that he did "not know particularly what the objects are, which Congress have in contemplation in this [Upper Ohio] command."[40] Previous thereto he had relied upon militia as being "from inclination as well as ability, peculiarly adapted"[41] to withstand sporadic Indian attacks, and daring and brilliant achievements of individual militiamen were accordingly rewarded by promotions and otherwise. For example, for transporting gunpowder from New Orleans to forts on the upper Ohio George Gibson was made a colonel in the Continental Army.

Available sources do not indicate Washington's possible and probable interest and tacit participation in George Rogers Clark's expedition for the conquest of the Northwest Territory. It was secretly planned by Patrick Henry, Clark, and others as a Virginia enterprise, but Washington knew about it. This conceded, it is a reasonable inference that the Sullivan expedition may have been "an effort to push the northwestern frontier nearer in line to Clark's conquest." Furthermore, as has been observed: "It is hardly possible . . . that his [Washington's] vision of the future of the western country did not have some weight in the decision to send out Sullivan's expedition. . . . The liberty of America was his thought and not victory for his own army alone."[42]

With the resumption of Indian hostilities throughout the Trans-Allegheny in 1777, and the Tory exodus thence to Canada in the following year,[43] it became necessary for Congress to give attention to frontier defense. Later the situation was complicated by Spanish designs upon the Trans-Allegheny and French connivance with Spanish plans for conquest, but despite these and other menaces Washington's choices of commanders for the Fort Pitt post were not always wise. General Edward Hand, the first commandant and a former resident, was too closely identified with the situation to avoid its entanglements.[44] "After much consideration" Washington, May 12, 1778, named General Lachlan McIntosh, a Georgian, to succeed Hand, but McIntosh knew too little about conditions to avoid intrigues.[45] Consequently he too, after less than a year's service, was recalled, but not before he had made a formidable showing against hostile Indians in what is now the state of Ohio, and not before he had carried the cause of independence in the Ohio Valley to its zenith. Although Washington could not understand the demands for McIntosh's recall, those making them were persistent, and Washington was practically forced to yield.

Under the control of Colonel Daniel Brodhead, successor to McIntosh, the military situation in and about Fort Pitt gradually became impossible. Covetous, intriguing, and accused of corruption, Brodhead was unable to coöperate with others. Under Washington's directions he did make an effective attack upon Indian enemies residing upon the upper Allegheny, thus preventing them from joining the Iroquois, when they were attacked by General Sullivan. Because of this and minor successes, together with Clark's victories on the lower Ohio, a number of Indian treaties were concluded in and around Fort Pitt in 1780; as a consequence the Americans gained control of the Indian situation along the entire Ohio frontier. Taking advantage of this opportunity, plans for attacking Detroit were revived and the possibility of dislodging the British from the lower Mississippi was also suggested, the objective being Natchez.

The proposed attack upon Natchez is informing not only because of the light it throws upon the scope of frontier operations, but also because of Washington's reactions. While not discouraging the undertaking "altogether," he did not hesitate to point out its difficulties. First and most important of all was the possibility of a counterattack upon Fort Pitt in the temporary absence of its defenders. Then too, no one among available leaders for the proposed enterprise understood the situation at Natchez, and finally, in the event of failure, Washington indicated that the return trip "against the current" would be difficult, exposing those making it to Indian attacks. He advised, however, that preparations looking to such an adventure be continued.[46]

Washington looked with greater favor upon the proposed attack upon Detroit. That frontier outpost then occupied a position relevant to the American Revolutionary frontier similar to that of Fort Duquesne during the greater part of the French and Indian War. As then, Washington was now in favor of removing "the cause." To this end, while not surrendering the prerogatives of Congress, he was willing to coöperate with the State of Virginia and offered assistance to George Rogers Clark, whom he did not know personally, for an attack upon Detroit. Stating that he had "ever had in view" the proposed attack and that he had wished "to carry [it] into execution by a Continental force," Washington, December 29, 1780, bespoke for the undertaking Brodhead's "countenance and assistance," and ordered him to turn over to Clark certain supplies which Governor Jefferson had requested. Even in the event of failure Washington was persuaded that "this most desirable object" would result in "much good" by creating "a diversion and giving the enemy employ[ment] in their own country."[47]

Despite these favorable harbingers and the prestige of its leader, the Detroit expedition came to naught. Shortly after it was launched the faithful Delawares went on the warpath; from beginning to end the expedition had the covert opposition of Brodhead; and meanwhile Washington and Congress became absorbed in common efforts to defend the South, where the British were trying to "roll up the scroll" and thus to end the Revolution to their advantage. As a result the West was again neglected; Clark was unable to collect a sufficient force for the Detroit expedition; and conditions in the upper Ohio Valley became demoralized. As has been truthfully said: "With all the Indian nations arrayed in complete hostility, with the army of defence honeycombed with dishonesty and intrigue, with discredit and discontent rife among the inhabitants, even the Herculean efforts of Clark were insufficient to restore the morale of the frontier."[48]

For his part in these developments, in November, 1781, Colonel Brodhead was superseded by Brigadier General William Irvine, and Colonel John Gibson was entrusted with the command at Fort Pitt during the short interim. Irvine found conditions there in a "wretched state"; troops presented a deplorable, even despicable figure; "indeed," said Irvine, "no man would believe from their appearance that they were soldiers; nay, it would be difficult to determine whether they were *white men.*" So hopeless was the situation that Irvine recommended the removal of the principal post on the upper Ohio from Fort Pitt to Chartier's Creek,[49] where Washington owned a considerable estate.

Although Irvine was able to effect a measure of rehabilitation in military conditions at Fort Pitt, his commander-in-chief could not forget the result of the Detroit expedition. Because it was undertaken with militia he was not surprised at its failure, but he was nevertheless sorry and convinced that the possession or destruction of that post was "the only means of giving peace and security to the western frontier." When the states had filled "up their regular battalions," he hoped for greater success.[50]

From the military standpoint conditions on the Ohio did not

improve greatly during the ensuing months. At the instance of Washington, Fort Pitt was reënforced and put in condition for defense, and for a time another attack upon Detroit was contemplated. From such an adventure Irvine hoped for "at least temporary ease to this country," but in time all thought of such an undertaking was given up. Even Washington approved this course, giving as his reasons the savage resentment produced by such excursions. An expedition against Sandusky had proved unsuccessful, fifty men losing their lives, among them Washington's friend and former surveyor, Colonel William Crawford, who in 1782, was burned at the stake;[51] the Moravian Indians on the Tuscarawas River in what is now the state of Ohio, were almost completely annihilated; and September 10, 1782, a second attack was made upon Fort Henry, now Wheeling, West Virginia, which proved all but successful. As a result of these developments Irvine concluded that "if this post [Fort Pitt] was evacuated, the bounds of Canada would be extended to the Laurel Hill in a few weeks."[52]

Thus at the termination of the Revolution, American frontier conditions were anything but favorable or creditable to the Americans. Everywhere north of the Ohio River, Indians were in hostile array; the Illinois was practically abandoned by Americans; Spain was in possession of lands along the Mississippi; the British had designs upon the Northwest Territory; and some states had not yet surrendered their claims to that coveted region and to other lands westward of the Alleghenies.

Although Washington may not have appreciated the full significance of this situation in its earlier phases, the refusal of the British to surrender posts in the Northwest Territory pending final peace negotiations aroused his suspicions. Acting under directions from Congress, in the summer of 1783, he named Baron Steuben a special commissioner to arrange for the transfer of these posts,[53] but the British, while treating Steuben politely, refused to negotiate to that end, even to permit him to visit the posts. In August, 1783, their assigned reason for this course was that peace had not been formally concluded. This action was in line with Washington's prediction of a year earlier to the effect that there would be *"no posts* to occupy," and as American traders penetrating the Northwest in the summer, encountered hostile Indians everywhere, he concluded they were being bribed and estranged by artful Britishers. This was true, and thus was laid the setting for another chapter of American history.

CHAPTER X

IN THE CRITICAL PERIOD

As A RESULT of the treaties acknowledging American independence, the United States secured all the territory westward of the Allegheny Mountains to the Mississippi River, between the northern boundary of Florida and a line passing centrally through the Great Lakes. Already effective in binding the states together in the Articles of Confederation and Perpetual Union, this domain continued to be a bond of union and became the touchstone of public policy. It was therefore largely because of his continued interest in the West that Washington was able to retain in peace that preëminence which he won in war. Thus the late Herbert B. Adams, in one of the most singular tributes ever paid by scholar to soldier and statesman, could say: "It would seem as though all lines of our public policy lead back to Washington as all roads lead to Rome."[1]

When they first acquired a public domain, the United States had difficulty to determine what to do with it. In September, 1783, when the Treaty of Paris was concluded, practically all claimant states had signified intention to cede their western lands to the Federal government.[2] As a consequence the solution of its territorial problems became imperative.

It was at this juncture that Washington formulated "the first definite *plan* for the formation of new States in the West," a service sometimes attributed to Thomas Jefferson. Together with a practical suggestion with reference to an Indian policy, Washington's plan was set forth in a letter to James Duane, chairman of the Congressional Committee on Indian Affairs. It provided for the formation of two new states, in shape and location resembling the present Ohio and Michigan. This general suggestion was adopted by Congress, October 15, 1783, "almost word for word"³ and later became the basis for the organization of the Northwest Territory.

Whatever Washington's post-Revolutionary solicitude for the American Indians may have been, it was not "consistent with the ease and tranquillity" to which he meant to devote the remainder of his life, to take an active and responsible part in effecting their civilization by spreading Christianity among them.⁴ This decision he made known to the Countess of Huntington, who sought to enlist his active service in this work. Evincing an entirely different attitude from that of French and Indian War days, when he regarded no Indian good but a dead Indian, Washington commended the plan of her Ladyship for settling Christian immigrants here and there among Indian Tribes as a means of advancing their civilization. In this plan he saw not only "humanity and charity" but also, and possibly more important to him, a means to "valuable political purposes" particularly the extension of the power and influence of the Confederation Congress. He therefore advised his friend, Richard Henry Lee, to suggest to the Countess that, instead of looking to the several states for suitable settlement sites, she should turn to Congress.⁵

At the close of the Revolution, Washington owned approximately 58,000 acres of land beyond the Alleghenies,⁶ 4695 acres of which were in Southwestern Pennsylvania, 9744 along the Ohio River, and 43,466 in the Great Kanawha Valley. His Ohio River lands were distributed as follows: 587 acres at "Round Bottom" a short distance below the present site of Moundsville, West Virginia; 2314 acres at "Washington Bottom" on the Ohio River below the mouth of the little Kanawha River; 2448 acres at or near the present site of Ravenswood, West Virginia; and 4395 acres a short distance below, at what is now Millwood. Beginning about three miles above its mouth, his Great Kanawha acreage extended along the meanderings of that stream, in some places on both sides, "from half a mile to a mile back" for a distance of approximately forty miles. It included 10,990 acres in what is now Mason County; 7276 acres in Putnam; and 2000 at St. Albans, 2950 at Dunbar, and a half interest in 250 acres at the Burning Spring, Kanawha County. His Pennsylvania holdings consisted of 2800 acres on Miller's Run near what is now Canonsburg; 1661 acres at Perryopolis on the Youghiogheny River; and 234 acres embracing the former site of Fort Necessity.

The larger part of these lands were still the domain of the forest primeval; the remainder were occupied by "squatters" and poor superintendents. Under the care of that "confounded fellow Simpson,"[7] Washington's mill at Perryopolis, one of the first west of the Alleghenies, had fallen into decay, and suits were being brought and others threatened to test the validity of his land titles. To give these matters personal attention, Washington in 1784 made another journey to the Trans-Allegheny.[8]

The major purpose of this visit did not, however, have to do directly with personal affairs, as some have supposed. Since 1769 Washington had been interested in the improved navigation of the Potomac River. In 1772, he had fathered the enactment of a law by the Virginia Assembly for that purpose and, when he left home for Cambridge in 1775, this improvement was in "a tolerable good train" and would have been in "an excellent way" but for the opposition it had encountered from certain Baltimore merchants interested in possible consequences to their city. Other jealousies had been removed by including the James River in the general plan of improvement, which, in 1784, embraced also the Ohio River and the two Kanawha rivers.[9]

With Thomas Jefferson, Washington believed "that not a moment ought to be lost in recommencing this business [the Potomac improvement]." He well knew that "the Yorkers will delay no time to remove every obstacle in the way of the other communication, so soon as the posts of Oswego and Niagara are surrendered."[10] He predicted also that they would build vessels for the navigation of the lakes, eliminating the coast traffic.[11] Thus it was as a promoter of internal improvement enterprises, the completion of which has since challenged the best engineering talent of America, that the "Father of his Country" visited the Trans-Allegheny for the sixth and last time.[12]

On this mission Washington left Mount Vernon, September 1, 1784, two days after General Lafayette had ended a two weeks visit with him. Again Washington was accompanied by his friend, neighbor, and physician, Dr. James Craik, who alone received a written invitation to make the trip, but as finally constituted, the party included also Washington's nephew, Bushrod Washington; William Craik, son of the doctor; and servants. As usual they traveled horseback, going this time by way of Leesburg, Snicker's Gap, Charles Town, Bath, and Old Town, to Cumberland. Because of the experience of their leader, they traveled light, taking, among other things, only a marquee, camp utensils, a few stores, medicines, hooks and lines.[13]

As commander-in-chief of the Revolutionary armies, in a region renowned for its patriotism and patriots, Washington was greeted with marked distinction on his way into the interior; bevies of friends, sometimes including relatives, awaited him here and there; and his journey was thus more eventful than it would otherwise have been. His first stop of importance was with his brother, Charles Washington, at "Happy Retreat" in Jefferson County, Virginia. Here, possibly by appointment, he met his cousin, Warner Washington, Ralph Wormley, General Daniel Morgan, and "many other Gentlemen."

Having finished his business with his tenants residing within reach of his brother, "so far at least as partial payments could put a close to it," and having provided a wagon for the transportation of his baggage thence to the Warm Springs, now Berkeley Springs, Morgan County, West Virginia, the extreme heat having caused his horses "to Rub and gaul," Washington reached the Springs the following day, September 5. Here he "was showed the Model of a Boat constructed by the ingenious Mr. Rumsey, for ascending rapid currents by mechanism."[14] Later he engaged this same "ingenious Rumsey" to build a dwelling house, a kitchen, and a stable upon his lots in the town of Bath. Thence he reached Cumberland, September 10, having stopped meanwhile to visit a tract of his land near the Springs. From the outset of this journey Washington showed far greater interest in internal improvement projects than in his own affairs. At Happy Retreat he learned from General Morgan that Berkeley, Frederick, and Hampshire counties would contribute "freely towards the extension of the Navigation of the Potomack; as well as towards opening a Road from East to West."[15]

On the way from Happy Retreat to Bath, Washington met Captain Stroads, "an intelligent man, who had been several times in the Western Country." With him Washington "held much conversation," as a result of which he gained additional information regarding approaches between the eastern and western waters and what was possibly his first suggestion regarding the possibility of connecting waters of the Monongahela with those of the Little Kanawha River, by a route wholly within the state of Virginia. This suggestion came indirectly from Captain Thomas Swearingen, and, although its possibilities were exaggerated, Washington reverted to them from time to time on this trip and subsequently.

From Fort Cumberland, Washington journeyed directly to Simpson's on the Youghiogheny, passing enroute the Great Meadows which, in the fourteen years since he had last seen them, had become "a very good stand for a Tavern." Thence in crossing the mountains he met "numbers of Persons and Pack horses going in with Ginseng; and for Salt and other articles at the Markets below." Arrived at Simpson's (Perryopolis), Washington first visited his mill and his several "tenements," all of which were disappointing. The mill was almost a wreck, and the tenements were in poor repair and improvement. As a consequence he was unable to sell the moiety of his "Co-partnership Stock" on the day appointed for that purpose, or even to get a bid on the mill, and that too, despite the fact that "many People were gathered," as Washington thought "more out of curiosity . . . than from other motives."[16] Finally, despairing of a "chance to get a good offer in money, for Rent," he leased the Simpson estate for five hundred bushels of wheat, payable annually at any place in the County he or his agents might direct. While not wholly satisfactory, this arrangement terminated the annoying and unprofitable partnership with Simpson. Upon terms to be inserted in future instructions, Washington then engaged Major James Freeman as superintendent of his "business over the Mountains."

In the week spent at Simpson's Washington made many contacts and gathered much information regarding conditions on the frontier. Squatters from his Miller's Run lands visited him in an attempt to establish their "fair and upright" intentions, and officers from Fort Pitt "confirmed reports of the discontented temper of the Indians and the Mischiefs done by some parties of them" in an effort to prevent white settlements north of the Ohio River. Indians were reported also to have attacked the Kentucky settlements and "a Party who had driven cattle to Detroit." For this reason Washington decided not to continue his "intended trip to the Great Kanawha."[17] Unable to get "a satisfactory acct. of the Navigation of the Cheat River, . . . nor any acct. of the distance and kind of Country between that, . . . and the Waters of Potomack—nor of the Country between the Little Kanawha and the Waters of the Monongahela," he resolved to return the way he came, or by "what is commonly called the Turkey foot Road."

On his Miller's Run lands, which he reached September 18, Washington encountered a trying situation. A large portion of these lands had been taken over by a Scotch-Irish sect of "Ceceders" whose *apparently* very religious" attitude was such that Washington did not suggest business matters to them on the Sunday following his arrival on Saturday. These people, living in log dwellings with "punchion" roofs, and with their more commodious barns and stables at no great distance, were bound together by common hardships and common religious principles into a sort of coöperative settlement and were unwilling "to separate or remove." Although he did not then wish to sell the lands occupied by them, their representations were such that Washington offered "the whole tract at 25 S[hillings] per Acre, the money to be paid at 3 annual payments with Interest," or he would have taken them as tenants of "999 year" leases at an annual rental of ten pounds per hundred acres. After a long consultation upon the former proposition both were declined by the "Ceceders" who, in true frontier fashion, resolved "to stand suit, and abide the Issue of the Law."[18]

After another visit to Simpson's, where he gave Major Freeman final instructions regarding the conduct of his business west of the mountains and made preparations for his return home, requesting Dr. Craik and his son William to return by way of the Turkey Foot Road "to make a more minute enquiry into the Navigation of Yohiogany Waters," Washington went to Beason Town, now Uniontown, Pennsylvania, to engage a lawyer to bring ejectment proceedings against the defiant settlers on his Miller's Run lands. While in Beason Town, he received information regarding the possibilities of connecting the navigable waters of the Monongahela with those of the Little Kanawha, and those of Cheat with those of the Potomac, which caused him again to change his plans for his return trip to the East. Still hopeful of finding a practical route of intercommunication between the eastern and western waters, wholly within the state of Virginia, he decided to explore Cheat River and to continue thence home by a route to the southward of the Turkey Foot Road.

In pursuance of this plan Washington left Beason Town, September 23, 1784, going direct to Colonel Theophilus Philips's sixteen miles distant, where he spent the night, near the mouth of Cheat River in the then county seat of Monongalia County, Virginia. In crossing this stream the following morning he was struck by its dark color which he readily attributed to the laurel, "among which it rises"; but he did not tarry. Thence, by way of the dividing ridge between Cheat and Monongahela rivers, he went directly to the office of Cap-

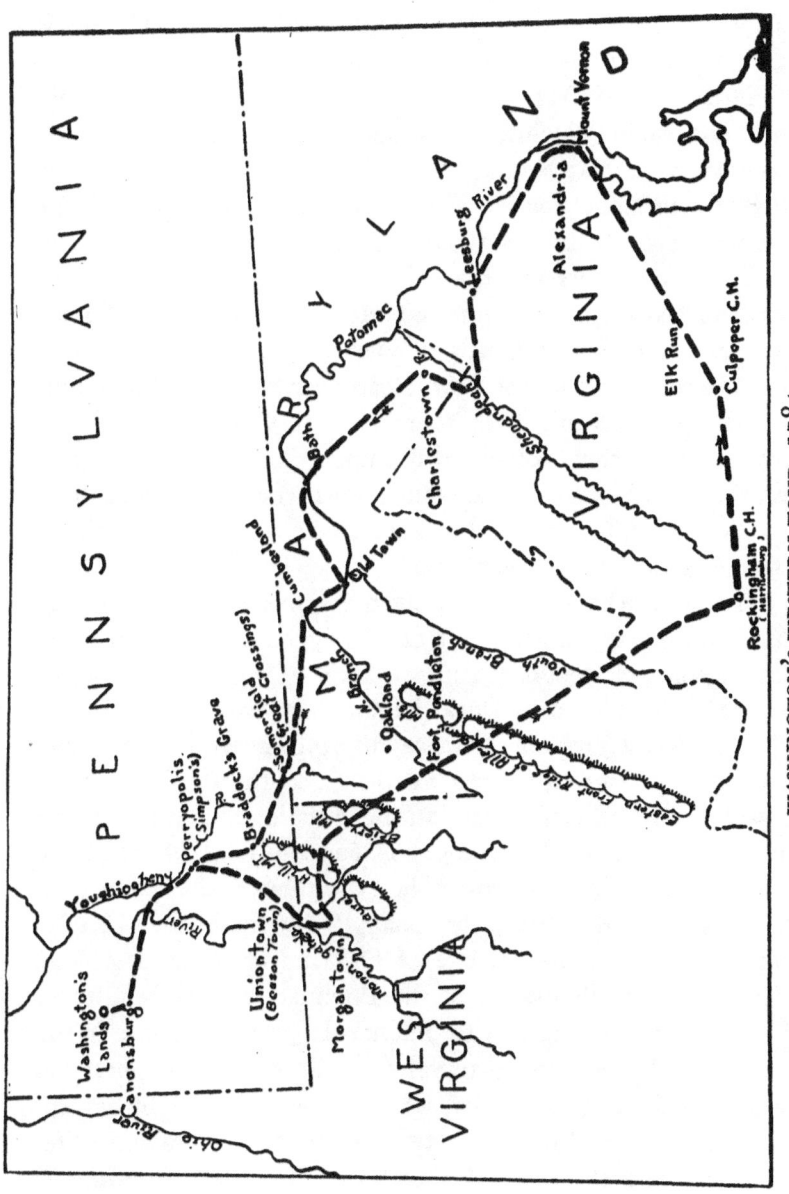

WASHINGTON'S WESTERN TOUR, 1784
From a drawing by Robert Merricks

tain Samuel Hanway, surveyor of Monongalia County. This office was at Peirpoint's on the present road between Ice's Ferry and Morgantown about five miles from the latter.

Here Zackquill Morgan, founder of the city which bears his name, and others, including Captain Hanway, discussed with Washington, at his request, many phases of inland navigation and intercommunication.[19] From them he learned that there were three routes between the region of the Cheat and the Youghiogheny rivers and that of the upper Potomac. One of these, the "New Road," connected Morgantown by way of Ice's Ferry and the Sandy Creek Glades with Braddock's Road; another branched from the New Road near Bruceton Mills, and followed McCulloch's Path to the North Branch of the Potomac; and the third connected the upper Tygart Valley River, near the present site of Clarksburg, with the North Branch at Fort Pendleton by way of Dunkard Bottom, one of the oldest settlements on Cheat River.

As none of these routes followed the meanderings of Cheat River, which was reported obstructed beyond Dunkard Bottom, Washington recrossed it at Andrew Ice's Ferry, going thence in an easterly direction over Cheat Mountain to what is now Bruceton Mills, West Virginia. Thence, in company with his nephew, Bushrod Washington, he proceeded in a southeasterly direction by way of McCulloch's Path, an old buffalo trail, through the sunny glades of the Youghiogheny (on the edge of which he spent the rainy night of September 25, without shelter other than his cloak), across Briery or Snaggy Mountain by Charles Friend's, near the present site of Oakland, Maryland, almost direct to the North Branch of the Potomac at Fort Pendleton, where he spent the night with Thomas Logston. Thence in the same general direction he traveled to Fort Pleasant upon the South Branch of the Potomac, where he spent the night of September 28, and the following day in the home of Abraham Hite, conversing with the Hites, Colonel John Neville, and others.[20]

Meanwhile, Washington had missed no opportunity to determine the general lay of the land and to gather other useful information. As a result, he was forced to the conclusion that some of the accounts given him had to be received with "great caution." This was particularly true "in the article of Roads; which (where they have been marked) seem calculated more to promote individual interest, than the public good."[21] Then as now, residents hoped that projected roads would pass by or near their doors, likely tavern sites being to them what service station and tourist camp sites are to present day landowners.

On the South Branch Washington again changed his plans for his homeward trip. Thence he was to have joined Dr. Craik at Colonel Warner Washington's near Charles Town, but finding that it would take only one day longer, he decided to go by the home of Thomas Lewis near Rockingham Court House, now Harrisonburg, Virginia. From Lewis, Washington hoped to get papers needed to prosecute ejectments of those who had settled on his Miller's Run lands in Pennsylvania and "a more distinct acct. of the communication between Jackson's River and the green Brier." Accordingly his nephew was sent to apprise the faithful Dr. Craik of Washington's change of plans, and September 29, accompanied by Captain Hite, Washington set out for Lewis's. Going by way of Roudebush's and Brock's Gap, he reached his destination the following day about sundown.

Washington's *Diary* for this period throws no light upon the immediate purpose of this side trip, but it is profuse regarding new possibilities for connecting and improving the eastern and western waters. With Gabriel Jones, a leading lawyer of the Shenandoah Valley and for a long time counsel for Lord Fairfax, Washington "had a good deal of conversation . . . on the Waters, and trade of the Western Country; and particularly with respect to the Navigation of the Great Kanawha and its communication with James and Roanoke Rivers." Although Mr. Lewis did not agree with them, thinking it possible to improve the New River and thus connect the headwaters of the Great Kanawha with those of the James, Jones confirmed Washington's conclusion "that the easiest and best communication between the Eastern and Western Waters is from the North branch of Potomack to Yohiogany or Cheat River; and ultimately that the Trade between the two Countries will settle in this Channel."[22] Thus to Washington, more perhaps than to any other person, may be given chief credit for seeing the trade possibilities of the general route now followed by the Baltimore and Ohio Railroad and the National Road.

"Having travelled on the same horses since the first day of September by the computed distances 680 Miles," Washington reached Mount Vernon, October 4, and at once committed to his *Diary* "Reflections" upon his journey, with which, notwithstanding his disappointment in being unable "to examine into the situation quality and advantages" of his lands upon the Ohio and the Great Kanawha rivers, then occupied by squatters and offered for sale in Philadelphia and in Europe by jobbers, he was well pleased. In the Shenandoah and South Branch rivers he discovered adequate water transportation "for all that fertile Country between the blue ridge and the Alligany Mountains." But immense and important as this area and its transportation were, Washington considered them "trifling when viewed upon that immeasurable scale," embracing the Ohio and the Great Lakes region. After indicating distances between Detroit and Alexandria, Richmond, Philadelphia, and New York, distances between Detroit and Alexandria being given for a route passing through Virginia and for another by way of Pittsburgh, Washington's exposition of the needs for and the benefits to be derived from an improvement of inland transportation, contained the highest order of statesmanship and patriotism. In this he set a goal that has never been fully attained, but in the proposed Lake Erie and Ohio Deep Water Canal and in the improved transportation of the Ohio River, this goal is more eagerly and confidently sought than ever before.

Other points of Washington's Reflections are worth while and in themselves would entitle their author to a place among American statesmen. Their chief concern was for the inhabitants of "the Western Country" immediately back of "the middle States," or in other words in the Ohio Valley. Flanked as these people were by enemies and detached from the East by mountain barriers, Washington saw that they stood "on a pivot" and that "the touch of a feather" would incline them almost any way. Accentuating this condition was their comparative freedom from labor and care, a condition made possible by the fact that their lands produced luxuriantly and that their surplus of flour could sometimes be marketed on the lower Mississippi at high prices. Without considering the tediousness of the return voyage or the time necessary to perform it, they floated to these markets as light-heartedly as they lived, but fortunately for the Union and for the settlers themselves, the Spaniards had "at times shut their ports against them altogether" and were at other times threatening.[23]

Washington's remedy for this situation was improved intercommunication between the East and the West. By extending inland navigation as far as possible and crossing portages by improved roads, he would have demonstrated to the western settlers "how easy it is to bring produce of their lands to our markets" to the great advantage of the country at large. In this way he would have dried up Spanish sources of trade; or if any part of that from the western settlements should continue to flow "down the Mississippi, from the Falls of the Ohio, in Vessels which may be built—fitted for the Sea—and sold with their Cargoes," he hoped at least to divert the proceeds "this way." As these settlements were already important and would in the future be composed largely of foreigners "who can have no predilection for us," Washington urged the necessity of immediate action, the more effectively to counteract the habit-forming influences of trade, which he regarded as almost unalterable. Great as were these considerations from an economic viewpoint, Washington regarded their political advantages as of "much greater importance."

Washington believed "a combination of circumstances" made "the present juncture more favorable than any other to fix the trade of the Western Country to our Markets." In the "jealous and untoward disposition of the Spaniards on the one side, and the private views of some individuals coinciding with the policy of the Court of G[reat] Britain on the other, to retain the Posts of Oswego, Niagara, Detroit," he saw an opportunity for Virginia to open her arms and bring the western settlements within her embrace. "The way is plain," said he, "and the expence, comparitively speaking deserves not a thought, so great would be the prize. The Western Inhabitants would do their part towards accomplishing it, weak as they now are, they would, I am persuaded meet us half way rather than be *driven* into the arms of, or be in any wise dependent upon, foreigners; the consequence of which would be, a seperation, or a War."[24]

In reply to arguments then being made that "the most direct Routs from the Lakes to the Navigation of Potomack are through the State of Pennsylvania" and that she would oppose an improvement by way of the Monongahela and Youghiogheny rivers, Washington answered that an application for this purpose, the proposed route by Cheat River proving impracticable, would place the legislature of the Pennsylvania Commonwealth in a very delicate situation. Admitting that such a proposition could not be wholly pleasing, he could not "readily conceive" that it would be rejected. On this point he continued:

"There is in that State, at least 100,000 Souls West of the Laurel hill, who are groaning under the inconveniences of a long land transportation. They are wishing, indeed looking, for the extension of inland Navigation; and if this can not be made easy for them to Philadelphia . . . they will seek a Mart elsewhere; and none is so convenient as that which offers itself through Yohiogany or Cheat River. . . . The certain consequence therefore of an attempt to restrain the extension of the Navigation of these Rivers, . . . or to impose any extra duties upon the exports, or imports, to or from another State, would be a seperation of the Western Settlers from the old and more interior government."[25]

Rumsey's discovery for "working boats against stream, by mechanical powers principally,"[26] a demonstration of which

Washington had witnessed at Bath only a few weeks previously, made a lasting impression on him. Upon his return to Mount Vernon he predicted that it "may not only be considered as a fortunate invention for these States in general," but that it would also be "one of those circumstances which have combined to render the present epoche favorable above all others for securing . . . a large portion of the produce of the Western Settlements, and of the Fur and Peltry of the Lakes." Accordingly, he regarded the economic and political importance of such an invention as "immense."

In the spirit of the foregoing "Reflections," and sometimes in their exact words, Washington set about at once following his return from the West, to interest fellow Virginians in the transportation needs and possibilities of that region and in the routes leading thereto. His letter of October 10, 1784, to Governor Benjamin Harrison on these subjects was admittedly "so much more explicit" than any Harrison could have written that he submitted it to the assembly with his approval and commendation. The legislators received the communication with such favor that it at once took rank among the most valuable Virginia state papers. More than anything else it set in motion those activities which resulted in her incorporation of the James River and the Potomac improvement companies. The difficulties encountered in the general situation, together with reasons for the two companies, were set forth in Washington's letter to Governor Harrison:

> The first and principal one is, the *unfortunate jealousy*, which ever has, and it is to be feared ever will prevail, lest one part [Potomac] of the State should obtain an advantage over the other parts, as if the benefits of the trade were not diffusive and beneficial to all. Then follows a train of difficulties, namely, that our people are already heavily taxed; that we have no money; that the advantages of this trade are remote; that the most direct route for it is through other States, over which we have no control; that the routes over which we have control are as distant as either of those which lead to Philadelphia, Albany, or Montreal; that a sufficient spirit of com-

merce does not prevade the citizens of this commonwealth; and that we are in fact doing for others, what they ought to do for themselves.[27]

Urging the reasonableness of Virginia's doing her part "towards opening the communication for the fur and peltry trade of the Lakes," and for the produce of the intervening country, which he predicted would "be settled faster than any other ever was, or any one could imagin," when once Congress had settled Indian matters and terms for disposing of public lands, Washington indicated the following advantages to be derived from an improved transportation between inland America and the Atlantic seaboard:

Without going into the investigation of a question, which has employed the pens of able politicians, namely, whether trade with foreigners is an advantage or disadvantage to a country, this State, as a part of the confederated States, all of which have the spirit of it very strongly working within them, must adopt it or submit to the evils arising therefrom without receiving its benefits. Common policy, therefore, points clearly and strongly to the propriety of our enjoying all the advantages, which nature and our local situation afford us; and evinces clearly, that, unless this spirit could be totally eradicated in other States as well as in this, and every man be made to become either a cultivator of the land or a manufacturer of such articles as are prompted by necessity, such stimulus should be employed as will *force* this spirit, by showing to our countrymen the superior advantages we possess beyond others, and the importance of being upon an equal footing with our neighbors.[28]

Meanwhile Washington had demonstrated something of the accuracy of his vision and the depth of his patrotism by taking the country at large into his confidence. This was accomplished in a letter of December 14, 1784, to Richard Henry Lee, President of Congress, in which it was suggested that that body "have the western waters well explored, the navigation of them fully ascertained, accurately laid down, and a complete and perfect map made of the country."[29] More important still was an accompanying suggestion that "all mines, minerals, and salt springs" be reserved in grants made from the public domain. In this way Washington would have benefited "the public, instead of the few knowing ones" and that too "without infringing any rule of justice"; for such a policy would, he thought, "inflict just punishment upon those, who in defiance" of their own laws, had dared to create enemies to disturb the public tranquillity by roaming "over the country, marking and surveying the valuable spots in it."[80]

Following the incorporation of the James River and the Potomac companies, Washington's public, or semi-public, activities were for some time given almost entirely to the organization and work of the latter. With a capital stock of approximately two hundred thousand dollars, it was organized May 17, 1785, with Thomas Johnson and Thomas Sim Lee of Maryland, who had joined in the enterprise, and John Fitzgerald and George Galpin of Virginia assisting the president, Washington, in the capacity of directors.[81] Soon thereafter work was commenced under the direction of "the ingenious Rumsey" and prosecuted rapidly. Washington and his associate directors gave it their personal attention at various times in 1785 and for some time thereafter.[82]

Meanwhile the Potomac had become associated with plans for immediate navigation by steam; John Fitch visited Washington in that interest;[83] and James Rumsey left his regular employment to perfect a steamboat.[84] Thus, in February, 1789, Washington was able to predict that the benefits of the improved navigation of the Potomac "will not be confined to narrower limits than the extent of the whole western territory of the United States,"[85] the presidency of which he was about to undertake.

In the organization of the James River and Potomac companies, Washington, with seeming unconsciousness and thus all the more effectively, found a rare opportunity to set an example for all well-meaning and truly patriotic Americans. With a view to rewarding his varied and valuable services, after a fashion then common in foreign lands, the Virginia Assembly offered him one hundred fifty shares of stock in these companies, but he declined them, modestly and considerately, but in the language of a true patriot opposed to the exploitation of a situation fraught with incalculable opportunities for favors and advantages. In this matter, as in others, he refused to subject himself to suspicions of sinister motives, preferring to remain "as free and independent as the air," and to be at liberty to express his sentiments and to suggest what occurred to him under the fullest conviction. This was his idea of loyalty to "the Union, and to this State [Virginia] in particular."[36]

During the years immediately following 1785, there were few phases of the western situation which escaped Washington's attention. Of most immediate concern was the road connecting the Potomac with Cheat River from the mouth of Savage River by way of the Glades to Dunkard Bottom, first surveyed in 1786 by Colonels Francis Deakins and John Neville.[37] Washington lost no opportunity to collect data upon Ohio Valley transportation and plans for connecting it with that of the Great Lakes region.[38] Because of a fear that it might be "disadvantageous" to the Union he opposed Connecticut's reservation of lands now within the State of Ohio.[39] In 1785 he would have established forts within the states to counteract British influences in the Northwest.[40] A year later he favored speaking "decisively" to those Kentuckians contemplating a Spanish alliance in the interest of trade,[41] but he was not averse to allowing Kentucky separate statehood in the Union.[42] Throughout these years his lands in southwestern Pennsylvania gave him no end of trouble,[43] but his lands on the Ohio and the Great Kanawha were rarely mentioned in his voluminous correspondence.

The settlements and proposed settlements north of the Ohio River, beginning with that at Marietta in 1788, met with Washington's unqualified approbation. Of the latter he said, "No colony in America was ever settled under such favorable auspices," and he rightly predicted that "information, property, and strength will be its characteristics."[44] This faith had its origin not only in the character of the promoters of the Marietta settlement, many of whom Washington knew personally, but also in the varied opportunities of their new environment. For similar reasons he predicted success for other proposed settlements in the Northwest Territory, notably that for which Joel Barlow was then gathering colonists in Europe. While advising him to locate westward of the mountains, Washington also commended the plans of a certain Richard Henderson bent upon establishing a colony in America, and he showed great versatility regarding local conditions, recommending to Henderson such works as Franklin's *Information for those who wish to remove to America,* Carey's *American Museum,* Morse's *American Geography,* and Jefferson's *Notes on Virginia.*[45]

On the absorbing subject of Mississippi navigation, then before the country in the famous Jay-Gardoqui Treaty, Washington's views were shaped largely by his plans for and his belief in the practicability of carrying the trade "of the Lakes, and of the Ohio River, as low down as the Great Kanawha if not to the Falls, . . . to the Atlantic ports easier and cheaper, taking the whole voyage together, than it can be carried to New Orleans."[46] Thus, in August, 1785, he was unable to divest himself of the opinion, however singular, "that the navigation of the Mississippi, *at this time,* ought to be no object with us." On the other hand, he thought it better to have this navigation temporarily obstructed, as that would allow time "to open and make easy the ways between the Atlantic States and the western territory."[47]

Furthermore in support of this position Washington said: "There is nothing which binds one country or one State to another but interest. Without this cement the western inhabitants, who more than probably will be composed in a great degree of foreigners, can have no predilection for us, and a commercial connection is the only tie we can have upon them."[48] In 1787, the activities of certain "ambitious and turbulent" spirits in Kentucky caused Washington to admit that the Mississippi navigation might be a "moot point to determine," but his sentiments with respect to it remained unchanged.[49] Adherence to the commercial and political advantages of this position enabled him to iron out controversies between Maryland and Virginia, and was a potent, possibly a determining factor, in his support of the movement to make a more perfect union, whose political traditions were largely Federalist and whose greatest potentialities were to be found in the West.

CHAPTER XI

IN THE FEDERALIST REGIME

WHILE PRESIDENT of the United States, Washington realized in a measure his hopes and expectations regarding the West. In keeping with his previously stated ideas, new states were carved out of the common territory and admitted to the Union on a basis of equality with the original states; Indian relations became comparatively peaceful and satisfactory; the frontier began to show obedience to and respect for the laws of the central government; foreign powers practically ceased to covet the American hinterland which, in keeping with Washington's predictions and to his great satisfaction, filled with an industrious and prosperous population; and by means of roads, post offices, river craft, and the Conestoga wagon, the West was being bound to the East by ties of interest.[1] More perhaps than any other person Washington foresaw these possibilities and was responsible for their consummation.

Inevitable as these achievements may now seem, they presented real problems in their day and cannot now be understood aside from their European background. Shortly after Washington became president, the French Estates General met, and soon thereafter France was in the throes of a revolution, the immediate effects of which extended through Europe and to America. Out of an archaic and semi-mediaeval condition a new France was born and, in its enthusiasm for its own achievements, began to extend its ideas and institutions to neighboring states and peoples. Not satisfied with this, the French planned to recover their former possessions in America, together with dependencies of decadent Spain to the south and the southwest.[2] It was to enlist Americans in this enterprise that "Citizen"

Genêt on April 8, 1793, landed in the United States as the agent of the French Republic.

In the accomplishment of his undertakings Genêt proposed to take the greatest possible advantage of the well-known hostility of American frontiersmen to Spain.[3] It is true that Spain as an ally of France, had assisted the United States to independence, but even in this service her selfishness was too thinly veiled to be disguised and, together with her subsequent course in refusing to withdraw from posts claimed by the United States eastward of the Mississippi River, had provoked bitter resentment. Moreover Spain continued to deny Americans the privilege of depositing goods at New Orleans, thus practically excluding them from the greatest possible benefits of the navigation of "the Father of Waters." Spain was also known to have intrigued with Indian tribes and was suspected of plotting treason with Kentucky and Tennessee malcontents. As a consequence American frontiersmen generally were threatening to descend upon New Orleans, to take it by force, and to hold it permanently for themselves and their children.[4]

By various means Washington kept in more or less intimate touch with this situation. For instance, a letter of January 25, 1790, from George Nicholas, a resident of Kentucky, to James Madison was referred by him to Washington. The letter brought the gratifying intelligence that Kentuckians were no longer seriously considering separating themselves from the Union and that neither the English nor the Spanish were then trying to persuade them to such a course; but it also told of efforts on the part of the Spanish to induce Kentuckians to settle within their territory, of their attempts to interfere with American trade, and of gross mismanagement of Indian affairs. More alarming still was the intelligence conveyed to the effect that the Spaniards had placed their affairs in and about Natchez in the hands of a capable administrator, de Lemos. Accordingly Nicholas advised that the United States take steps to win the affection of the westerners, that it determine at once its rights in Mississippi navigation, and that the Indians be made to understand that the United States was one country and not thirteen.[5]

In his dealings with Dr. James O'Fallon, agent of the South Carolina Yazoo Company, and incidentally James Wilkinson, "the most consummate artist in treason that the nation ever possessed,"[6] Washington was already alive to western conditions. On lands purchased from Georgia and still occupied by Indians, whose rights and interests the United States was bound by treaty to respect, O'Fallon planned to make a settlement in the Yazoo country in what is now western Mississippi.[7] Being assured that the proposed settlement would maintain its independence of Spain and remain a part of the United States, Kentuckians were willing to join in the enterprise, but, at the same time, the Spanish Governor, Estevan Miro, was told by O'Fallon, Wilkinson, and possibly others, of the desire of the would-be settlers "to be the slaves" of Spain. Alleging that the O'Fallon scheme was a violation of covenanted Indian rights and the laws and treaties of the United States and that it was also a menace to the peace and security of the frontier, Washington nipped it in the bud by a proclamation forbidding it and warning those "who have incautiously associated themselves with the said James O'Fallon."[8]

Despite the vigorous tone of this proclamation subsequent events on the frontier were not reassuring. In the increasing difficulties between lawless settlers and greedy land speculators on the one side and jealous Indians and their banditti on the other, Washington detected the ever-subtle hand of Spain and the double-dealing and perfidy of Alexander McGillivary in whom he had formerly confided.[9] When England and Spain, in the face of common dangers from revolutionary France, developed a measure of accord, Washington suspected them of "an understanding in all this business,"[10] but he did not even suspect Wilkinson. Instead he continued to praise his "great zeal and ability for the public weal" and through a mutual friend he informed Wilkinson of "the favorable light" with which his conduct was viewed in the Federal capital.[11]

It was into this whirlpool of treachery and discontent that

Genêt hoped to pour additional elements of revolution. In view of the offensive and defensive alliances still existing between his country and the United States he anticipated no serious objections on the part of Americans. In the event that any arose, he was prepared to offer them the Floridas as their portion of the spoils to be wrenched from Spain.[12] Thus fortified Genêt landed in Charleston, South Carolina, and, following an enthusiastic reception, proceeded thence to Philadelphia by an inland route through the Piedmont foothills, where the inhabitants were more in accord with his revolutionary sentiments and purposes than were those of the lowlands. On the way he took steps looking to the fitting out of armed expeditions against Spain and communicated with their prospective leaders. Everywhere he was greeted with enthusiasm, but despite all this he was effectively checked at Philadelphia by a proclamation of neutrality from Washington, in which he apprised his countrymen of the fact that the United States was then at peace with the warring powers of Europe and warned citizens of the United States against acts of hostility toward any of them.

Buoyed by the belief that American sovereignty rested in Congress, a mistake repeated by Europeans and others, Genêt soon recovered from the shock of Washington's neutrality proclamation and continued to plan for the consummation of his purposes.[13] Although confident of ultimate success, he nevertheless complained that "the old man [Washington]" was blocking him at every turn, and could not forgive his popularity with the people. Genêt even thought it might be necessary to press "secretly the convening of Congress." Openly he conferred with members of the opposition party and in Washington's absence at Mount Vernon, Genêt released the "Petite Democrate" to prey upon English commerce. Upon his return Genêt's acts met with Washington's unqualified disapproval, whereupon Genêt precipitated his own undoing by a threat to appeal from Washington to the American people.[14] As a result he was recalled, and Washington thus took another step to assert the dignity and the independence of the United States. At the same time he entrenched it in a policy of neutrality toward European affairs, which was maintained for more than a century.

Hoping to lull the United States into inertia by "wise delay and useful temporising," Genêt's successor, Jean-Antoine-Joseph Fauchet, continued thus to plan for the acquisition of Louisiana by France.[15] To that end Indian wars and the Whiskey Rebellion were watched by him and his successor, Pierre-Auguste Adet, in the expectation that some favorable turn would redound to the advantage of their country. The resulting suspicions had something to do with the accord that led the United States to negotiate the Jay Treaty of 1794 and the Pinckney Treaty of the year following.[16] By the latter Spain relinquished claim to lands eastward of the Mississippi River and north of the thirty-first parallel, and temporarily accorded to Americans the privilege of depositing goods at New Orleans.

These victories of the Washington administration only widened the breach between the United States and France. In 1795 the latter concluded with Spain the Treaty of Basel in the negotiations of which she made known her desire for Louisiana but did not press it. Had France then attained her pet American objective, the indications are that Washington would have taken a position not unlike that taken by Jefferson in 1802, in explanation of which he said: "There is on the globe one single spot, the possessor of which is our natural and habitual enemy. It is New Orleans. The day that France takes possession of New Orleans fixes the sentence which is to restrain her within her low water mark. . . . From that day we must marry ourselves to the British fleet and nation."[17] The fact that Washington leaned more and more toward the Federalists, beginning with 1794, did not nourish his old-time friendship for France. It is perhaps significant that in 1798 he accepted the chief command of the forces raised by the United States to fight France, her former ally.

In this as in other matters affecting French-American relations Washington was undoubtedly influenced somewhat by the presence in this country of "Democratic Societies" organized by

Citizen Genêt. These societies flourished in the Kentucky country and their existence was, in Washington's mind, always traced to the French. "Under a display of popular and convincing guises" he feared that they might destroy "the best fabric of human government and happiness, that has ever been presented to the experience of mankind." Voicing further his disapproval of their methods and purposes he said: "If the laws are to be so trampled upon with impunity, and a minority, a small one too, is to dictate to the majority, there is an end put, at one stroke, to republican government; and nothing but anarchy and confusion is to be expected hereafter."[18]

Meanwhile England had pursued a course in the Northwest not unlike that followed by Spain in the Southwest. Reluctant to yield the profits of the fur trade and the opportunities of an uncertain international situation, she had, on technical grounds, refused to surrender American posts in the region of the Great Lakes.[19] Washington's administration was only a few months old when he tried to determine her intentions in the matter,[20] but he was met by evasion. In fact, England had already resolved to keep the Trans-Allegheny region as distinct from the United States as possible and as closely connected with herself as possible. This policy was set forth in 1790, in a report of the Lords of Trade, in which they declared that it would be to England's best interest "to prevent Vermont and Kentucky and all other Settlements now forming in the Interior parts of the great Continent of North America, from becoming dependent on the Government of the United States, or on that of any other Foreign Country."[21] This policy of local autonomy mapped out by the English for the American frontier applied also to Indians and gave a measure of unanimity to their counsels and their dealings with the United States during the years immediately following.

When American settlements finally advanced beyond the Ohio River, 1788, the English policy of intermeddling could no longer be regarded complacently. By early 1791 their attitude in Indian affairs was such that Washington suspected them of intensifying and prolonging the campaign reluctantly undertaken by the United States to preserve "the peace and safety to the inhabitants of their frontier."[22] Realizing the dangers to which the United States was thus exposed, Washington shortly thereafter suggested to Jefferson the matter of an alliance between the United States and France. As Jefferson's heart was already set upon a French alliance, this suggestion caught his fancy, and, but for the unfortunate Genêt affair, it might have been followed up, thus altering completely the early course of American political history and foreign policy.

If Genêt's conduct dampened Washington's ardor for a French-American alliance and confirmed him in a policy of neutrality as between the United States and the warring powers of Europe, it did not diminish his concern regarding the British menace in the Northwest. During 1792 and 1793, conditions there were precarious, and the famous speech of February 10, 1794, made by Lord Dorchester, lately returned from England, did not help the situation. In this speech Dorchester conveyed to a disgruntled Indian delegation the possibilities of war between the United States and England. Moreover, the English seemed bent upon precipitating war when Governor Simcoe, with Dorchester's approval, built a fort at the Maumee Rapids in or near the course of General Wayne's proposed march against the Indians. The tenseness thus produced was heightened by the wide circulation given Dorchester's speech and the contention that the newly constructed fort was necessary for the protection of Detroit.[23]

Although partisans tried to explain away these incidents, alleging that the objectionable speech was spurious and that the construction of the fort on the Maumee was not fraught with sinister motives, Washington insisted that Dorchester had voiced the sentiments of the British cabinet,[24] and he characterized Simcoe's act as "the most open and daring, . . . of the British agents in America, though it is not the most hostile and cruel."[25] This he found in British-inspired "murders of helpless women and innocent children along our frontiers." In keeping with his policy of French and Indian War days, he was for removing the cause by aggressive action. Through Secretary of War Knox, he informed General Wayne that, if in the course of his campaign it should be necessary to dislodge the British garrison on the Maumee, it should be done. With a view to possible war with England, about the same time he requested information regarding the population and resources of Upper Canada and Lower Canada and regarding the temper and patriotic inclinations of their peoples.[26]

Fortunately the English government was not so warlike as were its representatives in Canada. Ever since England had become involved in war with France (1793), the English had in fact shown a disposition to amicable adjustments of differences with the United States.[27] As the United States was not averse to such an accord and also desired commercial concessions from England, Washington, April 6, 1794, named John Jay as special envoy to represent him in negotiations to these ends. The disadvantages thus occasioned by his playing into the hands of the Federalists and further alienating Jefferson's party were considered small in comparison with the advantages of averting a war with England, which might, through a concerted attack from Canada and the lower Mississippi, possibly in conjunction with Spain, have resulted in the loss to the United States of the entire Mississippi Valley.

The accord that followed, known as the Jay Treaty, was ratified by the United States Senate, June 24, 1795, and was at once given to the public, where it produced a veritable storm of indignation. Although gratified with the English surrender of the American posts along the lakes and with the free navigation of the Mississippi, which the English again conceded, the westerners opposed the commercial and other features of the Jay Treaty, in demonstrations of "a very unpleasant nature." While not entirely pleased with the treaty, Washington considered it better "than to suffer matters as they are, unsettled." In the face of protests against it he voiced the spirit of modern science when he said, "there is but one straight course, and that is to seek truth and pursue it steadily."[28]

While inextricably involved in foreign relations, Indian affairs both in the Southwest and in the Northwest had local aspects. In keeping with the policy of Congress to retain for itself exclusive control over territorial Indians, additional treaties were concluded in Washington's administration, but the whites openly violated them by wholesale encroachments upon Indian lands and by unscrupulous trade practices.[29] On the other hand, the Indians retaliated by murdering whites and destroying their property.[30] This was notably true in the Northwest and in regions now embraced in Georgia and Tennessee. Indians opposed the encroachment of white settlers north of the Ohio on the grounds that the Treaty of Fort Stanwix, 1784, and the Treaty of Fort Harmar, 1789, were fraudulent and void. Unwilling to concede these contentions, Washington sent armed forces against them with varying results. First General Josiah Harmar met with indifferent success, then came Governor Arthur St. Clair's inglorious defeat, which was followed in 1794 by General Anthony Wayne's victory at Fallen Timber. This was followed by the treaty of Greenville, as the result of which Indians ceded to the United States the larger part of what is now the state of Ohio. Meanwhile John Sevier and James Robertson had defeated the Cherokees and Chickamauguas thus opening to white settlement additional areas.

Washington was not, however, wholly satisfied with force as a means of dealing with the natives, whose comparative helplessness and ignorance he recognized and pitied. While rejoicing in Wayne's and Sevier's victories and deploring St. Clair's defeat, his desire for victory was only as a means to "a lasting peace upon terms of candor, equality, and good neighborhood."[31] As a father would advise his children, Washington admonished Indians to be good.[32] He offered a reward of $500 each for the arrest of whites accused of perpetrating outrages upon natives,[33] and although he considered trade indispensable as a means to political control of the Indians,[34] he advised that it be conducted on an honest basis and that profits be reasonable. While defending the practice of using gifts as a means of making compensations for injuries "not otherwise to be redressed," Washington agreed with Edmund Pendleton that "the plan of annual presents, in an abstract view, unaccompanied by other measures, is not the best mode of treating ignorant savages."[35] Forecasting a policy adopted almost one hundred years later, he would instead have layed greater stress upon the primary principles of civilization, education and husbandry.[36]

Although the Whiskey Rebellion, 1792-1794, was primarily a local affair, it had national, even international aspects. It was the last formidable stand in the Trans-Allegheny for unauthorized autonomy involving the power of the new Federal government, and it was closely watched by the agents of France, Spain, and England in the hope that it might eventuate in some favorable turn to their respective governments. Washington regarded it as "the first formidable fruit of the Democratic Societies"[37] and as a test of the Federal government. With him its suppression was therefore an act of patriotism fraught with far-reaching consequences, but his interest in the Rebellion can be best understood in the light of its historical background.

With a view to ascertaining the powers of the Federal government and raising revenues for its support, Congress, March 3, 1791, and May 8, 1792, authorized a general excise tax on spiritous liquors. As this tax was prying and sumptuary, it was resented generally, and in Trans-Allegheny Pennsylvania, where distilled spirits were produced and consumed in large quantities, opposition became intense. In the absence of roads and adequate water transportation, whiskey afforded the inhabitants of that region, mostly Scotch-Irish long accustomed to the use of strong drinks, a concentrated form for marketing and consuming their farm products to the greatest possible advantage. Thus any tax upon this staple was looked upon as an encroachment upon natural rights and was resented accordingly.[38]

Unlike other demonstrations against governmental authority, this one was slow in developing and was persistent and studied. An initial outbreak in the summer of 1792 was effectively suppressed by a proclamation from President Washington, admonishing and exhorting all persons against resistance to the laws and constituted authorities of their country,[39] but discontent continued to smoulder and in the summer of 1794 burst into open and formidable defiance. In Westmoreland, Washington, Fayette, and Allegheny counties federal inspectors and marshals were driven from their posts by armed mobs; other officers suffered violence; buildings were burned; and law was set at defiance.

Upon being notified of these happenings and of the impotency of the courts to prevent them, Washington, August 5, 1794, sent commissioners among the insurgents in an effort "to induce them to submit peacefully to the laws, and to prevent the necessity of using coercion to enforce their execution." To the same end two days later he issued a proclamation commanding all disaffected persons to cease opposition by September first of that year.[40] But as neither his commissioners nor his own entreaties were heeded, in the exercise of "that high and irresistible duty consigned . . . by the constitution," he called into action the militia of Pennsylvania, Virginia, Maryland, and New Jersey to enforce the laws of the United States. While not according "too much importance to the opposition," Washington intentionally authorized a force sufficiently large to make a formidable showing. The chief command was entrusted to his friend, Governor Henry Lee of Virginia.

By this demonstration of power, fifteen thousand strong, Washington hoped to "prevent the effusion of blood," as well as to make resistance futile. This was his conception of the best way to uphold the power and dignity of the central government.[41] That there might be no mistaking the latter purpose, he decided to give the mobilization of the militia his personal oversight. For this purpose, in company with Alexander Hamilton, Secretary of the Treasury, Washington left Philadelphia for Carlisle, Pennsylvania, September 30, 1794, the same day on which he received information of Wayne's victory over the Indians at Fallen Timbers. With this intelligence to brighten his way, he journeyed by Morris Town, Reading, and Lebanon and reached his destination four days later.

At Carlisle Washington received his first direct information concerning the insurrectionists and their purposes. Here he talked with William Findley and David Redick, representatives of a "Committee of Safety" of the "Whiskey Boys." Largely with a view to preventing an armed demonstration against their constituents, Findley and Redick begged Washington to discontinue military preparations and promised immediate obedience to the laws of Congress. But as neither could promise that Federal excise officers would be permitted to function in the disaffected areas, "except under the influence of the garrison," and as each admitted that the insurgents were opposed not only to the excise laws, but also to "all law and Government," and "the officers of Government,"[42] Washington ordered the preparations to continue and to be made effective. To the latter end he visited camps at Cumberland, Maryland, and at Bedford, Pennsylvania, and had the continuance of his presence in either been considered necessary, "it would not have been witholden."[43]

In his decision to give these preparations personal attention, Washington was doubtless motivated also by representations to the effect that the insurgents were "ignorant" to a degree beyond "anything he had any comprehension of." They were represented also as thinking themselves invulnerable to any power that could be sent against them. Rather than submit to the laws of the United States, some were reported to have sold their belongings preparatory to removal to Detroit. All this savored too much of border warfare and Revolutionary days to permit Washington to regard it complacently. He answered Findley's and Redick's requests in no unmistakable terms, the essence of which was "unequivocal proof" of their absolute submission to the laws of the United States. In reply to an inquiry regarding the character of the proof desired, Washington left it to them to determine "what was due to justice and example."[44]

The results of this firm stand are well known. In brief the insurgents vanished, a fact in which Washington found keen satisfaction, because their decision "demonstrated that our prosperity rests on solid foundations." According to Washington, it was also an "additional proof that his fellow-citizens understood the true principles of government and liberty; that they felt their inseparable union; that notwithstanding all the devices which have been used to sway them from their interest and duty, they were as ready to maintain the authority of the laws against licentious invasions as they were to defend their rights against usurpation." In the willingness of "the most and least wealthy" of citizens to stand in the same ranks as private soldiers, undeterred by a march of 300 miles over rugged mountains, by the approach of an inclement season, or by any other discouragement, Washington found another proof of the advantages of republican institutions.[45]

Both in respect to the "internal peace and welfare of this country, and because of the impression it made upon others, Washington considered the "great expense" of putting down the Whiskey Rebellion advantageous. Soon thereafter he suggested the enactment of a law for "devising and establishing a well regulated militia," which was postponed, with doubtful results, for more than a hundred years. Whatever may have been his opinion of militiamen in the French and Indian War and in the Revolution, he now conceded them "immortal glory" and saw in the spirit of their conduct a "conclusive refutation" of the assertion of Lord Sheffield, that "without the protection of Great Britain, we [United States] should be unable to govern ourselves, and would soon be involved in confusion." As a consequence of this demonstration, Washington hoped the British would understand "that republicanism is not the phantom of a deluded imagination."[46]

The announcement of final plans for the admission of Kentucky and Tennessee to separate statehood in the Union was a source of satisfaction to Washington. This was particularly true of Kentucky, the admission of which he said "would inspire the citizens of America with such confidence in it [Union], as effectively to do away [with] those apprehensions, which, under the former confederation, our best men entertain of division among ourselves."[47]

Meanwhile other matters, of primary concern to the West, did not escape Washington's attention. Among other things he approved the congressional plan for disposing of parts of the public domain in large tracts as a means of discharging the public debt.[48] In 1791 while on a tour of the South, he inspected the James River improvement,[49] and, three years later, he approved an act of the Virginia Assembly extending the time for the completion of the Potomac navigation.[50] Always he was interested in data regarding possible routes and distances for connecting the eastern and western waters, but, strange as it may seem to those who have suspected him of selfishness in his desires for a strong Union, his correspondence and papers are astonishingly free from reference to his own western lands. But for infrequent warnings to squatters and a few sale and rent notices,[51] evidences of such holdings are conspicuous by their absence.

Whatever Washington's early expectations regarding his western lands may have been, experience taught him that "distant property in land [was] more pregnant of perplexities than profit."[52] As opportunities seemed to favor from time to time during a period of more than twenty-five years, he alternately tried to rent and to sell his western holdings to advantage but with little or no success, certainly with none in the desired sales. Thus at his death, in addition to the tracts previously spoken of in this work, some of which had been increased in size by resurveys, he owned 3051 acres on the Little Miami in Ohio, and 5000 acres in Kentucky.[53] In 1796 he advertised his lands on the Ohio and Great Kanawha rivers as "among the most valuable on the western waters," but he was unable to sell them at prices ranging from three to six dollars per acre. At one time he was on the point of selling this entire acreage to a French gentleman, but because of revolutionary disturbances in his homeland, this prospective buyer was released from his contract.[54] After Washington's death these lands, with an estimated total valuation of approximately $300,000, were distributed among his heirs, some of whom later established homes upon them. His Ohio lands, valued at $15,251, were lost to his heirs in the legal contests which followed his death.[55]

The possession of Washington heirlooms by his relatives in the transmontane regions enriched their traditions almost as effectively as did the numerous sojourns and reputed sojourns of Washington himself.[56] This was notably true of his soldier relics, many of which were carried beyond the mountains following the distribution of his estate. With the injunction that they were not to be unsheathed "for the purpose of shedding blood, except it be for self-defense, or in defense of their country and its rights," five swords were inherited by as many nephews. William Augustine Washington received the sword given his uncle by Frederick the Great with the compliments of "the oldest general in the world to the greatest." This sword was inherited by Colonel John W. Washington and for years reposed in his home, Belle Air, near Harpers Ferry, where, together with a pistol presented to General Washington by Lafayette, it was captured by John Brown and used by him in his attack upon the United States Arsenal at Harpers Ferry, as a symbol of liberty. For a long time General Washington's "Spanish Dress" sword reposed also at Belle Air, but his famous "Battle" sword, the one carried by him during the periods of his military service, was carried to the banks of the Great Kanawha River, where it was a favorite possession in the home of Samuel W. Washington until 1843, when it was presented by its owner to "the Congress of the United States, in behalf of the nation." General Washington's "Sollingen" sword was carried directly to what is now Charles Town, West Virginia, where it remained until shortly after the Civil War. Thus the number and location of Washington trophies and mementoes in what is now West Virginia and its immediate environs could be multiplied almost indefinitely.[57]

From present West Virginia, descendants of Washington's brothers, carrying relics and mementoes of their distinguished relative, extended to many parts of the farther West. Outstanding among them was Lawrence Augustine Washington, Jr., son of Washington's nephew, Lawrence Augustine Washington (1774-1824), who died and was buried near Wheeling. In 1850, when flush times were on in Texas, the younger Washington, together with his family including a sister, Mary Dorcas, moved from their farm of 126 acres to the Lone Star state, whence his descendants extended to several western states.

Like others who set out from western Virginia to begin life anew in the West, Lawrence Augustine Washington, Jr. was well equipped. He was a graduate of the University of Virginia and of Jefferson Medical College, Philadelphia. He took with him one hundred Negro slaves; blooded stock of horses, sheep and cattle; hounds; a library; a grand piano; and some of the treasured George Washington relics. In 1919 most, if not all of these, were turned over to the Mount Vernon Association, at an appropriate service held at the Dallas Scottish Rite Temple, Dallas, Texas.[58]

Although Washington's predilections for the West were strong, justifying the commemoration of his name in hundreds of its governmental units and natural features, he did not expect or wish for it a growth and development distinct from that of the other sections of the Union. This was clearly revealed in his farewell address, 1796, in which he warned against dangers of sectional strife and forcefully presented the reciprocal advantages of harmony and accord among the great sections of his country. Following a presentation of such advantages to the North and to the South, he predicted that "The *East* in a like intercourse with the *West*," had already found, and would continue to find through progressive improvement of internal communications "a valuable vent for the commodities which it brings from abroad or manufactures at home." On the other hand and of perhaps "still greater consequence" he was convinced that the West "must of necessity owe the *secure* enjoyment of indispensable *outlets* for its own productions to the weight, influence, and the future maritime strength of the Atlantic side of the Union, directed by an indissoluble community of interest as *one nation*."[59]

After he left the presidency, Washington's suggestions regarding the West were as wholesome and constructive as they had ever been. Forecasting an arrangement which has survived for one hundred and fifteen years as a model for the world, he advised that neither the United States nor Great Britain in times of peace, keep armed vessels "on the Lakes."[60] Because of its central location, he preferred a site in the vicinity of Louisville instead of Natchez, for a proposed army observation post,[61] and he was largely responsible for the choice of Harpers Ferry as a federal arsenal site. Factors recommending this location attest the same sort of realism in the "Father of his Country" as he displayed in his boyhood. First was the proximity of Harpers Ferry to furnaces and forges of the best iron; moreover, it had fine shipping facilities by water both east and west; and finally, it was on the great highway "to the country of the Ohio River."[62]

Although Washington's suggestions regarding the West were forward-looking, the extent of his vision of its future cannot of course be definitely determined. Unlike Jefferson, he put no time limits upon the possible extension of white settlements westward of the Mississippi River, if indeed he contemplated such a thing, which he doubtless did. Both by personal contacts and through plans for its settlement and government he was familiar with the Trans-Allegheny to the Mississippi. He had seen settlement extend itself throughout almost the entire area, and probably more than most men of his time, he reckoned with the possible effect of an improved transportation. He must therefore have realized that the Trans-Allegheny, like the older sections to the eastward, would become too small for the white man and that he would push farther the relentless course of empire.

As respects the Trans-Allegheny Washington's plans for tying it to the East by ties of interest are perhaps his greatest claims to statesmanship. In them he laid the basis for the future development of the country whose independence he had done most to win, but in doing so he doubtless had a view to the growth of American democratic ideals as well. Washington's writings afford abundant evidences of the fact that he appreciated the democratizing influences and possibilities, as well as the loyalty of the West. It will be recalled that his settlement on the Great Kanawha was to have both civil and religious liberty, and in the event of failure elsewhere, he was prepared to make a last stand for independence in the mountains of West Augusta, where after the manner of a Scotch Highlander, he was determined to carry on the fight until his efforts were crowned with victory. Thus his subsequent plans to lay low the hills and exalt the valleys of the Appalachian range were not due to his fear of democracy but rather to his confidence in and devotion to it. In this way he laid the basis for the Federalist party in the West long before that party was born. If the seeds of Jeffersonian democracy grew best in that virgin soil, the way was meanwhile being paved there for Henry Clay and the American System.

Whatever may be said of Washington's interest in western lands, particularly the amount of his holdings and the method and purpose of acquiring them, these considerations never blinded him to the public interest, as has been implied by those who espouse the economic interpretation of American history in its narrowest sense. Those of Washington's lands which did not come to him as compensation for services, were purchased from fellow soldiers, usually as personal favors and at their earnest request. Through several decades these lands were held at great sacrifice and were offered for sale at moderate prices. If as a young man he had illusions about getting rich through his western holdings, these illusions were dissipated long before the

Federal Constitution was made, for already according to his own words, he had learned that "distant property in land [was] more pregnant with perplexities than with profit." Nevertheless, his interest for the public good would permit no limits upon our western boundary.

After all the most informing phase of Washington's personal interests in the West was the readiness and completeness with which he forgot them when the public was involved. While he was fighting for the independence of America, his settlement on the Great Kanawha River was destroyed; his mill at Perryopolis, Pennsylvania, went to rack; and squatters occupied the select sites of his other landed holdings. Yet forgetful of the fact that he had meanwhile served his country without monetary compensation, there are those who mischievously magnify the personal phase of his visit of 1784 to the West. For all such as well as for others, it is well to recall that, while on that visit, Washington in the eagerness of his search for road and canal sites did not even visit his lands on the Ohio and Great Kanawha rivers as he had set out to do, and that shortly thereafter he recommended to Richard Henry Lee, President of the Continental Congress, that "all mines, minerals, and salt springs," be reserved for public uses in future grants from the public domain. Reflecting his own growth and earnestness in the public interest over a period of years, was his accompanying statement to the effect that choice natural resources should not become the property of those who in childish fashion, claimed them because they happened to be the first to see them.

Finally and despite his intense love for the West, Washington was the father of the entire country. As such, like a loving and indulgent parent, his vision rose above sections and factions. In fact, his chief objection to the latter was that they would become sectional and destroy the Union. Thus not only was he "first in the hearts of his countrymen," but they, all of them, were first in his heart, a fact which has added an element of sacredness to his name among leaders of all parties and all sections. Moreover, unlike the prophets of old, this attitude was shown him before he died and by those who knew him best. Indeed, it is doubtful whether it has grown much through the succeeding ages. Accordingly the conclusion: Whatever the vicissitudes of American government, the present indications are that succeeding systems, even a possible more socialistic regime, will be proud to acknowledge Washington's paternity of the United States.

APPENDIX A

THE BATTLE OF FORT NECESSITY
JULY 3, 1754

I. Contemporaneous Newspaper Accounts

1. *Maryland Gazette* (Annapolis) for July 25, 1754, quoting the *Virginia Gazette* (Williamsburg) for July 19, 1754, summarizing unofficial reports attributed to Colonel George Washington and Captain James Mackay.

"Williamsburg, July 19, [1754]

"On Wednesday last arrived in Town, Colonel George Washington and Captain James Maccay, who gave the following Account to his Honour the Governor, of the late Action between them and the French, at the Great Meadows in the Western Parts of this Dominion.

"The third of this Instant July, about 9 o'Clock, we received Intelligence that the French, having been reinforced with 700 Recruits, had left Monongehela, and were in full March with 900 Men to attack us. Upon this, as our Numbers were so unequal, (our whole Force not exceeding 300) we prepared for our Defence in the best Manner we could, by throwing up a small Intrenchment, which we had not Time to perfect, before our Centinel gave Notice, about Eleven o'Clock, of their Approach, by firing his Piece, which he did at the Enemy, and as we learned afterwards killed three of their Men, on which they began to fire upon us, at about 600 Yards Distance, but without any Effect: We immediately called all our Men to their Arms, and drew up in Order before our Trenches; but as we looked upon this distant Fire of the Enemy only as an Artifice to intimidate, or draw our Fire from us, we waited their nearer Approach before we returned their Salute. They then advanced in a very irregular Manner to another Point of Woods, about 60 Yards off, and from thence made a second Discharge; upon which, finding they had no Intention of attacking us in the open Field, we retired into our Trenches, and still reserved our Fire; as we expected from their great Superiority of Numbers, that they would endeavour to force our Trenches; but finding they did not seem to intend this neither, the Colonel gave Orders to fire, which was done with great Alacrity and Undauntedness. We continued this unequal Fight, with an Enemy sheltered behind the Trees, ourselves without Shelter, in Trenches full of Water, in a settled Rain, and the Enemy galling us on all Sides incessantly from the Woods, till 8 o'Clock at Night, when the French called to Parley: From the great Improbability that such a vastly superior Force, and possessed of such an Advantage, would offer a Parley first, we suspected a Deceit, and therefore refused to consent that they should come among us; on which they desired us to send an Officer to them, and engaged their Parole for his Safety; we then sent Captain Van Braam, and Mr. Peyronee, to receive their Proposals, which they did, and about Midnight we agreed that each Side should retire without Molestation, they back to their Fort at Monongehela, and we to Wills's Creek: That we should march away with all the Honours of War, and with all our Stores, Effects and Baggage. Accordingly the next Morning, with our Drums beating, and our Colours flying, we began our March in good Order, with our Stores, &c. in Convoy; but we were interrupted by the Arrival of a Reinforcement of 100 Indians among the French, who were hardly restrained from attacking us, and did us considerable Damage by pilfering our Baggage. We then proceeded, but soon found it necessary to leave our Baggage and Stores; the great Scarcity of our Provisions obliged us to use the utmost Expedition, and having neither Waggons nor Horses to transport them. The Enemy had deprived us of all our Creatures, by killing, in the Beginning of the Engagement, our Horses, Cattle, and every living Thing they could, even to the very Dogs. The Number of the Killed on our Side was 30, and 70 wounded; among the former was Lieutenant Mercier, of Capt. Maccay's Independent Company; a Gentleman of true military Worth, and whose Bravery would not permit him to retire, tho' dangerously wounded, 'til a second Shot disabled him, and a third put an End to his Life, as he was carrying to the Surgeon. Our Men behaved with singular Intrepidity, and we determined not to ask for Quarter, but with our Bayonets screw'd, to sell our Lives as dearly as possibly we could. From the Numbers of the Enemy, and our Situation, we could not hope for Victory; and from the Character of those we had to encounter, we expected no Mercy, but on Terms that we positively resolved not to submit to. The Number killed and wounded of the Enemy is uncertain, but by the Information given by some Dutch in their Service to their Countrymen in ours, we learn that it amounted to above 300; and we are induced to believe it must be very considerable, by their being busy all Night in burying their Dead, and yet many remained the next Day; and their Wounded we know was considerable, by one of our Men, who had been made Prisoner by them after signing the Articles, and who, on his Return told us, that he saw great Numbers much wounded and carried off upon Litters. We were also told by some of their Indians after the Action, that the French had an Officer of distinguishable Rank killed. Some considerable Blow they must have received, to induce them to call first for a Parley, knowing, as they perfectly did, the Circumstances we were in.

"Col. Washington, and Capt. Maccay, left Capt. Clarke at Winchester, on the 11th last, and his Men were not then arrived there. Thus have a few brave Men been exposed, to be butchered, by the Negligence of those who, in Obedience to their Sovereign's Command ought to have been with them many Months before; and it is evidently certain, that had the Companies from New York been as expeditious as Capt. Maccay's from South Carolina, our Camp would have been secure from the Insults of the French, and our brave Men still alive to serve their King and Country. Surely, this will remove the Infatuation that seems to have prevailed too much among our Neighbours, and inforce a late ingenious Emblem well worthy of their Attention and Consideration."

2. *Maryland Gazette*, August 1, 1754, quoting letter of Colonel James Innes, in command of North Carolina troops, to Governor James Hamilton of Pennsylvania.

"Having notice of a Person going to your Province immediately, I thought it proper, on this Occasion, to give you a short Detail of what hath lately happen'd.

"After having regulated the March, and the Transportation of the *North Carolina* Regiment, I immediately proceeded to *Williamsburg*, and by my Commission from Governor *Dinwiddie*, as Commander in Chief of this Expedition, I set out for *Winchester*, where I arrived on the 30th of *June*, in order to take the Command upon me, and to bring up the *New York* two independent Companies, with those of the *North Carolina* Regiment then upon their March from *Alexandria* for this *Town*.

"Col. W*ashington*, with the *Virginia* Regiment, and Captain Maccay, with the *South Carolina* Independent Company, together, did consist but of Four Hundred Men, of which a good many were sick, and out of Order.

"On the third of *July* the *French*, with about Nine Hundred Men, and considerable Body of Indians, came down upon our Incampment, and continued to fire, from all Quarters, from Eleven in the Morning till Night, when the *French* called out to our People, they would give them good Conditions, if they would capitulate, a Copy of which I here inclose you.

"After the Capitulation the *French* demolished the Works, and in some Time after retir'd to the *Ohio*, taking two Captains as Hostages along with them. We all know the *French* are a people that never pay any Regard to Treaties longer than they find them consistent with their Interest; and this Treaty they broke immediately, by letting the *Indians* demolish and destroy every Thing our People had, especially the Doctor's Box, that our wounded should meet with no Relief. In this Action it is said that we had about 100 Men killed and wounded, a Third whereof supposed to be killed; and it is reported we kill'd double the Number of the *French*. If this does not alarm the neighbouring Governments, nothing can; and I make no Doubt but the *French* will soon claim this fine Body of Land, as their right by Conquest, if we do not immediately raise a sufficient Force to convince them of the contrary. What I can learn of their Force, is, that they had 700 Men in their first Division; 800 in the next, and 500 in the last, not as yet joined; which, with their *Indians*, make a considerable Body.

"Colonel *Washington* and Captain *Maccay*, told me, there were many of our Friend *Indians* along with the *French*, sundry of which came up, and spoke to them, told them they were their Brothers, and ask'd them how they did; particularly, *Susquehanna Jack,* and others, who distinguished themselves by their Names; and it is also said, that some of the *Delawares* were there. We had not an *Indian* to assist when the Engagement commenced or ended.

"It is my real Opinion, that nothing will secure to us the *Indians* now in our Friendship, if we allow ourselves to be baffled by the *French;* as it is very natural and common for a more polite People than the *Indians* to side with the strongest: So that there is a Necessity either to go into the Affair in Dispute heartily at once, or to give it up entirely."

3. *Maryland Gazette* for August 29, 1754, quoting letter from Captain Adam Stephen to "a Gentleman in this Province [Pennsylvania]."

"June 29, we received certain Intelligence, that the French were reinforced with 300 White Men, and the same Number of Indians, and that they intend to march immediately to attack us; Whereupon Col. Washington call'd a Council of War, wherein it was resolved to send an Express to hasten the Independents to join us, and that in the mean Time we should set about fortifying ourselves, as well as the Time would permit, and there wait the arrival of Cap. Lewis, and Mr. Polson, who were out on Detachments, and to whom Orders were sent to join us with the utmost Expedition. Captain Maccay arrived at our Camp at Gist's House, in the Night, and we were joined by our Detachment next Forenoon: when a Council of War was again call'd, wherein it was unanimously resolved to retreat immediately, carrying all public Stores with us; and as we had but two very indifferent Teams, and few Horses, the Officers loaded their own Horses with Ammunition, and left part of their Baggage behind; Col. Washington setting them an Example, by ordering his Horse to be loaded first, and giving four Pistoles to some Soldiers to carry his necessary Baggage. We had nine Swivels, which were drawn by the Soldiers of the Virginia Regiment twelve Miles, of the roughest and most hilly Road of any on the Alleghany Mountains. The independents refused to lend a Hand to draw the Guns, or help off with the Ammunition; nor would they do Duty as Pioneers, which had an unhappy Effect on our Men, who no sooner learned that it was not the proper Duty of Soldiers to perform these Services, than they became as backward as the Independents. This was one great Reason why we had not completeated [*sic*] our Works before the Attack.

"July 1st, we arrived very much fatigued at the Meadows, and had continued our Retreat, but for want of Horses and Conviences to carry our Ammunition. Our Men had been eight Days without Bread, and instead of a large Convoy, which we had long expected, there arrived only a few Bags of Flour: They were so harassed with working on the Fortifications at Gist's, and with marching, that they were not able to draw the Swivels. This being the Case, and having certain Intelligence that the Yorkers had arrived at Alexandria about twenty Days before, a fatal Stay! and a flying

Report, that they had got to Will's Creek on their March to join us, it was thought most advisable to fortify ourselves in the best Manner possible, and wait our Convoys and Reinforcements, which we daily expected.

"In the mean Time an Express was sent to inform them of our Station, and hasten them to our Assistance. We set about clearing the Woods nearest to us, and carrying in the Logs, to raise a Breastwork, and enlarge the Fort. July 3d, by Break of Day, we were alarmed by one of our Centries, who was shot in the Leg by the Enemy; and about nine, we received Intelligence, by some of our advanced Parties, that the Enemy were within four Miles of us, that they were a heavy numerous Body, and all naked. We continued to fortify, and prepare ourselves for their Reception. They came up with us before eleven o'Clock, and by their furious Attacks and superior Numbers, we expected that they would have attempted to storm us directly, and therefore answered them only with Musket Shot now and then, as we could make sure of an active Fellow. The keeping up our Fire made the Enemy more secure, and expose themselves the more, which was a principal Reason of their losing so many Men on that Occasion. At Night, they call'd to Parly, and we suspecting Deceit took but little Notice of it, until they repeated the same frequently, and then Mr. Van Braam was sent to speak with them, who soon returned to assure us that they were in earnest. This was no disagreeable News to us, who had received no Intelligence of the approach of our Convoys or Reinforcements, and who had only a Couple Bags of Flour and a little Bacon left for the Support of 300 Men. We had intended to have killed the Milch Cows which were our greatest Dependence before the Engagement, but had no Salt to preserve them, and they soon bcame the property of a superior Enemy. By the continued Rains, and Water in the Trenches, the most of our Arms were out of Order, and we had only a Couple of Screws in the whole Regiment to clean them. But what was still worse, it was no sooner dark, than one-half of our Men got drunk. Under these disadvantageous Circumstances, we agreed to the Articles of Capitulation, which no Doubt you have seen, with the Difference which I shall remark, and which I think very Material. Mr. Peyronie was dangerously wounded, and we much regretted to the Loss of his Services on this Occasion.

"When Mr. Van Braam returned with the French Proposals, we were obliged to take the Sense of them by word of Mouth: It rained so heavily that he could not give us a written Translation of them; we could scarcely keep the Candle light to read them; they were wrote in a bad Hand, on wet and blotted Paper so that no Person could read them but Van Braam who had heard them from the mouth of the French Officer. Every Officer then present, is willing to declare, that there was no such word as Assassination mentioned; the Terms expressed to us were 'the Death of Jumonville.' If it had been mentioned, we could have got it altered, as the French seemed very condenscending, and willing to bring Things to a Conclusion; during the whole course of the Interview: Upon our insisting on it they altered what was more material to them, the Article relating to Ammunition, which they wanted to detain; and that of the Cannon, which they agreed to have destroyed, instead of reserved for their Use. Another Article, which appears to our Disadvantage, is that whereby we obliged ourselves not to attempt an Establishment beyond the Mountains: This was translated to us, 'Not to attempt Buildings or Improvements, on the Lands of his Most Christian Majesty.' This we never intended; but denied that he had any Lands there, and therefore thought it needless to dispute that Point.

"The Article, which related to the Hostages, is quite different from the Translation of it given to us; they are mentioned for the Security of the Performance of the Tready, as well as for the Return of the Prisoners: There was never such intention on our Side, nor mention of it made on theirs by our Interpreter. Thus by the evil Intention or Negligence of Van Braam, our Conduct is blamed by a busy World, fond of finding Fault without considering Circumstances, or giving just Attention to Reasons which might be offered to obviate their Clamours. Let any of these brave Gentlemen, who fight so many successful Engagements over a Bottle, imagine himself at the Head of 300 Men, and laboring under all the Disadvantages abovementioned, and would not accept of worse Terms than Col. Washington agreed to? Which were, all the Honours of War, without the mention of '*Assassination*' or any other Expression objected to in the abovementioned Articles. It appears to me, that if he did not, he might justly be said to be Accessary to the Destruction of so many Men, which would have been the inevitable Consequence of his mistaken Courage, or Obstinacy. You have no Reason to doubt but the whole Affair was well conducted, when the French, who had first orders to give no Quarter, and to pay the Indians with our Scalps and Spoils, were the first who discovered an Inclination to Treat. That they had such Orders and intended no Quarter, is certain, from the Mouth of one of their own Officers."

II. Articles of Capitulation

Capitulation granted Mons. De Villier, captain and commander of infantry and troops of his most Christian Majesty, to those English troops actually in the fort of Necessity which was built on the lands of the King's dominions July the 3rd, at eight o'clock at night, 1754.

As our intention has never been to trouble the peace and good harmony which reigns between the two friendly princes, but only to revenge the assassination which has been done on one of our officers, bearer of a summons, upon his party, as also to hinder any establishment on the lands of the dominions of the King, my master; upon these considerations, we are willing to grant protection or favor, to all the English that are in the said fort, upon the conditions hereafter mentioned.

1. We grant the English Commander to retire with all his garrisons, to return peaceably into his own country, and we promise to hinder his receiving any insult from us French, and to restrain as much as shall be in our power the Savages that are with us.

2. He shall be permitted to withdraw and to take with him whatever belongs to them excepting the artillery, which we reserve for ourselves.

3. We grant them the honors of war; they shall come out with drums beating, and with a small piece of cannon, wishing to show by this means that we treat them as friends.

4. As soon as these Articles are signed by both parties they shall take down the English flag.

5. Tomorrow at daybreak a detachment of French shall receive the surrender of the garrison and take possession of the aforesaid fort.

6. Since the English have scarcely any horses or oxen left, they shall be allowed to hide their property, in order that they may return to seek for it after they shall have recovered their horses; for this purpose they shall be permitted to leave such number of troops as guards as they may think proper, under this condition that they give their word of honor that they will work on no establishment either in the surrounding country or beyond the Highlands during one year beginning from this day.

7. Since the English have in their power an officer and two cadets, and, in general, all the prisoners whom they took when they assassinated Sieur de Jumonville they now promise to send them with an escort to Fort Duquesne, situated on Belle River, and to secure the safe performance of this treaty article, as well as of the treaty Messrs. Jacob Van Braam and Robert Stobo, both Captains shall be delivered to us as hostages until the arrival of our French and Canadians herein before mentioned.

We on our part declare that we shall give an escort to send back in safety the two officers who promise us our French in two months and a half at the latest.

Made out in duplicate on one of the posts of our blockhouse the same day and year as before.

       Signed
         JAMES MACKAY
         GO. WASHINGTON
         COULON DE VILLIER

III. ROSTER OF VIRGINIA OFFICERS AND PRIVATES[1]

[1] The Roster of Captain James Mackay's command consisting of South Carolina troops, is not available. The spelling used is that found in the reports made at Wills Creek, July 9, 1754.

FIELD OFFICERS OF THE VIRGINIA REGIMENT

Colonel George Washington, Commanding
Lieutenant Colonel George Muse
Major Adam Stephen
Ensign William Peyronie, Adjutant
Ensign James Craik, Surgeon

CAPTAIN STOBO'S COMPANY

Captain Robert Stobo—hostage	Sergeant Robert Tunstill
Lieutenant William Polson	Corporal Nathan Lewis
Sergeant Thomas Langdon	Drummer James Carson

218   WASHINGTON AND THE WEST

Private Charles Smith
Private John Jones
Private John Goldson
Private John Ritson—killed
Private William Coffland
Private David Welch (Daniel)
Private Michael McGrath—wounded
Private John Franklin
Private Michael Reilly—wounded
Private Daniel McClaren—killed
Private Adam Jones
Private John Carroll
Private Thomas Fisher—killed
Private Patrick Durphy—wounded
Private James Good—wounded
Private William Stallons
Private Robert McCulroy
Private Jesse Morris
Private Joseph Gibbs
Private Anthony Kennedy
Private John Tranton—killed
Private Charles Waddy
Private Henry Bayly
Private William Deveeny
Private Alexander Stewart—wounded

Private Nicholas Foster
Private Isaac Moore
Private Peregrin Williams—wounded
Private James Welch
Private Joseph Casterton
Private Henry Bowman
Private Henry Neill
Private John Bryan
Private Jacob Gowing
Private John Brown
Private James Milton
Private William Swallow
Private Robert McCulroy—wounded
Private Edward Graves
Private Richard Morris
Private Ware Rocket
Private Dennis Kinton
Private Daniel Staple
Private John Allen
Private James Batty
Private Thomas Ogden
Private Benjamin Gause
Private Richard Smith
Private John Capshaw
Private John Harwood

CAPTAIN HOG'S COMPANY

Captain Peter Hog
Lieutenant James Towers
Ensign William Bronaugh
Sergeant Edmond Waggoner
Sergeant Richard Trotter
Corporal James Thomas
Corporal Nicholas Morgan
Private Robert Jones—wounded
Private James Heyler—wounded
Private Jesse May
Private James Samuel
Private Joseph Milton
Private Benjamin Hamilton
Private Mathew Cox
Private John Martin
Private Mathew Durham—wounded
Private Michael Scully
Private Joshua Burton—wounded
Private William Johnston

Private Abner Hazlip
Private William Coleman
Private Argyle House—wounded
Private Thomas Kitson
Private Thomas Moss
Private David Gorman—wounded
Private John Ogilby
Private John Roe
Private Southy Hazlip
Private Peter Effleck
Private Duncan Farguson
Private Thomas Chaddock
Private Robert Elliot—wounded
Private John Ramsay
Private Andrew Fowler
Private Samuel Hyden—wounded
Private Zachariah Smith
Private Thomas Napp
Private Bibby Brooke

APPENDIX A

Private Thomas Slaughter
Private Joseph Gatewood
Private Briant Page
Private John Chapman—wounded
Private John Mears
Private Matthew Nevison
Private William Underhill
Private Thomas Harris
Private Edward Goodwin—wounded
Private James Ford—wounded
Private Joseph Scott
Private Marshal Pratt
Private William Dean
Private James Letort
Private Dominick Moran
Private Dudley Skinner—wounded
Private Andrew Clark
Private John Stephens
Private Philip Gatewood
Private James Meggs
Private Thomas Sellars

CAPTAIN LEWIS'S COMPANY

Captain Andrew Lewis—wounded
Lieutenant John Savage—wounded
Sergeant John McCulley—wounded
Sergeant Robert Graham
Corporal Thomas Stedman
Corporal Josias Baker
Drummer Abraham Mashaw
Drummer David Wilkinson
Private John Whitman
Private Thomas Scott—killed
Private John Smith
Private William Harbinson
Private James Fullham—wounded
Private Robert Grymes
Private John Poor
Private John Rodgers—wounded
Private Garrett Clark—killed
Private William Poor
Private Michael McCannon
Private John Maston
Private Thomas Bird—wounded
Private Edward Cahell—wounded
Private Arthur Watts—wounded
Private John Biddlecome
Private Thomas Pearson
Private Edward Bayley
Private John Powers
Private James Faugesson
Private Nehemiah Tendall—wounded
Private James Rowe
Private John Mulholand
Private Patrick Coyle
Private John Ramsay—killed
Private John Smith
Private John Durham—wounded
Private John Rodgers
Private Mathew Jones
Private Joseph Baxter
Private James Ludlow
Private Thomas Foster
Private Thomas Burney
Private Thomas Nicholson—wounded
Private John Burk
Private Nathan Chapman—wounded
Private Cornelius Henley
Private William Carnes
Private Tarance Swinney
Private Philip Connerley—wounded
Private James Smith
Private John Field
Private Robert Murphey
Private James Tytus
Private George McSwine—wounded
Private John McEntire
Private Bartholemew Burns
Private Patrick McPick
Private John Truston
Private Daniel Malatte
Private James McCommac

CAPTAIN VAN BRAAM'S COMPANY

Captain Jacob Van Braam—hostage
Lieutenant Thomas Wagener
—wounded
Ensign John Mercer
Sergeant Major John Hamilton
—wounded

Sergeant Rudolph Brickner—wounded
Sergeant Thomas Carter
Corporal Nicholas Major
Corporal John Allan
Drummer Ezekiel Richardson
Private John Robinson—killed
Private Wile Johnston—wounded
Private William Gerrard
Private Robert Bell
Private Richard Bolton
Private Thomas Donahough
Private Michael Franks
Private William Simmons—killed
Private William Knowls
Private James Black
Private John Brown
Private Godfry Bomgardner
Private Christopher Byerley
Private George Taylor—wounded
Private William Mitchell
Private John Stewart
Private John Potter—wounded
Private John McGuire
Private Charles Allbury
Private George Malcomb
Private Francis Self
Private John Johnson
Private John Campbell
Private William Bayley—killed
Private Joseph Powell—wounded
Private Edward King
Private John Coin
Private Charles Dunn
Private Patrick Gallaway
Private Jacob Funkhouser
Private Bernard Draxeller
Private George Gobell
Private William Carter
Private John Thomson
Private Thomas Hennesey
Private Francis Rogers
Private Benjamin Spiser
Private Demsey Simmons—wounded
Private Edward Whitehead
Private Hugh Paul
Private Angus McDonald
Private Arthur Howard
Private Mathias Sharp
Private Edward Minor
Private William Hogan

CAPTAIN MERCER'S COMPANY

Captain George Mercer—wounded
Sergeant Mark Hollis
Sergeant James Tyrrell
Corporal Hugh McCoy
Corporal John Boyd
Drummer Edward Evans
Private James Dewey
Private James Gwin
Private Robert Bennett
Private Robert Stewart—wounded
Private David Montgomery
Private William Lowry
Private Samuel Arsdale
Private Timothy Conway—wounded
Private John Bisnor—missing
Private Nathaniel Barrett
Private William Field
Private William Holland—missing
Private John Ferguson
Private George Gibbons
Private Jacob Myer
Private Frederick Rupart
Private Barnaby McKan—killed
Private Henry Earnest
Private Alexander Pierry
Private Thomas Burk
Private Adam Leonard
Private Hugh Stone
Private Christopher Bombgardner
Private Claud Dallowe
Private William Gardner—wounded
Private Christopher Helsley
Private William Pullen—killed
Private Mathew Howard—missing
Private John Biyans
Private Thomas Burris
Private John Farmer
Private Jacob Arrens—captured by the enemy
Private John McGuire

APPENDIX A

Private Philip Waters
Private Robert Bennett
Private Joshua Jordan—wounded
Private Michael Walker
Private William Broughton
Private Henry Bristowe
Private Hugh McKoy
Private James Daily
Private John May

Private John Gollahorn
Private John Clements
Private John Huston
Private William McIntire
Private Hugh Ratchford
Private Gasper Moorhead
Private William Tyan
Private Bryan Conner

APPENDIX B

THE BATTLE OF THE MONONGAHELA

I. Account of the march and first report of the battle as given in extracts from letters, the first from Little Meadows, June 18, 1755, and the second from Great Meadows, July 1, 1755, and printed in the *Pennsylvania Gazette* for July 24, 1755.

1. "I have nothing material since my last: There is a Party gone this Day of near 500 Men, and To-morrow the General marches with 1000 of the choicest Men: They take but four Hawitzers, four Twelve-pounders, twelve Cohorns, and thirty Waggons, with the best Horses, and spare Ones, and the Remainder of their Provisions to be carried on Horses Backs; and they expect to be at the French Fort in less than ten Days; and Colonel Dunbar, with the Remainder of the Forces, Carriages, &c. are to march next Monday, so that I hope my next will give you an Account of our being in Fort Du Quesne. The General has sent a Captain and 150 Men to cover your Workmen at the Roads, so that we hope the so much wished for Communication with Philadelphia will soon be opened. We are already greatly distressed for fresh Provisions, all our Hopes are on you."

2. "On the 9th of last Month, the whole Army (except 600 Men, with Sir John St. Clair, who marched two Days before) went from Wills's-Creek, and with infinite Difficulty, through the worst Roads in the World, arrived ten Days afterwards at the Little Meadows, where an Abbatis was made by Sir John and two Engineers, incircling the whole Camp. Here the Whole halted three Days; then the Baronet with his Party moved forwards, and the second Day after the General with four Hawitzers, four 12 Pounders, 13 Artillery Waggons, besides Ammunition Carts, followed him, and have kept marching ever since, and this Evening it is expected his Excellency will be within 25 Miles of the Fort. Colonel Dunbar, with the Remainder of the Army, four Artillery Officers, 84 Carriages, with Ordnance Stores, and all the Provision Waggons, form the Rear, amongst whom I am.

"The Night before last we were alarmed four different Times by the skulking Indians, on whom our Out-Guards and Centries fired. 'Tis said this Morning the General has had Advice, that 500 Regulars are in full March to the Fort, which is the Reason he is determined to be there before them. As we have had but very little fresh Provisions since we left the Fort at Wills's Creek, the Officers as well as private Men have been, and still are, extremely ill of the Flux, many have died. To-morrow Morning we march again, and are to encamp on the western Side of the Great Meadows; from whence we are to proceed after the General, but am fearful it will not be before we have built some Fortification there, and leave a strong Party of Men, with a great Deal of Provisions and Artillery Stores, our Horses being so weak, for want of Food and Rest, that it is impossible for the whole Rear to join the Front in Five and Twenty Days.

"We are sorry to acquaint our Readers, that by Variety of Accounts from the Frontiers it appears, that General Braddock, with 1500 Men, being on the Ninth Instant within a few miles of Fort Du Quesne, was attacked by the French and their Indians, who fought in the Indian Manner from behind Trees, taking Aim, firing and retiring; but the English kept together in a Body, firing in the European Manner; and after an Engagement of near three Hours, they were obliged to retreat, with the Loss of Part of the Artillery and the Baggage; a great Number of Officers and Soldiers being killed and wounded. The Remainder had joined Colonel Dunbar, who with his Regiment was bringing up the Rear with the heavy Baggage, some Artillery Stores, Provisions, &c. and the whole marched back on the Twelfth for Fort Cumberland, where it was expected they might arrive about the Twentieth. 'Tis said the General had three Horses shot under him, and himself and Sir John St. Clair, are both wounded, but it was hoped not mortally. That the Officers behaved extremely well, but the Soldiers could not be kept in Order. In these Circumstances most of the Accounts agree; but there is a great Variety in other Respects, and therefore, as more authentick Accounts are hourly expected, we chuse to def[er] other Particulars till we have better Authority for inserting them.

"It is hoped that these Southern Colonies, by a vigorous Exertion of their Strength, will soon have a Body of Men upon the Frontiers, capable of repairing our late Loss, and asserting their Right to the Country the French have taken Possession of."

II. The battle and participating officers as given in an "Extract of a Letter from an Officer" at Fort Cumberland, July 18, 1755, and printed in the *Pennsylvania Gazette*, No. 1388, July 31, 1755.

"The 9th Inst. we passed and repassed the Monongahela, by advancing first a Party of 300 Men, which was immediately followed by another of 200. The General, with the Column of Artillery, Baggage, and the main Body of the Army, passed the River the last Time about One a Clock. As soon as the whole had got on the Fort Side of the Monongahela, we heard a very heavy and quick Fire in our Front; we immediately advanced in order to sustain them; but the Detachment of the 200 and 300 Men gave Way, and fell back upon us, which caused such Confusion, and struck so great a Panick among our Men, that afterwards no military Expedient could be made use of that had any Effect upon them: The Men were so extreamly deaf to the Exhortations of the General, and the Officers, that they fired away, in the most irregular Manner, all their Ammunition, and then run off, leaving to the Enemy the Artillery, Ammunition, Provision and Baggage; nor could they be persuaded to stop till they got as far as Gist's Plantation, nor there only in

Part, many of them proceeding as far as Colonel Dunbar's Party, who lay six Miles on this Side.

"The Officers were absolutely sacrificed by their unparallelled good Behaviour, advancing sometimes in Bodies, and sometimes separately, hoping by such Example to engage the Soldiers to follow them, but to no Purpose.

"The General had five Horses killed under him, and at last received a Wound thro' his Right Arm into his Lungs, of which he died the 13th Instant. Secretary Shirley was shot thro' the Head; Capt. Morris wounded; Mr. Washington had two Horses shot under him, and his Clothes shot thro' in several Places, behaving the whole Time with the greatest Courage and Resolution. Sir Peter Halket was killed upon the Spot. Col. Burton, and Sir John St. Clair wounded; and enclosed I have sent you a List of the Killed and Wounded, according to as exact Account as we are yet able to get.

"Upon our proceeding with the whole Convoy to the Little Meadows, it was found impracticable to advance in that Manner; the General therefore advanced with Twelve Hundred Men, with the necessary Artillery, Ammunition and Provisions, leaving the main Body of the Convoy under the Command of Col. Dunbar, with Orders to join him as soon as possible.

"In this Manner we proceeded with Safety and Expedition, till the fatal Day I have just related; and happy it was, that this Disposition was made, otherwise the whole must either have starved, or fallen into the Hands of the Enemy, as Numbers would have been of no Service to us, and our Provision was all lost.

"As our Number of Horses was so much reduced, and those extreamly weak, and many Carriages being wanted for the wounded Men, occasioned our destroying the Ammunition and superfluous Part of the Provision left in Col. Dunbar's Convoy, to prevent its falling into the Hands of the Enemy.

"As the whole of the Artillery is lost, and the Troops are so extreamly weakened by Deaths, Wounds and Sickness, it was judged impossible to make any farther Attempt; therefore Col. Dunbar is returning to Fort Cumberland, with every Thing he is able to bring up with him.

"By the particular Disposition of the French and Indians, it was impossible to judge of the Numbers they had that Day in the Field.

"A List of the Officers who were present, and of those killed and wounded in the Action on the Banks of Monongahela, the ninth Day of July, 1755.

STAFF

His Excellency Edward Braddock, Esq; General and Commander in Chief of all his Majesty's Forces in North America. Died of his Wounds.

Robert Orme, Esq; ⎫
Roger Morris, Esq; ⎬ Aid de Camps. wounded.
George Washington, Esq; ⎭ wounded.

William Shirley, Esq; Secretary, killed.
Sir John St. Clair, Deputy Quarter-Master General, wounded.
Matthew Lesly, Gent. Assistant to the Q. Master General, wounded.
Francis Halket, Esq; Major of Brigade,

APPENDIX B

44TH REGIMENT

Sir Peter Halket, Colonel, killed.
Lieutenant Colonel Gage, slightly wounded.
Capts. Tatton, killed.
    Hobson,
    Beckworth,
    Gethins, killed.
Lieuts. Falconer,
    Litteler, wounded.
    Bailey,
    Dunbar, wounded.
    Pottinger,

Halket, killed.
Treeby, wounded.
Allen, killed.
Simpson, wounded.
Lock, wounded.
Disney, wounded.
Kennedy, wounded.
Townsend, killed.
Preston,
Nartlow, killed.
Pennington, wounded.

48TH REGIMENT

Lieut. Col. Burton, wounded.
Major Sparks, slightly wounded.
Capts. Dobson,
    Cholmley, killed.
    Bowyer, wounded.
    Ross, wounded.
Capt. Lieut. Morris,
Lieuts. Barbut, wounded.
    Walsham, wounded.
    Crimble, killed.
    Wideman, killed.
    Hansard, killed.
    Gladwis, wounded.

Hathorn,
Edmeston, wounded.
Cope,
Brereton, killed.
Hart, killed.
Montrefeur, wounded.
Dunbar,
Harrison,
Cowhart,
M'Mullen, wounded.
Crow, wounded.
Stirling, wounded.

ARTILLERY

Capt. Orde,
Capt. Lieut. Smith, killed.
Lieut. Buchannan, wounded.

Lieut. M'Cloud, wounded.
Lieut. M'Culler, wounded.

DETACHMENT OF SAILORS

Lieut. Spendelow, killed.
Mr. Haynes, Midshipman,
Mr. Talbot, Midshipman, killed.

Capt. Stone, of General Lascell's Regiment, killed.
Capt. Floyer, of General Warburton's Regiment, wounded.

INDEPENDENT COMPANIES OF NEW-YORK

Capt. Gates, wounded.
Lieut. Soumain, killed.
Lieut. Miller,

Lieut. Howarth, of Capt. Demerie's Independent Company, wounded.
Lieut. Gray, of the same Company, wounded.

VIRGINIA TROOPS

Capts. Stephens, wounded.	Lieuts. Woodward,
Waggoner,	Wright, killed.
Polson, killed.	Splitdorff, killed.
Peronie, killed.	Stuart, wounded.
Stewart,	Waggoner, killed.
Lieut. Hamilton, killed.	M'Neale,

According to the most exact Return we can as yet get, about 600 Men killed and wounded."

NOTES

Chapter I

1. For more detailed information on the early life of George Washington see: S. W. Mitchell, *Youth of Washington*, chaps. 1-10; J. C. Fitzpatrick, *Washington Himself*, chaps. 1-3; Woodrow Wilson, *Washington*, pp.3-49; R. A. Pryor, *Mother of Washington and Her Times*; United States George Washington Bicentennial Commission, *History of the George Washington Bicentennial Celebration*, I, 5-15, 205-35 (hereafter cited as Bicentennial Commission, *History*); Charles Moore, *Family Life of George Washington;* Grace King, *Mount Vernon on the Potomac;* M. D. Conway, *George Washington and Mount Vernon,* and *Barons of the Potomac and the Rappahannock;* G. W. P. Custis, *Recollections and Private Memoirs of Washington;* Rupert Hughes, *George Washington*, I, chaps. 1-2.
2. Fitzpatrick, *op. cit.*, pp. 17-19; Hughes, I, 1-38.
3. Bicentennial Commission, *History*, I, 230-34.
4. *Ibid.*, p. 233.
5. P. L. Ford, *The True George Washington*, pp. 17-19; Hughes, *op. cit.*, I, 13-15.
6. Ford, *op. cit.*, pp. 17-22; Custis, *op. cit.*, p. 303.
7. Hughes, *op. cit.*, II, 46.
8. Bicentennial Commission, *History*, I, 230.
9. H. C. Lodge, *George Washington*, I, chap. 2, "The Washingtons."
10. Hughes, *op. cit.*, I, 12; William Meade, *Old Churches, Ministers and Families of Virginia*, II, 167.
11. Hughes, *op. cit.*, I, 12; Fitzpatrick, *op. cit.*, p. 17; Washington, *Writings* (ed. by W. C. Ford), XIV, 391-96.
12. Fitzpatrick, *op. cit.*, pp. 19-20, 517 n.
13. *Ibid.*, p. 19.
14. *Ibid.*
15. *Ibid.*, p. 20.
16. *Ibid.*, p. 25.
17. *Ibid.*
18. *Ibid.*, p. 26.
19. For instances and alleged instances in the early life of Washington, see Conway, *George Washington and Mount Vernon;* Moore, *op. cit.;* Hughes, *op. cit.*, I, chap. 2; and W. R. Thayer, *George Washington*, chap. 1.
20. Fitzpatrick, *op. cit.*, p. 21.
21. See J. M. Toner, *Washington's Rules of Civility and Decent Behavior;* Conway, *George Washington's Rules of Civility;* Fitzpatrick, *op. cit.*, p. 518 n.
22. *Ibid.*, p. 28.
23. *Ibid.*, p. 43.
24. *Ibid.*, pp. 35, 518 n; Hughes, *op. cit.*, I, 35.

Chapter II

1. Thomas Fairfax (October 22, 1693-December 9, 1781), sixth Baron of Cameron, was born at Leeds Castle, County Kent, England. On his mother's side he was a direct descendant from the Culpepers. In physique and in character, Fair-

fax was indeed said to be a Culpeper. At the age of sixteen he succeeded to his family peerage and entered Oriel College, Oxford, where, except for a single contribution to Addison's *Spectator*, Fairfax's career was uneventful. In 1719 following the death of his mother, from whom he inherited his Virginia estate, a large part of his heritage in England going to pay the debts of his spendthrift father, Fairfax secured a commission in King George's Army and later became Treasurer of the Royal Household. While thus engaged his chief concern was to arrange a marriage to untangle an inherited litigation involving his claims to the Fairfax estates in Yorkshire. Disappointed in this and possibly also in love, he abandoned a career and withdrew to Leeds Castle to devote his time to fox hunting and breeding hounds. See Fairfax Harrison, "Thomas Fairfax," *Dictionary of American Biography*, VI, 255-57; J. E. Cooke, *Fairfax, or The Master of Greenway Court*, and *Stories of the Old Dominion*, pp. 94-110; Wilson, *George Washington*, pp. 48-59; George Washington Bicentennial Commission, *History*, I, 5-16; Samuel Kercheval, *History of the Valley of Virginia*; O. F. Morton, *Story of Winchester in Virginia*, chap. 3; Fairfax Harrison, "The Proprietors of the Northern Neck," in *The Virginia Magazine of History and Biography*, XXXIII; Washington, *Diaries* (ed. by J. C. Fitzpatrick), I, 3-12; C. E. Kemper, "Early Westward Movement of Virginia," in *Virginia Magazine of History and Biography*, XII-XIII; T. K. Cartmell, *A History of Frederick County Virginia*, chap. 47; Ford, *The True George Washington*; S. N. Robins, *Love Affairs of Famous Virginians*; Hughes, *George Washington*, I, chaps. 3-5.

2. As the late S. Weir Mitchell understood Washington's boyhood environment and the boy Washington as well as, or perhaps better than, any of the numerous writers on those subjects, the following imaginary letter from his fertile pen but purporting to be from Lord Fairfax to Washington's mother, is informing:

"BELVOIR

"HONORED MADAM: You are so good as to ask what I think of a temporary residence for your son George in England. It is a country for which I myself have no inclination, and the gentlemen you mention are certainly renowned gamblers and rakes, which I should be sorry your son were exposed to, even if his means easily admitted of a residence in England. He is strong and hardy, and as good a master of a horse as any could desire. His education might have been bettered, but what he has is accurate and inclines him to much life out of doors. He is very grave for one of his age, and reserved in his intercourse; not a great talker at any time. His mind appears to me to act slowly, but, on the whole, to reach just conclusions, and he has an ardent wish to see the right of questions—what my friend, Mr. Addison, was pleased to call 'the intellectual conscience.' Method and exactness seem to be natural to George. He is, I suspect, beginning to feel the sap rising, being in the spring of life, and is getting ready to be the prey of your sex, wherefore may the Lord help him, and deliver him from the nets those spiders, called women, will cast for his ruin. I presume him to be truthful because he is exact. I wish I could say that he governs his temper. He is subject to attacks of anger on provocation, and sometimes without just cause; but as he is a reasonable person, time will cure him of this vice of nature, and in fact he is, in my judgment, a man who will go to school all his life and profit thereby.

"I hope, madam, that you will find pleasure in what I have written, and will rest assured that I shall continue to interest myself in his fortunes.

"Much honoured by your appeal to my judgment, I am, my dear madam, your obedient humble servant, FAIRFAX."

3. Harrison's "The Proprietors of the Northern Neck," in *Virginia Magazine of History and Biography*, XXXIII; Kercheval, *History of the Valley of Virginia*;

Cartmell, *op. cit.*, chap. 47; F. V. Aler, *History of Martinsburg and Berkeley County*, chap. 5; W. W. Hening, *Statutes at Large*, IV, 514.

4. Thomas Lewis and Peter Jefferson, father of Thomas Jefferson, were the leading surveyors of this party. See Thomas Lewis's *Journal*, September 10, 1746-February, 1747.

5. Harrison, "Thomas Fairfax," *Dictionary of American Biography*, VI, 255-57; Cooke, *Fairfax; or, The Master of Greenway Court*.

6. Washington, *Writings* (ed. Fitzpatrick), I, 6; Washington, *Diaries* (ed. Fitzpatrick), I, 3-4.

7. Washington, *Writings* (ed. Fitzpatrick), I, 11; Washington, *Diaries* (ed. Fitzpatrick), I, 9.

8. Washington, *Writings* (ed. Fitzpatrick), I, 11; Washington, *Diaries*, (ed. Fitzpatrick), I, 9-10.

9. *Ibid.*, p. 11.

10. *Ibid.*, p. 7; Washington, *Writings* (ed. Fitzpatrick), I, 9; A. C. Myers, *The Boy George Washington*.

11. Washington, *Diaries* (ed. Fitzpatrick), I, 5; Washington, *Writings* (ed. Fitzpatrick), I, 7.

12. Washington, *Diaries* (ed. Fitzpatrick), I, 6.

13. *Ibid.*, p. 4.

14. By subsequent purchases, one of 456 acres in 1750, and another of 552 acres in 1752, Washington's realty holdings were increased to 1558 acres, all of which were paid for from his own holdings.

15. Mitchell, *op. cit.*, chap. 13; Lodge, *George Washington*, I, 55-60; Washington, *Writings* (ed. Fitzpatrick), I, 13-18.

16. *Ibid.*, p. 17.

17. Hughes, *George Washington*, I, 43.

18. Rev. Jonathan Boucher, *Reminiscences of an American Loyalist*, p. 49.

19. Moore, *Family Life of Washington*, p. 34.

20. For detail of voyage see Washington, *Diaries* (ed. Fitzpatrick), I, 17-36.

21. Fairfax Harrison's "George Washington's First Commission," in *Virginia Magazine of History and Biography*, XXXI, 271-73.

22. His pay was 100 pounds a year. "The Official Records of Robert Dinwiddie. . . ," *Virginia Historical Collections*, I, 390. (Hereafter cited as *Dinwiddie Papers*.)

23. Fitzpatrick, *Washington Himself*, p. 49.

Chapter III

1. Suggested readings: Hayes Baker-Crothers, *Virginia and the French and Indian War*; L. K. Koontz, "The Virginia Frontier, 1754-1763," *Johns Hopkins University Studies*, XLIII, 11-186; Mitchell, *The Youth of Washington;* A. B. Hulbert, *Historic Highways of America*, III; C. W. Alvord, *The Mississippi Valley in British Politics*, I and II; A. T. Volwiler, *George Croghan and the Western Movement*, 1741-1782; R. G. Thwaites, *France in America*; Hughes, *George Washington*, I, chap. 6; W. J. Showalter, "The Travels of George Washington," *The National Geographic Magazine*, LXI, 1-63.

2. C. W. Alvord and Lee Bidgood, *The First Explorations of the Trans-Alleghany*, p. 28.

3. Thwaites, *op. cit.*, chap. 5; Baker-Crothers, *op. cit.*, chap. 1; Volwiler, *op. cit.*, pp. 20-30.

4. Francis Parkman, *Montcalm and Wolfe*, I, 48. See also Hughes, *op. cit.*, I, 79.

5. Volwiler, *op. cit.*, pp. 21-25; Baker-Crothers, *op. cit.*, pp. 3-6; C. A. Hanna, *The Wilderness Trail*, I, 2-24; Christopher Gist, *Journal* (ed. Darlington), pp. 44-45; Justin Winsor, *The Mississippi Basin*, p. 249.

6. Hanna, *op. cit.*, I, 2-6; Baker-Crothers, *op. cit.*, pp. 39-40, 73-77, 93-95, 154-55.

7. Kemper, "The Early Westward Movement of Virginia," *Virginia Magazine of History and Biography*, XII and XIII; Alvord and Bidgood, *op. cit.*, pp. 17-249; Fairfax Harrison, "The Virginians of the Ohio and the Mississippi in 1742," *Virginia Magazine of History and Biography*, XXX, 203-22.

8. Cartmell, *History of Frederick County Virginia*, p. 250.

9. *Dinwiddie Papers*, I, 17 n; Baker-Crothers, *op. cit.*, pp. 8-11, 27-28; Koontz, *op. cit.*, p. 39.

10. *Journal* (ed. Darlington).

11. Washington, *Diaries* (ed. Fitzpatrick), I, 35.

12. This appointment carried a competence of one hundred pounds per annum. In November of the following year Washington was made adjutant of the Northern Neck and Eastern Shore. In this position his duties were to muster the militia, inspect their equipment, and witness drills. Fitzpatrick, *Washington Himself*, pp. 47-48.

13. Kemper, *op. cit.*, XIII, 140-50.

14. Alvord, *op. cit.*, I, 89-90.

15. Washington, *Writings* (ed. Fitzpatrick), I, 22-30; *Diaries* (ed. Fitzpatrick), I, 43-67. See also Gist's, "Journal," *Massachusetts Historical Society Collections*, V, 102-8.

16. Washington, *Diaries*; *Writings* (ed. Ford), I, 43-44.

17. *Diaries* (ed. Fitzpatrick), I, 44.

18. *Writings* (ed. Fitzpatrick), I, 24; *Diaries* (ed. Fitzpatrick), I, 45.

19. *Ibid.*, p. 46.

20. *Ibid.*, pp. 47-49.

21. *Ibid.*, p. 48.

22. *Ibid.*, p. 49.

23. *Writings* (ed. Fitzpatrick), I, 25; *Diaries* (ed. Fitzpatrick), I, 50.

24. *Ibid.*, p. 52.

25. *Ibid.*, p. 55.

26. Hulbert, *op. cit.*, III, 108; Washington, *Diaries* (ed. Fitzpatrick), I, 58.

27. *Ibid.*, p. 59.

28. Hulbert, *op. cit.*, p. 108; Hughes, *op. cit.*, I, 89; *Pennsylvania Gazette*, March 26, 1754.

29. *Diaries* (ed. Fitzpatrick), I, 60.

30. *Ibid.*, p. 67; Hughes, *op. cit.*, I, 94.

31. *Dinwiddie Papers*, I, 75; Boucher, *Reminiscences of an American Loyalist*, p. 49. Quoting a letter dated January 16, 1754, from "a Gentleman in Virginia to his Friend here [Annapolis]," the *Maryland Gazette* for February 14, 1754, carried this naive notice of Washington's safe return from his journey to the French:

"Mr. Washington, the Ambassador sent to the Indian Country, is returned, which affords us new Conversation. It is undoubtedly offered for Truth, that the French have settled and fixed several Forts near the Ohio Tract, especially one upon French River, which Mr. Washington was at, and that proper Officers and Five Hundred Men, are in each Fort, chiefly French, and that they have twelve Cannon mounted on each of them, and great Numbers of French and Indians close at Hand, to assist at a smal warning. Mr. Washington was received in a polite genteel Manner by the Commandant of the Fort, who read and answered our Governor's Letter, and at the same Time told Mr. Washington, that it was his Instructions from the King his Master, to keep Possession, and to advance farther and fight those who shall oppose them, &c. and added that he had expected an Army to be sent for twelve Months past by the English, and that they were prepared for them, for he supposed they must knock it out, and he did not care how soon. Mr. Washington is gone to Williamsburg, and 'tis supposed the Assembly will meet immediately, and that Men will be rais'd, &c."

Generally local newspapers printed in full Washington's *Journal* of his journey to the French. It occupied a large portion of each issue of the *Maryland Gazette* for March 21 and March 28, 1754.

Chapter IV

1. *Dinwiddie Papers*, I, 22, 55, 56; Washington, *Writings* (ed. Fitzpatrick), I, 20 n, 30.
2. Washington, *Diaries* (ed. Fitzpatrick), I, 43-65.
3. *Dinwiddie Papers*, I, 59.
4. *Ibid.*, pp. 96, 107, 111, 115, 118; *Maryland Gazette*, August 22, 1754.
5. Koontz, "The Virginia Frontier, 1754-1763," *Johns Hopkins University Studies*, XLIII, 53.
6. *Dinwiddie Papers*, I, 75.
7. *Pennsylvania Gazette*, January 23, 1754; *Ibid.*, May 16, 1754.
8. *South Carolina Gazette*, June 4-11, 1754. Under the same date this newspaper printed the following appeal and facts sustaining it from "a gentleman residing in one of the colonies to the Northward:"

"April 8, 1754

"I AM extremely sorry to hear, that the governments of Pennsylvania and Maryland, have not view'd the incroachments of the French in their proper light; or, if they have, that they won't exert themselves at this time of imminent danger. Should the French once gain a settlement on Ohio, they will then have great advantages over the Southern colonies, as must be obvious to every person the least acquainted with their situation. In time of peace between the two crowns, they will be continually spiriting on the Indians in their alliance, to murder and scalp the inhabitants of your back counties in order to prevent the extension of your back settlements; and, in time of war, how easy will it be for a number of troops, collected from their several forts, or perhaps sent from Old France for that purpose, to make a descent upon some or other of the colonies. What then must be the consequence! Unarmed, and disunited as you are, will you be able to repel the invaders, or prevent their ravaging or laying waste your country, or hinder them from committing their too well known barbarities on such of your inhabitants as may fall within their power? The evil day may be a while put off, but sooner or later it will surely come, unless you rouze from the lethargy you seem at present in, and make use of those means to protect yourselves which the almighty has put in your power; the most proper way of doing which is, to obstruct those incendiaries, the French and their Indians, from settling in your frontiers. By an hearty union of the colonies, and proper management, we might, with little assistance from our mother country, not only dislodge the French from Ohio, but from Quebec itself. But to send 3 or 400 men against 5 times their number, can answer no other end than to expose us to the contempt of our Indian allies, who will think themselves obliged to quit the interest of those that seem unable to protect them.

"You desire me to acquaint you with what I hear that may be depended on, concerning the designs of the French, in sending so large a number of troops from Canada as they did the last summer. In answer to which I can inform you, that I have lately seen Mr. B———r, who was at Oswego at the time their forces passed by that fort; who says, he learnt by sundry deserters, and others, that Mons. du Quisne, the new governor general of Canada, a young gentleman formerly captain of a man of war, declares, he will have a French fort on each of the waters that empty themselves into St. Lawrence, or Mississippi; that he believes the late governors of Canada have been all asleep, but that he will make every officer under him know his duty, and do it. That 4 or 5 detachments were, during the last summer, sent from Canada to the Ohio, making in the whole about 2000, besides Indians, under the command of Mons. Morin (or Morang, as some call him) whose knowledge of the Indians recommended him to the new governor for that office. The detachment that accompanied Morin, consisted of about 40 or 50 large bateaus, and canows, many of them supposed to carry more than 30 men; they sailed within musket shot of Oswego, without ever striking their colours, and had their trumpets blowing, drums beating, &c. This was in sight of many of the six Nations, and foreign Indians, who could not sufficiently express their surprise at such an armament, and asked whether the English and French were not at peace.

"Some of these troops returned to Canada during the winter, to quarters, but great part of them were left, as is supposed, at the forts on and near the lakes, to be ready to go down the Ohio early in the spring: Those that returned had with them the Pennsylvania Indian traders so often mentioned to be taken by the French on Ohio; these poor wretches were in irons, and lodged a night within a few miles of Oswego. One of the famous chiefs of the Cahuga nation, proposed to some of the traders to attack the French, and recover the prisoners, but they could not muster a sufficient party to do this. Mons. Morin built 2 or 3 forts, but many disputes arising between him and his officers, together with a severe fit of the gout, obliged him to desire to quit his command; for which purpose an express was last September sent to Canada, and I suppose the gentleman who writes to governor Dinwiddie was made his successor, who if he exceeds Morin as much in humanity, as he does in politeness and good sense, may be of service to those who may have the misfortune of being taken prisoners in that country.

"I saw Morin and his son, some years ago in Canada; they have all the vain airs of the French, joined with the savageness of the Indians, without the least of the politeness of the former, or native simplicity and grandeur of the latter. The father commanded when the brave Donahew, Captain of one of the Boston sloops, was decoyed ashore and killed; the son was one of his party: As trophies of their victory, the old man shewed me a tobacco pouch, which he, and the young brute, let me know was made of the skin of poor Donahew's arm: The father had also Donahew's ring, which the son, acquainted me he cut off the finger to get, as it would not come off easily. After this, I saw some of Donahew's men who were prisoners, they not only confirmed the above, but assured me, the brutish father did himself cut off several pieces of their dead captain's flesh, and threw them into the fire, and encouraged the Indians to do the like; and when they were roasted, the cannibal son, and sundry Indians, tore them with their teeth. This may serve as a specimen of the neighbours you are like to have."

9. Baker-Crothers, *Virginia in the French and Indian War*, chap. 3; Koontz, *op. cit.*, chap. 3.

10. Washington, *Writings* (ed. Fitzpatrick), I, 32; *Dinwiddie Papers*, I, 92.

11. Alvord, *Mississippi Valley in British Politics*, I, 105-7; G. L. Beer, *British Colonial Policy, 1754-1756*, pp. 132-59; Baker-Crothers, *op. cit.*, pp. 6-8; *South Carolina Gazette*, 1754 passim.

12. Baker-Crothers, *op. cit.*, pp. 40-45.

13. *Dinwiddie Papers*, I, 81.

14. Washington, *Writings* (ed. Fitzpatrick), I, 37-38; Washington, *Diaries* (ed. Fitzpatrick), I, 73; *Dinwiddie Papers*, I, 59.

15. Washington, *Journal of 1754* (ed. Toner), pp. 14, 17; Fitzpatrick, *Washington Himself*, p. 57; *Dinwiddie Papers*, I, 59.
16. *Maryland Gazette*, March 14, 1754.
17. *Ibid.*
18. Washington, *Diaries* (ed. Fitzpatrick), I, 74; Washington, *Writings* (ed. Fitzpatrick), I, 38.
19. Lodge, *George Washington*, I, 69.
20. As given in the *Maryland Gazette* for May 23, 1754, quoting a dispatch from Philadelphia, dated May 9, Washington made the following report of events and conditions on the frontier:

"Friday last an Express arrived here from Major Washington with Advice that Mr. Ward, Ensign of Captain Trent's Company, was compelled to surrender his small Fort in the Forks of Monongahela to the French, on the 17th past; who fell down from Venango with a fleet of 360 Battoes and Canoes, upwards of 1000 Men, and 18 Pieces of Artillery, which they planted against the Fort; and Mr. Ward, having but 44 men and no Cannon to make a proper Defence, was obliged to surrender on Summons, capitulating to march out with their Arms, &c. and they had accordingly joined Major Washington, who was advanced with three Companies of the Virginia Forces, as far as the New Store near the Allegheny Mountains, where the Men were employed in clearing a Road for the Cannon, which were every Day expected with Col. Fry, and the Remainder of the Regiment. We hear farther, that some few of the English Traders on the Ohio escaped, but 'tis supposed the greater Part are taken, with all their Goods, and Skins, to the Amount of near 20,000 £. The Indian Chiefs, however, have dispatched Messages to Pennsylvania, and Virginia, desiring that the English would not be discouraged, but send out our Warriors to join them, and drive the French out of the Country before they fortify; otherwise the Trade will be lost, and to their great Grief, an eternal Separation made between the Indians and their Brethren the English. 'Tis farther said, that besides the French that came down from Venango, another Body of near 400, is coming up the Ohio; and that 600 French Indians of the Chippeways and Ottoways are coming down Siota River, from the Lake, to join them; and many more French are expected from Canada; the design being to establish themselves, settle their Indians, and build Forts just on the Back of our Settlements in all our Colonies; from which Forts, as they did from Crown-Point, they may send out their Parties to kill and scalp the Inhabitants, and ruin our Frontier Counties. Accordingly, we hear, that the Back Settlers in Virginia, are so terrif'd by the Murdering and Scalping a whole Family last Winter, and the taking of this Fort, that they begin already to abandon their Plantations, and remove to Places of more Safety. The Confidence of the French in this Undertaking seems well grounded on the present disunited State of the British Colonies, and the extreme Difficulty of bringing so many different Governments and Assemblies to agree in any speedy and effectual Measures for our common Defence and Security; while our Enemies have the very great Advantage of being under one Direction, with one Council and one Purse. Hence, and from the great Distance of Britain, they presume that they may with Impunity violate the most solemn Treaties subsisting between the two Crowns, kill, seize and imprison our Traders, and confiscate their Effects at Pleasure (as they have done for several Years past) murder and scalp our Farmers, with their Wives and Children, and take an easy Possession of such Parts of the British Territory as they shall find most convenient for them; which if they are permitted to do, must end in the Destruction of the British Interest, Trade and Plantations in America."

21. Captain de Contrecoeur with six hundred men established a camp where Pittsburgh now stands on April 16. See C. W. Dahlinger, *Marquis Duquesne*, p.

48; Gist, *Journal* (ed. Darlington), p. 275; F. X. Garneau, *History of Canada*, I, 467; Washington, *Diaries* (ed. Fitzpatrick), I, 52, 75-76.

22. *Ibid.*, p. 77.
23. *Ibid.*, pp. 79-82.
24. Washington, *Writings* (ed. Fitzpatrick), I, 48; *Dinwiddie Papers*, I, 170.
25. *Ibid.*, pp. 171-72.
26. Washington, *Writings* (ed. Ford), I, 59-63.
27. Washington, *Diaries* (ed. Fitzpatrick), I, 83-84.
28. Washington, *Writings* (ed. Ford), I, 82; Washington, *Diaries* (ed. Fitzpatrick), I, 87; *Dinwiddie Papers*, I, 179; Washington, *Writings* (ed. Fitzpatrick), I, 63-64; *Alexandria Gazette*, July 19, 1754; N. B. Craig, *Washington's First Campaign, Death of Jumonville, and the Taking of Fort Necessity*, p. 5; I. D. Rupp, *Early History of Western Pennsylvania*, p. 74; and Washington, *Writings* (ed. Sparks), II, Appendix, p. 447.
29. Washington, *Journal of 1754* (ed. Toner), pp. 14, 17, 89; James Veech, *Monongahela of Old*, p. 47.
30. Fitzpatrick, *op. cit.*, p. 62; *Pennsylvania Gazette*, June 27, 1754; *Maryland Gazette*, June 13, 1754.
31. *Ibid*; *Pennsylvania Gazette*, June 27, 1754; Washington, *Writings* (ed. Fitzpatrick), I, 63-64.
32. For French accounts see G. R. de Flassan, *Histoire de la Diplomatie Française*, VI, 28; Lacretelle Le Jeune, *Histoire de France*, II, 234; Abbé G. H. R. de Montgaillard, *Histoire de France*, V, 297.
33. *Mémoire contenant le précis des faits, avec leur pièces justificatives, pour servir de répose aux observations envoyées, par les ministers d'Angleterre, dans les course de l'Europe*. In 1757 this work was published in English at Philadelphia. See also N. B. Craig, *Olden Time*, II, 140-277; and Hughes, *George Washington*, I, 141.
34. Washington, *Journal of 1754* (ed. Toner), p. 17; Fitzpatrick, *op. cit.*, p. 62. Reputable American historians, mostly local, have accepted the French accounts of the Jumonville affair as in the main correct. For example, the English accounts failed to satisfy Samuel W. Pennypacker, see his *Pennsylvania in American History*, p. 152; and Winthrop Sargent in his *History of an Expedition against Fort Du Quesne, in 1755*, p. 43, states that "considering all that we can learn, it is to be regretted that there seems some cause to believe the truth of this [the French] story."
35. Antoine L. Thomas, *Oeuvres Diverses*, I, 2-10; Dahlinger, *op. cit.*, pp. 52-53.
36. Dr. William Hindman, pastor of the Presbyterian Church, Uniontown, Pennsylvania, and chairman of the local committee in charge of the reconstruction of Fort Necessity, first suggested the possible use of this information to the present author.
37. *Dinwiddie Papers*, I, 180.
38. Rupp, *op. cit.*, p. 84; Washington, *Journal of 1754* (ed. Toner), p. 8. See Appendix A, II.
39. Washington, *Writings* (ed. Fitzpatrick), I, 69.
40. *Maryland Gazette*, August 29, 1754. See Appendix A, I, 2.
41. *Pennsylvania Gazette*, June 27, 1754.
42. Washington, *Writings* (ed. Fitzpatrick), I, 70; Washington, *Writings* (ed. Fort), I, 89-90.
43. Lodge, *George Washington*, I, 74-75.

Chapter V

1. *Writings* (ed. Fitzpatrick), I, 58.
2. *Ibid.*, p. 67.

3. *Ibid.*
4. *Ibid.*, p. 69.
5. *Ibid.*, p. 73.
6. *Ibid.*, pp. 71-74.
7. Washington, *Diaries* (ed. Fitzpatrick), I, 91; Washington, *Journal of 1754* (ed. Toner), p. 102. A dispatch summarizing a report by Christopher Gist quoted in the *Pennsylvania Gazette* for June 27, 1754, said:

"Colonel Fry's Illness has greatly retarded the March of the Division under his Command, which would otherwise have been long ago at the Camp, where we hourly expected to hear of their Arrival, and that of the Company from South Carolina. . . . And on Tuesday Evening last, the above-mentioned Twenty-one Prisoners arrived in this City [Winchester], under a strong Guard, amongst whom are four Officers, who acquaint us that their Commander Captain Dijonville [sic] was killed in the Action [Jumonville skirmish].

"We are likewise certainly assured by the Gentlemen who escorted the Prisoners, of the Death of Joshua Fry, Esq; Colonel of the Virginia Regiment, and Commander in Chief of the Expedition to Ohio. He was born in Somersetshire, and bred at Oxford, where he made a very eminent Proficiency in all the solid and useful Learning of that noble Place; and particularly excelled in the Mathematical Sciences. He was first Grammar-Master, and then Professor of Mathematicks at William and Mary College; but having quitted those Posts, he has since gone through various publick Employments in this Country, with acknowledged Ability, and unblemished Honour and Reputation. He was a Man of so clear a Head, so mild a Temper, and so good a Heart, that he never failed to engage the Love and Esteem of all that knew, or were concerned with him, and therefore died universally lamented."

8. Washington, *Writings* (ed. Fitzpatrick), I, 74.
9. Washington, *Diaries* (ed. Fitzpatrick), I, 92.
10. Washington, *Writings* (ed. Fitzpatrick), I, 80.
11. *Ibid.*, p. 76.
12. *Ibid.*, pp. 80-81.
13. *Ibid.*, p. 83.
14. *Ibid.*, pp. 81-82.
15. *Dinwiddie Papers*, I, 218; Washington, *Writings* (ed. Fitzpatrick), I, 82 n.
16. *Ibid.*, pp. 84-88; *Diaries* (ed. Fitzpatrick), I, 99, 93-101; *Journal of 1754* (ed. Toner), p. 126.
17. *Diaries* (ed. Fitzpatrick), I, 99-100.
18. Rupp, *Early History of Western Pennsylvania*, pp. 75-76. See Appendix A, I, 3.
19. *South Carolina Gazette*, September 26, 1754; *Maryland Gazette*, August 29, 1754.
20. The name "Fort Necessity" was first used in the "Articles" of its capitulation.
21. Villiers, "Journal," in Craig, *Olden Time*, II, 212; C. H. Sipe, *Indian Wars of Pennsylvania*, p. 161; *Colonial Records of Pennsylvania*, VI, 142, quoting letter from Captain Robert Stobo.
22. Rupp, *op. cit.*, pp. 75-76, 84-86; *Alexandria Gazette*, July 19, 1754; *Dinwiddie Papers*, I, 233, 240.
23. Washington, *Journal of 1754* (ed. Toner), p. 165.
24. Parkman, *Montcalm and Wolfe*, I, 1; Thayer, *George Washington*, p. 19.
25. G. M. Wrong, *Rise and Fall of New France*, II, 751.
26. Craig, *Olden Time*, II, 211-13; *Maryland Gazette*, July 25, 1754. See also Appendix A, I, 1.
27. Rupp, *op. cit.*, p. 84.

28. Villiers, "Journal" in Craig, *Olden Time*, II, 212.

29. Villiers reached Fort Duquesne from Montreal, June 26, and set out the following day. See "Journal" in *Memorial Containing a Summary View of Facts*, p. 173; F. H. Severance, "An Old Frontier of France," in *Buffalo Historical Society Publications*, XX; and Dahlinger, *Marquis Duquesne*, p. 55.

30. For accounts of the Battle of Fort Necessity see *Dinwiddie Papers*, I, 239-43; Rupp, *op. cit.*, pp. 85-88; *Colonial Records of Pennsylvania*, VI; *Maryland Gazette*, July 25, 1754; *Virginia Gazette*, July 19, 1754; Craig, *Olden Time*, II, 211-13.

31. Probably as far from the truth as was Washington's estimate, based largely upon reports given him by Indians, was that by Villiers placing his casualties at two killed and a few slightly wounded. Craig, *Olden Time*, II, 213; Appendix A, I, 1.

32. Rupp, *op. cit.*, pp. 74-77; *Virginia Gazette*, July 19, 1754.

33. These "Articles" are printed in French in Washington, *Writings* (ed. Ford), I, 120-21; see also Washington, *Writings* (ed. Sparks), II, Appendix, p. 464. See Appendix A, II.

34. Villiers carried this flag to Canada, and one of the Virginia colors. Dahlinger, *op. cit.*, p. 56.

35. "Journal" in Craig, *Olden Time*, II, 212.

36. Arthur Hassall, *The Balance of Power, 1715-1789*, chap. 8, "The Diplomatic Revolution."

37. *Mémoire Contenant de Précis des Faits*, p. 147; Rupp, *op. cit.*, p. 83; Craig, *Olden Time*, II, 212.

38. Rupp, *op. cit.*, pp. 84-85; *South Carolina Gazette*, September 19, 1754; *Ibid.*, September 26, 1754.

39. "Journal" in Craig, *Olden Time*, II, 213.

40. *South Carolina Gazette*, September 19, 1754; *Ibid.*, September 26, 1754.

41. Sipe, *op. cit.*, p. 166.

42. *Maryland Gazette*, April 17, 1755; *Ibid.*, August 29, 1754.

43. *History of the United States*, III, 78 (Century edition, Boston, 1879).

44. Quoted in Hughes, *George Washington*, I, 159.

45. Harry R. Blackford, C. E., *The Reconstruction of Fort Necessity*. A pamphlet.

46. Lodge, *George Washington*, I, 74-75.

47. *Writings* (ed. Fitzpatrick), I, 54.

48. *Dinwiddie Papers*, I, 230; Rupp, *op. cit.*, pp. 75, 84; *South Carolina Gazette*, September 19, 1754.

49. *Dinwiddie Papers*, I, 228, 287-89.

50. Van Braam was taken to Canada, where he was detained six years. During most of this time he was subjected to great hardships. Among other things he was forced to subsist on bread and water with a limited allowance of horse meat. For sketch see Washington's *Journal of 1754* (ed. Toner), pp. 21-24.

Captain Stobo escaped shortly after his arrival in Canada and had many adventures before his return to Virginia. His *Memoirs* were published at Pittsburgh in 1854. Both Van Braam and Stobo were given land grants by Virginia. For sketch of Stobo see Washington's *Journal of 1754* (ed. Toner), p. 81.

51. Washington, *Writings* (ed. Sparks), II, 447; Hughes, *George Washington*, I, 10; Lodge, *George Washington*, I, 76.

52. Craik was Washington's physician and accompanied him on most of his journeys and campaigns.

CHAPTER VI

1. Suggested readings: Sargent, *History of an Expedition against Fort Du Quesne*, the standard secondary account of the Braddock expedition; Boyd Crumrine, *History*

of Washington County [Pennsylvania]; W. H. Lowdermilk, *History of Cumberland [Maryland]*; Baker-Crothers, *Virginia and the French and Indian War*, pp. 58-81; Koontz, "The Virginia Frontier, 1754-1763," *Johns Hopkins University Studies*, XLIII, 68-75; Lodge, *George Washington*, I, 75-85; Hughes, *George Washington*, I, 12-14; Volwiler, *George Croghan and the Westward Movement, 1741-1782*; Thwaites, *France in America*, chaps. 9-11.

2. The local newspaper press carried many comments on religious liberty. One of the most informing to come to the attention of the present writer being that from Philo Hugo, "Shenandoe," Virginia, telling of the hardships endured by French Protestants in 1686 and 1687 following the revocation of the Edict of Nantes. See *Maryland Gazette*, August 29, 1754.

3. Koontz, *op. cit.*, pp. 42-48; Baker-Crothers, *op. cit.*, chap. 3.
4. Horatio Sharpe, *Correspondence*, I, 104-6; *Maryland Gazette*, April 14, 1755.
5. *Dinwiddie Papers*, I, 310.
6. Hulbert, *Historic Highways*, IV, 25.
7. *Ibid.*, pp. 53-58.
8. Lodge, *George Washington*, I, 78.
9. *Writings* (ed. Ford), I, 138-39; Hughes, *op. cit.*, I, 173-74.
10. *Writings* (ed. Ford), I, 140.
11. Hulbert, *op. cit.*, IV, 36-38; Hughes, *op. cit.*, I, 195-204.
12. *Dinwiddie Papers*, I, 511. The *Maryland Gazette* for March 20, 1755, quoting a dispatch from Williamsburg, Virginia, made the following announcement of Braddock's arrival in America: "February 28. The Three Ships of War arrived at Hampton, are the Centurian, Commodore Keppel, the Norwich, the Honourable Captain Barrington and the Syren, Capt. Proby; in the Norwich came passengers, the Honourable Major General Braddock, Commander of all the Forces in North America; Capt. Orme, Aid-de-Camp, and Mr. Shirley, Secretary, who came to this City last Sunday, where they await the arrival of the Forces, who are every Day expected."
13. Baker-Crothers, *op. cit.*, chap. 4.
14. *Ibid.*, pp. 63-64; Volwiler, *op. cit.*, pp. 95-98; Hulbert, *op. cit.*, IV, 112-14.
15. *Ibid.*, p. 58.
16. Washington, *Writings* (ed. Fitzpatrick), I, 109-14; S. M. Hamilton (ed.), *Letters to Washington*, I, 57; N. W. Stephenson, "The Romantics and George Washington," *American Historical Review*, XXXIX, 281-82.
17. *Writings* (ed. Fitzpatrick), I, 109; *Writings* (ed. Ford), I, 141-44.
18. *Ibid.*, p. 152; Hughes, *op. cit.*, I, 204; *South Carolina Gazette*, July 25, 1754.
19. *Writings* (ed. Ford), I, 152.
20. Sharpe, *op. cit.*, I, 203-4; Baker-Crothers, *op. cit.*, pp. 70-71; *Dinwiddie Papers*, I, 496; *Maryland Gazette*, April 14, 1754.
21. Hughes, *op. cit.*, I, 210-11; Hulbert, *op. cit.*, IV, 58-60.
22. Sargent, *op. cit.*, pp. 193-96; Crumrine, *op. cit.*, pp. 48-52.
23. *Writings* (ed. Fitzpatrick), I, 139; *Writings* (ed. Ford), I, 161 n.
24. Hulbert, *op. cit.*, IV, 67-75, quoting Braddock's letters of June 5, 1755, to Sir John Robinson.
25. Hughes, *op. cit.*, I, 212-13.
26. *Ibid.*, pp. 214-15; Sargent, *op. cit.*, pp. 168-76; *Dinwiddie Papers*, I, 484; Baker-Crothers, *op. cit.*, p. 63; Koontz, *op. cit.*, p. 70.
27. Washington, *Writings* (ed. Fitzpatrick), I, 133; Hughes, *op. cit.*, I, 209, quoting Watson's *Annals of Philadelphia and Pennsylvania*, (1857), II, 140.
28. The following is perhaps the best description of this historic highway, certainly the best description of it in the process of making:

"In the forests it is easy to conjure up the scene when this old track was opened —for it was cut through a 'wooden country,' to use an expression common among the pioneers. Here you can see the long line of sorry wagons standing in the road when the army is encamped; and though many of them seem unable to carry their loads one foot further—yet there is ever the ringing chorus of the axes of six hundred choppers sounding through the twilight of the hot May evening. It is almost suffocating in the forests when the wind does not blow, and the army is unused to the scorching American summer which has come early this year. The wagon train is very long, and though the van may have halted on level ground, the line behind stretches down and up the shadowy ravines. The wagons are blocked in all conceivable positions on the hillsides. The condition of the horses is pitiful beyond description. If some are near to the brook or spring, others are far away. Some horses will never find water tonight. To the right and left the sentinels are lost in the surrounding gloom.

"And then with those singing axes for the perpetual refrain, consider the mighty epic poem to be woven out of the days that have succeeded Braddock here. Though lost in the Alleghenies, this road and all its busy days mirror perfectly the social advance of the western empire to which it led. Its first mission was to bind, as with a strange, rough, straggling cincture the East and the West."—Hulbert, *op. cit.*, IV, 206.

29. *Writings* (ed. Fitzpatrick), I, 143; *Writings* (ed. Ford), I, 166; Hughes, *op. cit.*, I, 227-28.

30. *Writings* (ed. Ford), I, 168.

31. *Writings* (ed. Fitzpatrick), I, 145-46; *Writings* (ed. Ford), I, 170-71; Hughes, *op. cit.*, I, 229.

32. *Writings* (ed. Fitzpatrick), I, 146; *Writings* (ed. Ford), I, 170; Hulbert, *op. cit.*, IV, 111.

33. Sargent, *op. cit.*, p. 217.

34. *Ibid.*, pp. 221-32; Crumrine, *op. cit.*, p. 44.

35. Washington's account of the Battle of the Monongahela to his mother, written the same day as that to Dinwiddie, is less formal than the latter and may be interesting for purposes of comparison, if for nothing else. In part, he wrote:

"We March'd on to that place with't any considerable loss, having only now and then a stragler pick'd up by the French Scoutg. Ind'nd. When we came here, we were attack'd by a Body of French and Indns. whose number, (I am certain) did not exceed 300 Men; our's consisted of abt. 1,300 well arm'd Troops; chiefly of the English Soldiers, who were struck with such a panick, that they behav'd with more cowardice than it is possible to conceive; The Officers behav'd Gallantly in order to encourage their Men, for which they suffer'd greatly; there being near 60 kill'd and wounded; a large proportion out of the number we had! The Virginia Troops shew'd a good deal of Bravery, and were near all kill'd; for I believe out of 3 Companys that were there, there is scarce 30 Men left alive; Capt. Peyrouny and all his Officer's down to a Corporal was kill'd; Capt. Polson shar'd near as hard a Fate; for only one of his was left: In short the dastardly behaviour of those they call regular's expos'd all others that were inclin'd to do their duty to almost certain death; and at last, in dispight of all the efforts of the Officer's to the Contrary, they broke and run as Sheep pursued by dogs; and it was impossible to rally them.

"The Genl. was wounded; of w'ch he died 3 Days after; Sir Peter Halket was kill'd in the Field where died many other brave Officer's; I luckily escap'd with't a wound, tho' I had four Bullets through my Coat, and two Horses shot under me; Captns. Orme and Morris two of the Genls. Aids de Camp, were wounded early in the Engagem't. which render'd the duty hard upon me, as I was the only person then left to distribute the Genl's. Orders which I was scarcely able to do, as I was not half recover'd from a violent illness, that confin'd me to my Bed, and a Waggon, for above 10 Days; I am still in a weak and Feeble cond'n; which induces me to halt here, 2 or 3 Days in hopes of recov'g. a little Strength, to enable me to proceed homewards; from whence, I fear I shall not be able to stir till towards Sept., so that I shall not have the pleasure of seeing you till then, unless it be in Fairfax; please to give my love to Mr. Lewis and my Sister, and Compts. to Mr. Jackson and all other Fds. that enquire after me. I am, Hon'd Madam Yr. most dutiful Son."—*Writings* (ed. Fitzpatrick), 151-52. See also Appendix B.

36. For July 31, 1775 the *Pennsylvania Gazette* said: "Mr. Washington had two Horses shot under him, and his Clothes shot thru' in several Places, behaving the whole Time with the greatest courage and Resolution."

CHAPTER VII

1. Hughes, *George Washington*, I, 277-78; Parkman, *Montcalm and Wolfe*, I, 341. Letters from Carlisle, Pennsylvania, extracts of which were printed in the *Pennsylvania Gazette* for July 31, 1755, confirmed in part these claims with respect to that colony. That dated July 22 told of murdered families and of others "coming on this Side the Mountain" and continued:

"We are now in the utmost Confusion, not knowing what Hand to turn to, being more afraid of the Indians (whom we doubt were the late Murderers on the new Road) than of the French. Our Back Settlers are in general fled, and are likely to be ruined for the Loss of their Crops and Summer's Labour; several of them on Juniata having left some Part of their Household Furniture in the Flight, and since, going back to fetch or hide it, have found every Thing broken and destroyed by the Indians, and their Horses in the Corn-fields."

2. Wrong, *Rise and Fall of New France*, II, 755.
3. *Writings* (ed. Fitzpatrick), I, 156-57; *Writings* (ed. Ford), I, 179.
4. *Writings* (ed. Fitzpatrick), I, 159-63; *Writings* (ed. Ford), I, 181.
5. *Writings* (ed. Fitzpatrick), I, 159; *Writings* (ed. Ford), I, 181.
6. Hamilton, *Letters to Washington*, I, 79-81.
7. *Dinwiddie Papers*, II, 135.
8. Hening, *Statutes at Large*, VI, 521-30, 550-52; Baker-Crothers, *Virginia in the French and Indian War*, pp. 84-85; Washington, *Writings* (ed. Ford), I, 181 n.
9. *Dinwiddie Papers*, II, 139-40; *Pennsylvania Gazette*, July 31, 1755. See Appendix B, II.
10. Koontz, "The Virginia Frontier, 1754-1763," *Johns Hopkins University Studies*, XLIII, 72-73; *Dinwiddie Papers*, II, 112-13.
11. *Pennsylvania Gazette*, July 1, 1756.
12. *Ibid.*, May 20, 1756; *Ibid.*, July 1, 1756.
13. *Ibid.*, September 16, 1756.
14. *Ibid.*
15. Washington, *Writings* (ed. Fitzpatrick), I, 201; *Dinwiddie Papers*, II, 236-42.
16. *Writings* (ed. Fitzpatrick), I, 202-7; *Dinwiddie Papers*, II, 237, 242; Washington, *Writings* (ed. Ford), I, 194-95, 201.
17. *Writings* (ed. Fitzpatrick), I, 197; *Dinwiddie Papers*, II, 243.
18. *Ibid.*, p. 243.
19. *Ibid.*, pp. 318, 325, 331, 338; Washington, *Writings* (ed. Ford), I, 229-34; Washington, *Writings* (ed. Sparks), I, 77.
20. Hughes, *op. cit.*, I, 294-301.
21. Washington, *Writings* (ed. Fitzpatrick), I, 289-91, 293-96; William Shirley, *Correspondence* (ed. C. H. Lincoln), II, 412.

22. Washington, *Writings* (ed. Fitzpatrick), I, 285-86; Koontz, *op. cit.*, p. 86.
23. *Writings* (ed. Fitzpatrick), I, 355; *Writings* (ed. Ford), I, 277.
24. *Writings* (ed. Fitzpatrick), I, 324-25; *Writings* (ed. Ford), I, 249-52; See also Hughes, *op. cit.*, I, 308.
25. *Writings* (ed. Fitzpatrick), I, 302-3; Washington, *Writings* (ed. Ford), I, 238 n; Hughes, *op. cit.*, I, 302-3.
26. *Dinwiddie Papers*, II, 381.
27. *Writings* (ed. Fitzpatrick), I, 317; *Writings* (ed. Ford), I, 245-55.
28. *Dinwiddie Papers*, II, 407.
29. *Writings* (ed. Ford), I, 335.
30. Fitzpatrick, *Washington Himself*, p. 92; Koontz, *op. cit.*, p. 85.
31. Baker-Crothers, *op. cit.*, p. 102.
32. Washington, *Writings* (ed. Fitzpatrick), I, 423, 487-92; Beer, *British Colonial Policy*, p. 254; Baker-Crothers, *op. cit.*, p. 106.
33. For names, location, and description of eighty-one forts built on the Virginia frontier at this time see Koontz, *op. cit.*, Appendix I.
34. *Dinwiddie Papers*, II, 523.
35. *Writings* (ed. Fitzpatrick), I, 487-90, 491 n, 511-14; *Dinwiddie Papers*, II, 552; Washington, *Writings* (ed. Ford), I, 312; Koontz, *op. cit.*, pp. 80-81.
36. *Writings* (ed. Fitzpatrick), I, 471; Hughes, *op. cit.*, I, 314-18.
37. *Writings* (ed. Fitzpatrick), I, 528-29; *Writings* (ed. Ford), I, 404-5.
38. *Writings* (ed. Fitzpatrick), I, 531-33; *Writings* (ed. Ford), I, 406-9.
39. *Writings* (ed. Fitzpatrick), II, 22; *Writings* (ed. Ford), I, 431-32.
40. Koontz, *op. cit.*, pp. 82-83.
41. *Dinwiddie Papers*, II, 703.
42. Washington, *Diaries* (ed. Fitzpatrick), I, 110; R. T. Barton, "The First Election of Washington to the House of Burgesses," in *Virginia Historical Society Collections*, XI, 115.
43. Quoted in Hughes, *op. cit.*, I, 342.
44. *Writings* (ed. Fitzpatrick), II, 166-67.
45. *Writings* (ed. Fitzpatrick), II, 251; Hughes, *op. cit.*, I, chap. 25; Barton, *op. cit.*, p. 115; Fitzpatrick, *Washington Himself*, p. 119.
46. Baker-Crothers, *op. cit.*, chap. 7.
47. Hughes, *op. cit.*, I, 376.
48. *Writings* (ed. Fitzpatrick), II, 260, 276-82; *Writings* (ed. Ford), II, 72.
49. Quoted in Hughes, *op. cit.*, I, 383. See also Hulbert, *Historic Highways*, V, 113.
50. Washington, *Writings* (ed. Fitzpatrick), II, 283; Hening, *op. cit.*, VII, 171; Baker-Crothers, *op. cit.*, p. 136.
51. Washington, *Writings* (ed. Fitzpatrick), II, 290-93; *Writings* (ed. Ford), II, 101-2; Parkman, *op. cit.*, II, 160.
52. Hughes, *op. cit.*, I, 424.
53. *Writings* (ed. Fitzpatrick), II, 308-10; *Writings* (ed. Ford), II, 116-18.

Chapter VIII

1. Hughes, *George Washington*, II, 80.
2. P. L. Haworth, *George Washington, Country Gentleman*, pp. 60-90; Hughes, *op. cit.*, II, 90-105.
3. R. B. Cook, *Washington's Western Lands*, chaps. 3-7.
4. *Writings* (ed. Fitzpatrick), II, 414-18, 430, 442; *Writings* (ed. Ford), II, 189, 200, 207; Haworth, *op. cit.*, p. 286.
5. Hughes, *op. cit.*, II, chap. 4.

6. This condition is perhaps adequately described in the following extract from a review by Daniel Grinnan of Professor A. O. Craven's *Soil Exhaustion as a Factor in the Agricultural History of Virginia and Maryland*, in *Virginia Magazine of History and Biography*, July, 1927:

"He [Virginia Farmer] had to struggle to earn his bread. England, his only permitted market for his tobacco, his single crop, was 3,000 miles away across a stormy sea, and when the tobacco, after the sweat and toil of raising and curing it had been endured, and the expenses of putting it on a ship in the river had been paid, it then was plucked by so many harpies, that there was but little left to the credit of the planter; and this small balance went into the purchase of English articles at swollen prices that were shipped to him at heavy cost across the same wild sea.

"The proud Virginian was really regarded as a helot that was useful only for the crop he raised. It is difficult to enumerate the charges that the tobacco had to bear: there were charges for freight, insurance, drayage, English tariff taxes for coming in and for going out, charges for handling, warehouse charges, inspection charges, factor's charges and some others. Being across the wide ocean the planter had to accept any statement that his factor chose to render, and being always in debt to the factor there was an interest charge; and for the purchase of the articles that were shipped to Virginia there was another factor's charge and the prices paid for articles as shown by the factor's statement had to be accepted as correct solely on faith. In addition, the price of tobacco fluctuated and was often so low that the planter received only a pittance and sometimes received nothing but a debit entry. He was cut off from trade of all kinds with other countries than England, and the value of tobacco stored in England that could not be sold or exported to the Continent was soon consumed by warehouse charges."

7. *Writings* (ed. Ford), XII, 360; Haworth, *op. cit.*, p. 68 ff.
8. *Journals of the House of Burgesses of Virginia*, 1758-1776.
9. *Diaries* (ed. Fitzpatrick), passim.
10. Hughes, *op. cit.*, II, chap. 8.
11. *Writings* (ed. Ford), II, 179.
12. Alvord, *Mississippi Valley in British Politics*, II, 92-93, 119, 189; H. B. Adams, "Maryland's Influence upon the Land Cessions of the United States," in *Johns Hopkins University Studies*, III, 12.
13. *Writings* (ed. Fitzpatrick), II, 365; Cook, *op. cit.*, p. 157.
14. G. H. Alden, "New Governments West of the Allegheny Mountains before 1780," in *University of Wisconsin Bulletin*, II, 1-74; Washington, *Writings* (ed. Sparks), II, 479; Benjamin Franklin, *Writings*, IV, 233; Alvord, *op. cit.*, II, 116.
15. C. H. Ambler, *History of Transportation in the Ohio Valley*, p. 32; Volwiler, *George Croghan and the Westward Movement*, pp. 180-90, 200-5; Washington, *Writings* (ed. Fitzpatrick), II, 468-69.
16. Ambler, *op. cit.*, pp. 28-33.
17. *Writings* (ed. Fitzpatrick), II, 458-59; *Writings* (ed. Ford), II, 213-18. See also Hughes, *op. cit.*, II, 651-56.
18. *Writings* (ed. Fitzpatrick), II, 467-70; *Writings* (ed. Sparks), II, 346-50.
19. *Writings* (ed. Fitzpatrick), II, 470-71; *Writings* (ed. Sparks), II, 349.
20. C. W. Butterfield, *Washington-Crawford Letters*, pp. 5-10.
21. Alvord, *op. cit.*, I, 314, 318.
22. *Writings* (ed. Fitzpatrick), III, 9, 26, 66, 76, 157, 183; Alden, *op. cit.*, pp. 22-36; Alvord, *op. cit.*, II, 116, 165; Washington, *Writings* (ed. Ford), II, 351-54; Hughes, *op. cit.*, II, Appendix III.
23. Butterfield, *op. cit.*, p. 11.

24. *Writings* (ed. Fitzpatrick), III, 22; *Writings* (ed. Ford), II, 366-72; Fitzpatrick, *Washington Himself*, p. 142.
25. *Writings* (ed. Fitzpatrick), III, 26; *Diaries* (ed. Fitzpatrick), I, 404-6.
26. *Diaries* (ed. Fitzpatrick), I, 409-10.
27. *Ibid.*, p. 411.
28. *Ibid.*
29. *Ibid.*, p. 426.
30. *Ibid.*, p. 423.
31. *Ibid.*, pp. 426-29.
32. *Ibid.*, p. 431.
33. *Ibid.*, p. 447.
34. *Writings* (ed. Fitzpatrick), III, 9-12; *Writings* (ed. Ford), II, 272-76, 366-72; *Writings* (ed. Sparks), II, 355-59; Butterfield, *op. cit.*, p. 23.
35. *Writings* (ed. Fitzpatrick), III, 47-50; *Journals of the House of Burgesses of Virginia*, 1770-1772, pp. xii, xxvi; Alvord, *op. cit.*, II, 181-83; *Writings* (ed. Ford), II, 465-69.
36. *Writings* (ed. Fitzpatrick), III, 68.
37. *Ibid.*, III, 86; *Writings* (ed. Sparks), II, 357-60; *Writings* (ed. Ford), II, 394-96; *Journals of the House of Burgesses, Virginia*, 1770-1772, pp. xx, xxi.
38. *Writings* (ed. Ford), II, 366-72, 351-54, 465-69; Hughes, *op. cit.*, II, chap. 12.
39. Volwiler, *op. cit.*, p. 297; Hamilton, *Letters to Washington*, IV, 294.
40. Hughes, *op. cit.*, II, 138; R. G. Thwaites and Louise P. Kellogg, *Documentary History of Dunmore's War, 1774*, p. 66 passim; Alvord, *op. cit.*, II, 188-89.
41. Butterfield, *op. cit.*, pp. 25, 35, 37; Hamilton, *op. cit.*, IV, 294. On July 5, 1775, to avoid further trouble, Lord Dunmore issued Washington a military patent for his lands on Miller's Run. Cook, *op. cit.*, p. 118.
42. Some idea of the location and extent of Washington's western lands as of 1773, may be had from the following advertisement which appeared in the *Baltimore Advertiser* for August 20 of that year:

MOUNT VERNON IN VIRGINIA,
July 15, 1773.

"The Subscriber having obtained Patents for upwards of TWENTY THOUSAND ACRES of LAND on the *Ohio* and *Great Kanhawa* (Ten Thousand of which are situated on the banks of the first-mentioned river, between the mouths of the two *Kanhawas*, and the remainder on the *Great Kanhawa*, or *New River*, from the mouth, or near it, upwards, in one countinued survey) proposes to divide the same into any sized tenements that may be desired, and lease them upon moderate terms, allowing a reasonable number of years rent free, provided, within the space of two years from next October, three acres for every fifty contained in each lot, and proportionably for a less quantity, shall be cleared, fenced, and tilled; and that, by or before the time limited for the commencement of the first rent, five acres for every hundred, and proportionably, as above, shall be enclosed and laid down in good grass for meadow; and moreover, that at least fifty good fruit trees for every like quantity of land shall be planted on the Premises. Any persons inclinable to settle on these lands may be morefully informed of the terms by applying to the subscriber, near *Alexandria*, or in his absence, to MR. LUND WASHINGTON; and would do well in communicating their intentions before the 1st of October next, in order that a sufficient number of lots may be laid off to answer the demand.

"As these lands are among the first which have been surveyed in the part of the country they lie in, it is almost needless to premise that none can exceed them in luxuriance of soil, or convenience of situation, all of them lying upon the banks either of the *Ohio* or *Kanhawa*, and abounding with fine fish and wild fowl of various kinds, as also in most excellent meadows, many of which (by the bountiful hand of nature) are, in their present state, almost fit for the scythe. From every part of these lands water carriage is now had to *Fort Pitt*, by an easy communication; and from *Fort Pitt* up the *Monongahela*, to *Redstone*, vessels of convenient burthen, may and do pass continually; from whence, by means of *Cheat River*, and other navigable branches of the *Monongahela* it is thought the portage to *Potowmack* may, and will, be reduced within the compass of a few miles, to the great ease and convenience of the settlers in transporting the produce of their lands to market. To which may be added, that as patents have now actually passed the seals for the several tracts here offered to be leased, settlers on them may cultivate and enjoy the lands in peace and safety, notwithstanding the unsettled counsels respecting a new colony on the *Ohio*; and as no right money is to be paid for these lands, and quitrent of two shillings sterling a hundred, demandable some years hence only, it is highly presumable that they will always be held upon a more desirable footing than where both these are laid on with a very heavy hand. And it may not be amiss further to observe, that if the scheme for establishing a new government on the *Ohio*, in the manner talked of, should ever be effected, these must be among the most valuable lands in it, not only on account of the goodness of soil, and the other advantages above enumerated, but from their contiguity to the seat of government, which more than probable will be fixed at the mouth of the *Great Kanhawa*. GEORGE WASHINGTON." See also Washington, *Writings* (ed. Fitzpatrick), III, 144.

43. *Ibid.*, p. 151; Butterfield, *op. cit.*, pp. 29-32. In 1798 Washington purchased from Henry Lee 5000 acres of land in what is now Grayson County, Kentucky. See W. R. Jillson, *Land Adventures of George Washington*, pp. 34-38.

44. Washington, *Writings* (ed. Fitzpatrick), III, 124-29, 151; *Writings* (ed. Ford), II, 371-74.

Chapter IX

1. Washington to Henry Riddell, February 22, 1774, quoted in Hamilton, *Letters to Washington*, IV, 337-39; Washington, *Writings* (ed. Ford), II, 407.
2. *Writings* (ed. Fitzpatrick), III, 190; Hamilton, *op. cit.*, IV, 339.
3. *Ibid.*, pp. 357-59.
4. Alvord, *Mississippi Valley in British Politics*, II, 187.
5. Hughes, *George Washington*, II, 148.
6. *Writings* (ed. Fitzpatrick), III, 212; *Writings* (ed. Ford), II, 408 n, 412.
7. Hamilton, *op. cit.*, IV, pp. 337-39 n; Washington, *Writings* (ed. Sparks), III, 94-95; Cook, *Washington's Western Lands*, pp. 44-45. For Washington's instructions to Crawford see *Writings* (ed. Fitzpatrick), III, 199-204.
8. Butterfield, *Washington-Crawford Letters*, pp. 96-97.
9. E. D. Branch, *Westward*, chap. 7, "The Wilderness Road"; F. L. Paxson, *American Frontier*, 1763-1893, pp. 26-32; Thwaites and Kellogg, *Dunmore's War*, introduction; Alvord, *op. cit.*, II, chap. 5.
10. *Ibid.*, pp. 188-89.
11. V. A. Lewis, *History of the Battle of Point Pleasant*.
12. Washington, *Writings* (ed. Fitzpatrick), III, 229-33, 237-38; for copy of "Fairfax Resolves," see Peter Force (ed.), *American Archives*, I, 597-600. (Hereafter cited as *American Archives*.)
13. Thwaites and Kellogg, *op. cit.*, p. 93.
14. Butterfield, *op. cit.*, p. 54.
15. *Writings* (ed. Fitzpatrick), III, 268-72; *Writings* (ed. Ford), II, 454, 462; *Diaries* (ed. Fitzpatrick), II, 187.

16. *Writings* (ed. Fitzpatrick), III, 268-72.
17. Cook, *op. cit.*, pp. 47-50, quoting letters from James Cleveland to Washington.
18. *Ibid.*, p. 52.
19. Butterfield, *op. cit.*, p. 74.
20. *Journals of the House of Burgesses of Virginia*, 1773-1776, XIII, 282; *American Archives*, II, 1240.
21. See chapter 5 of this work.
22. For copy of treaty see Thwaites and Kellogg, *Revolution on the Upper Ohio*, pp. 25-127.
23. *Writings* (ed. Sparks), IV, 232, 254, 257, 550-52; Hughes, *op. cit.*, II, 554.
24. *American Archives*, I, 962-63; Thwaites and Kellogg, *Dunmore's War*, p. 311; W. Va. Legislature, *Hand Book and Manual* (1926), pp. 468-73; A. S. Withers, *Chronicles of Border Warfare*, p. 179.
25. *Writings* (ed. Sparks), III, 4-5.
26. Shortly after Morgan reached Cambridge, Washington's forces were augmented, August 11, 1775, by a company from Virginia led by Captain Hugh Stephenson. See Bedinger's "Journal" in Danske Dandridge, *Historic Sheperdstown*, chap. 8. See also "Alphabetical List of Officers and Privates connected with Shepherdstown, or recruited in its Neighborhood, during the Revolution," in Dandridge, *op. cit.*, pp. 298-359, Appendix A; Washington, *Writings* (ed. Fitzpatrick), III, 507. See also Morton, *Story of Winchester in Virginia*, p. 87; P. A. Bruce, *The Virginia Plutarch*, chap. 18.
27. Quoted in Hughes, *op. cit.*, II, 246.
28. R. H. Lee, *Letters* (ed. Ballagh), I, 150. See also Hughes, *op. cit.*, II, 225-26.
29. Quoted in *Ibid.*, p. 552.
30. Henry Howe, *Historical Collections of Virginia*, p. 183. See *Ibid.*, p. 454.
31. *Writings* (ed. Fitzpatrick), III, 498; *Writings* (ed. Sparks), III, 94-95.
32. *Ibid.*, p. 94.
33. Hughes, *op. cit.*, II, 145-46, quoting the *London Morning Post*, June 7, 1779.
34. Washington's New York lands embraced the site of Fort Schuyler and were known as the "Oriskany tract." Ford, *True George Washington*, p. 132; Cook, *op. cit.*, p. 139.
35. *Writings* (ed. Sparks), III, 92-94.
36. *Ibid.*, V, 118-20.
37. *Ibid.*, VI, 384.
38. Hughes, *op. cit.*, III, 490; S. A. Drake, *Aboriginal Races of North America*, p. 609.
39. J. A. James, "Pittsburgh a Key to the West During the American Revolution," in *Ohio Archaeological and Historical Quarterly*, XXII, 64-79.
40. *Writings* (ed. Sparks), V, 382.
41. *Ibid.*, IV, 138.
42. Fitzpatrick, *Washington Himself*, p. 364; J. A. James, *The Life of George Rogers Clark*, pp. 114-15; James, *George Rogers Clark Papers*, LIV and chap. 7; Louise P. Kellogg, *Frontier Advance on the Upper Ohio*, pp. 17-19; Hening, *Statutes at Large*, IX, 375.
43. Thwaites and Kellogg, *Frontier Defense on the Upper Ohio*, pp. 51-53, 249-56; Kellogg, *op. cit.*, pp. 13-14, 49-51; C. H. Van Tyne, *The Loyalist in the American Revolution*.
44. Kellogg, *op. cit.*, pp. 14, 45, 54, 60, 128.
45. *Ibid.*, pp. 27-28, 238-39, 253, 262.
46. *Writings* (ed. Sparks), VI, 434.

47. *Ibid.*, VII, 343-45.
48. Kellogg, *Frontier Retreat on the Upper Ohio*, p. 34.
49. C. W. Butterfield (ed.), *Washington-Irvine Correspondence*, pp. 75, 78.
50. *Ibid.*, p. 83.
51. See biographical sketch of William Crawford, Butterfield, *Washington-Irvine Correspondence*, pp. 114-17.
52. *Ibid.*
53. *Writings* (ed. Sparks), VIII, 452-64, 465 n.

Chapter X

1. Quoted in A. B. Hulbert, *Washington and the West*, p. 3. See also Adams, "Maryland's Influence," in *Johns Hopkins University Studies*, III, 7-127; Justin Winsor, *The Westward Movement*, chaps. 7-8.
2. Adams, *op. cit.*, pp. 9-54.
3. *Ibid.*, pp. 41-42.
4. *Writings* (ed. Sparks), IX, 86, 91, 111.
5. *Ibid.*, p. 93.
6. For locations, surveys, and plats see Cook, *Washington's Western Lands*, chaps. 3-7.
7. *Ibid.*, p. 114; *Writings* (ed. Sparks), XII, 264, 275.
8. Washington, *Diaries* (ed. Fitzpatrick), II, 279-316.
9. See "Washington and the Potomac: Manuscripts," in *American Historical Review*, XXVIII, 497-520, 705-23; Washington, *Writings* (ed. Sparks), IX, 30-34.
10. *Ibid.*, p. 32.
11. *Ibid.*
12. For a splendid résumé of this journey and its objectives see Hulbert, *Washington and the West*, pp. 107, 199. See also Adams, *op. cit.*, pp. 72-74; Cook, *op. cit.*, pp. 161-63.
13. *Diaries* (ed. Fitzpatrick), II, 299, 279-328.
14. *Ibid.*, p. 282.
15. *Ibid.*, p. 280.
16. *Ibid.*, p. 292. Washington's Mill at Simpson's (Perryopolis, Pennsylvania,) was built in 1774-1776 and ceased to run in 1918.
17. *Ibid.*, pp. 290-93.
18. *Ibid.*, p. 298.
19. *Ibid.*, pp. 302-4.
20. This route may have passed by or near the site recently marked by a West Virginia Commission as the birthplace of Nancy Hanks, the mother of Abraham Lincoln, but there is no evidence that Washington stopped there.
21. *Diaries* (ed. Fitzpatrick), II, 310.
22. *Ibid.*, p. 315.
23. *Ibid.*, p. 325.
24. *Ibid.*, p. 327.
25. *Ibid.*, p. 328.
26. *Ibid.*, pp. 327-28.
27. *Writings* (ed. Sparks), IX, 61, 58-68; Hulbert, *Washington and the West*, pp. 175-86.
28. Washington *Writings*, (ed. Sparks), IX, 61-62.
29. *Ibid.*, p. 80.
30. *Ibid.*, p. 81.
31. Washington, *Diaries* (ed. Fitzpatrick), II, 377 n; 376.
32. *Ibid.*, pp. 336, 352, 376, 394.

33. *Ibid.*, p. 432.
34. E. M. Turner, *James Rumsey: Pioneer in Steam Navigation*, pp. 110-11, 123.
35. *Writings* (ed. Sparks), IX, 470.
36. At the solicitation of friends he accepted this gift as a trust for the state of Virginia. Later one hundred shares were given to Liberty Hall Academy, now Washington and Lee University. The remaining fifty shares were left to endow a university in the District of Columbia, embracing as it then did a part of what is now Virginia. See Washington, *Writings* (ed. Sparks), XI, 19-24, 172-73.
37. *Diaries* (ed. Fitzpatrick), III, 84.
38. *Writings* (ed. Sparks), IX, 214, 291-92, 302-3, 326-27, 445.
39. *Ibid.*, pp. 178-79.
40. *Ibid.*, p. 109.
41. *Ibid.*, p. 180.
42. *Ibid.*, p. 134.
43. Washington, *Writings from Original Manuscript Sources*, reports from his agent, Tobias Lear, 1791-1799.
44. *Writings* (ed. Sparks), IX, 385.
45. *Ibid.*, pp. 384-86.
46. *Ibid.*, p. 119.
47. *Ibid.*
48. *Ibid.*
49. *Ibid.*, p. 261.

Chapter XI

1. Suggested readings: F. J. Turner, "The Origin of Genet's Projected Attacks on Louisiana and the Floridas," *American Historical Review*, III, 650-71; F. J. Turner, "The Policy of France toward the Mississippi Valley in the Period of Washington and Adams," *American Historical Review*, X, 249-80; J. S. Bassett, *The Federalist System*, chaps. 4-8; A. C. McLaughlin, "The Western Posts and the British Debts," *Annual Report of the American Historical Association*, 1894, pp. 412-14; Winsor, *The Westward Movement*, chaps. 13-24; S. F. Bemis, *Jay's Treaty*.
2. F. J. Turner, "The Policy of France toward the Mississippi Valley. . . ," *American Historical Review*, X, 259-63; F. J. Turner, "The Origin of Genet's Projected Attacks. . . ," *American Historical Review*, III, 650. "Selection from the Draper Collection in the possession of the State Historical Society of Wisconsin to elucidate the proposed French expedition under George Rogers Clark against Louisiana, in the years, 1793-94," *Annual Report of the American Historical Association*, 1896, I, 930-1107; "Correspondence on Genet's Projected Attack, 1793-94," *Annual Report of the American Historical Association*, 1897, pp. 567-679; "Correspondence of Genet," *Annual Report of the American Historical Association*, 1903, II, 201-86.
3. F. J. Turner, "The Origin of Genet's Projected Attacks. . . ," *American Historical Review*, III, 650-51.
4. Ambler, *History of Transportation in the Ohio Valley*, pp. 71-72.
5. Washington, *Diaries* (ed. Fitzpatrick), IV, 74-77.
6. F. J. Turner, "The Origin of Genet's Projected Attacks. . . ," *American Historical Review*, III, 652; R. O. Shreve, *The Finished Scoundrel*.
7. C. H. Haskins, "Yazoo Land Companies," *American Historical Association Papers*, V, 69-72.
8. J. D. Richardson, *Messages and Papers of the Presidents*, I, 102; Washington, *Diaries* (ed. Fitzpatrick), IV, 126-27, 157; F. J. Turner, "The Origin of Genet's Projected Attacks. . . ," *American Historical Review*, III, 652.
9. *Writings* (ed. Sparks), X, 267-78.

10. *Ibid.*, p. 280.
11. *Ibid.*, p. 265.
12. F. J. Turner, "The Origin of Genet's Projected Attacks...," *American Historical Review*, III, p. 664; Jefferson, *Writings* (ed. Ford), VI, 206.
13. F. J. Turner, "The Origin of Genet's Projected Attacks...," *American Historical Review*, III, 665-67; Bemis, *op. cit.*, p. 145.
14. Bassett, *op. cit.*, pp. 92-96.
15. F. J. Turner, "The Policy of France toward the Mississippi Valley...," *American Historical Review*, X, 265.
16. Bassett, *op. cit.*; Bemis, *op. cit.*
17. F. J. Turner, "The Origin of Genet's Projected Attacks...," *American Historical Review*, III, 669; Bemis, *op. cit.*, p. 123.
18. *Writings* (ed. Sparks), X, 426, 427-30, 435-54.
19. F. J. Turner, "The Policy of France toward the Mississippi Valley...," *American Historical Review*, X, 256.
20. *Diaries* (ed. Fitzpatrick), IV, 17.
21. F. J. Turner, "The Policy of France toward the Mississippi Valley...," *American Historical Review*, X, 256.
22. *Writings* (ed. Sparks), X, 153.
23. F. J. Turner, "The Policy of France toward the Mississippi Valley...," *American Historical Review*, X, 259; Jefferson, *Writings* (ed. Ford), I, 212.
24. Bemis, *op. cit.*, p. 195 n; Bassett, *op. cit.*, chap. 4; Winsor, *Westward Movement*.
25. *Writings* (ed. Sparks), X, 434.
26. *Ibid.*, 395; Bemis, *op. cit.*, p. 72.
27. F. J. Turner, "The Policy of France toward the Mississippi Valley...," *American Historical Review*, X, 265-68.
28. *Writings* (ed. Sparks), XI, 51.
29. *Ibid.*, p. 73; Richardson, *op. cit.*, I, 65.
30. *Ibid.*, p. 82.
31. *Ibid.*, p. 167.
32. *Writings* (ed. Sparks), X, 130-31, 210-14.
33. Richardson, *op. cit.*, I, 137.
34. *Ibid.*, p. 76.
35. *Writings* (ed. Sparks), XI, 12.
36. Richardson, *op. cit.*, I, 122; Washington, *Writings* (ed. Sparks), X, 132.
37. *Ibid.*, p. 429. See official papers relating to the Whiskey Rebellion in *Annals of Congress*, 4th Congress, 2791-2866. See also *American State Papers, Military Affairs*, I. For contemporary accounts see William Findley, *History of the Insurrection in the Four Western Counties of Pennsylvania* and H. M. Brackenridge, *History of the Western Insurrection in Western Pennsylvania*.
38. Washington, *Diaries* (ed. Fitzpatrick), IV, 209; Bassett, *op. cit.*, chap. 7.
39. Richardson, *op. cit.*, I, 124-25; *Writings* (ed. Sparks), X, 297.
40. Richardson, *op. cit.*, I, 158-60, 162-66.
41. *Diaries* (ed. Fitzpatrick), IV, 212-13.
42. *Ibid.*, pp. 214-16.
43. Richardson, *op. cit.*, I, 165.
44. *Diaries* (ed. Fitzpatrick), IV, 213-15.
45. Richardson, *op. cit.*, I, 166.
46. *Writings* (ed. Sparks), XI, 11.
47. *Ibid.*, X, 137.
48. Richardson, *op. cit.*, I, 83.

49. *Diaries* (ed. Fitzpatrick), IV, 158.
50. *Writings* (ed. Sparks), XI, 6-7.
51. *Ibid.*, X, 200.
52. Cook, *Washington's Western Lands*, p. 124.
53. *Ibid.*, pp. 107-11; Bicentennial Commission, *History*, I, 477; Jillson, *Land Adventures of George Washington*, p. 58.
54. Cook, *op. cit.*, p. 125.
55. *Ibid.*, pp. 130, 107-11; Bicentennial Commission, *History*, I, 477; Jillson, *op. cit.*, chap. 2.
56. See Boyd B. Stutler, "The Swords of Washington," *West Virginia Review*, IX, 346-47.
57. Washington's most famous swords now repose in widely separated places. The "Frederick the Great" sword was all but destroyed in the fire of the New York Capitol, 1911, where it still reposes, a piece of bent and twisted steel. The "Spanish Dress" sword, the "Sollingen" sword, and the sword said to have been used by him when he surrendered command of the Continental Army, are now at Mount Vernon. His "Battle" sword is in the United States National Museum at Washington, D. C., and the sword presented him by General William Darke, a resident of what is now Jefferson County, West Virginia, is in the Washington Headquarters of the Washington Association of New Jersey, at Morristown, New Jersey. See Stutler, *op. cit.*, 346-47.
58. *Wheeling Sunday News*, February 17, 1935.
59. *Writings* (ed. Sparks), XII, 219-20; Richardson, *op. cit.*, I, 215-16.
60. *Writings* (ed. Sparks), XI, 456.
61. *Ibid.*, pp. 453-54.
62. *Ibid.*, p. 457.

SELECT BIBLIOGRAPHY

GENERAL PREFATORY NOTE

For the most part, this work is based upon printed sources, the most important of which are Washington's *Diaries* and his *Writings*. Inasmuch as a select critical "Washington Bibliography" is easily available in the *History of the George Washington Bicentennial Celebration*, A, Volume I, Literature Series, pages 185-99, a "Select Bibliography" is adequate to all reasonable requirements for this volume. The "Washington Bibliography" was prepared by a special committee of the American Library Association and is comprehensive. The present writer makes particular acknowledgments to Dr. Roy Bird Cook, *Washington's Western Lands*. It contains not only locations and exact extent of surveys but plats as well.

PRINTED SOURCES

American State Papers. Documents, legislative and executive of the United States Congress. 38 vols. Washington, 1832-1861.

Annals of Congress. 1st Congress, 1st Session, to 18th Congress, 1st Session, 1789-1824.

Bedinger, Henry. "Journal," in Danske Dandridge's *Historic Shepherdstown*. Charlottesville, Va., 1910.

Boucher, Jonathan. *Reminiscences of an American Loyalist, 1738-1789.* Boston, 1925.

Brooke, Walter E., editor. *Agricultural Papers of George Washington.* Boston, 1912.

Burnaby, Andrew. *Travels through the Middle Settlements in North-America, in the Years 1759 and 1760.* London, 1775; New York, 1904.

Butterfield, Consul W., editor. *Washington-Crawford Letters.* Being the correspondence between George Washington and William Crawford, from 1767 to 1781, concerning western lands. Cincinnati, 1877.

────── editor. *Washington-Irvine Correspondence.* The official letters which passed between Washington and Brigadier-General William Irvine and between Irvine and others concerning military affairs in the west from 1781 to 1783, arranged and annotated with an introduction containing an outline of events occurring previously in the Trans-Allegheny country. Madison, Wis., 1882.

Byrd, William. *Writings.* Edited by John S. Bassett. New York, 1901.

Champlain, Samuel de. *Works.* 6 vols. Champlain Society Publications. Toronto, Canada, 1929.

Colonial Records of Pennsylvania. Edited by Samuel Hazard. 16 vols. Harrisburg, 1851-1853.

"Correspondence of Genêt," *Annual Report of the American Historical Association*, 1903 (2 vols.), II, 201-86.

"Correspondence on Genêt's Projected Attack," *Annual Report of the American Historical Association*, 1897, pp. 567-679.

Custis, George W. P. *Recollections and Private Memoirs of Washington*. Philadelphia, 1859.

Darlington, William M., editor. *Christopher Gist's Journal* with historical, geographical and ethnological notes and biographies of his contemporaries. Pittsburgh, 1893.

Dinwiddie, Robert. "The Official Records of Robert Dinwiddie, Lieutenant-governor of Virginia, 1751-1758." Edited by R. A. Brock, in *Virginia Historical Society Collections*, new series. 16 vols. Richmond, 1883-1884.

Fitzpatrick, John C. *George Washington's Accounts of Expenses*. Boston, 1917.

Force, Peter., editor. *American Archives*, 9 vols. Washington, 1837-1853.

Franklin, Benjamin. *Writings*. Edited with a life and introduction by Albert H. Smyth. 10 vols. New York, 1905-1907.

Gallatin, Albert. *Writings*. Edited by Henry Adams. 3 vols. Philadelphia, 1879.

Gist, Christopher. "Journal," in *Massachusetts Historical Society Collections*, 3rd series, V (1836), 102-8.

—————— *Journal*. See Darlington, W. M., editor.

Hamilton, Stanislaus M., editor. *Letters to Washington and Accompanying Papers*. 5 vols. Boston, 1898-1902.

Hazard, Samuel, editor. *Register of Pennsylvania*. 16 vols. Philadelphia, 1828-1836.

Hening, William W. *The Statutes at Large, Being a Collection of the Laws of Virginia, 1619-1792*. 13 vols. Philadelphia, 1823.

James, James A. *George Rogers Clark Papers, 1771-1781. Illinois State Historical Library Collections* (Vol. III, Virginia Series), VIII (1912).

Jefferson, Thomas. *Writings*. Library edition, 20 vols. Washington, 1903-1904.

—————— *Writings*. Edited by Paul L. Ford. 10 vols. New York, 1892-1899.

—————— *Notes on the State of Virginia*. Philadelphia, 1787.

Journals of the Continental Congress, 1774-1789. Complete edition, 29 vols. Washington, 1904-1933.

Journals of the House of Burgesses of Virginia, including the records of the committee of correspondence. Edited by H. R. McIlwaine and J. P. Kennedy. 13 vols. Richmond, 1905-1915.

Kellogg, Louise P. *Frontier Advance on the Upper Ohio, 1778-1779. Wisconsin State Historical Society Collections* (Vol. IV, Draper Series), 1916.

—————— *Frontier Retreat on the Upper Ohio, 1779-1781. Wisconsin State Historical Society Collections* (Vol. V, Draper Series), 1917.

Lee, Richard H. *Letters*. Edited by J. C. Ballagh. 2 vols. New York, 1911-1914.

Lewis, Thomas. *Journal, September 10, 1746-February, 1747*. New Market, Va., 1925.

Madison, James. *Writings.* Edited by Gaillard Hunt. 9 vols. New York, 1900-1910.

Marshall, John. *Life of George Washington,* commander-in-chief of the American forces during the war which established the independence of his country, and first president of the United States. 5 vols. Philadelphia, 1804-1807.

O'Callaghan, E[dmund] B. *Documentary History of the State of New York.* 4 vols. Albany, 1849-1851.

Pennsylvania Archives. Edited by Samuel Hazard. 12 vols. Philadelphia, 1852-1856.

Richardson, James D., editor. *A Compilation of the Messages and Papers of the Presidents.* 10 vols. Washington, 1896.

Saunders, William L., editor. *Colonial Records of North Carolina.* 10 vols. Raleigh, 1886-1890.

Sharpe, Horatio. *Correspondence, 1750-1771.* Edited by W. H. Browne. 3 vols. (Vols. VI, IX, XIV of *Maryland Historical Society Archives*) Baltimore, 1888-1895.

Shirley, William. *Correspondence.* Edited by Charles H. Lincoln. 2 vols. New York, 1912.

Stobo, Robert. *Memoirs.* Pittsburgh, 1854.

Thomas, Antoine L. *Oeuvres Diverses.* One vol. in 2 parts. Amsterdam, 1762.

Thwaites, Reuben G., and Kellogg, Louise P. *Documentary History of Dunmore's War, 1774,* compiled from the Draper manuscripts in the library of the Wisconsin Historical Society. Madison, 1905.

——— *Revolution on the Upper Ohio, 1775-1777,* compiled from the Draper manuscripts in the library of the Wisconsin Historical Society. Madison, 1908.

——— *Frontier Defense on the Upper Ohio, 1777-1778,* compiled from the Draper manuscripts in the library of the Wisconsin Historical Society. Madison, 1912.

Villiers. "Journal," in Craig, *Olden Time.* 2 vols. Pittsburgh, 1847.

Washington, George. *Calendar of the Correspondence of George Washington, Commander-in-Chief of the Continental Army.* Edited by John C. Fitzpatrick. 5 vols. Washington, 1906-1915.

——— *Diaries.* Edited by John C. Fitzpatrick. 4 vols. Boston, 1925.

——— *Journal of 1754.* Edited by Joseph M. Toner. Albany, 1893.

——— *Letters and Recollections of George Washington.* Edited by Louisa Lear Eyre. New York, 1906.

——— *Writings.* Edited by Worthington C. Ford. 14 vols. New York, 1889-1893.

——— *Writings.* Edited by Jared Sparks, together with a biographical sketch. 12 vols. Boston, 1834-1837.

——— *Writings from the Original Manuscript Sources.* Now being published by the George Washington Bicentennial Commission under editorship of John C. Fitzpatrick. Available at date of present writing, 11 vols. Washington, 1931-1934.

Washington-Crawford Letters. See Butterfield, C. W.
Washington-Irvine Correspondence. See Butterfield, C. W.

NEWSPAPERS

Annapolis: *Maryland Gazette*, 1753-1758. Files incomplete.
Charleston: *South Carolina Gazette.* Files of 1754.
Philadelphia: *Philadelphia Gazette*, 1753-1774. Files fairly complete.
Williamsburg: *Virginia Gazette*, 1753-1758. Files incomplete.

SECONDARY WORKS
Books
BIOGRAPHIES

Adams, Henry. *The Life of Albert Gallatin.* Philadelphia, 1879.
Baker, William S. *Washington after the Revolution.* Philadelphia, 1898.
Bowers, Claude G. *Jefferson and Hamilton: the Struggle for Democracy in America.* Boston, 1925.
Carrington, Henry B. *Washington the Soldier.* New York, 1899.
Conway, Moncure D., editor. *George Washington and Mount Vernon.* Long Island Historical Society. Brooklyn, 1889.
Cooke, John E. *Fairfax; or, The Master of Greenway Court.* A chronicle of the valley of the Shenandoah. New York, 1868.
Corbin, John. *Unknown Washington: Biographic Origins of the Republic.* New York, 1930.
Dahlinger, Charles W. *The Marquis Duquesne sieur de Menneville, Founder of the City of Pittsburgh.* Pittsburgh, 1932.
Dictionary of American Biography. Edited by Allen Johnson and Dumas Malone under the auspices of the American Council of Learned Societies, Abbe-Seward. 16 vols. New York, 1928-1934.
Fay, Bernard. *George Washington, Republican and Aristocrat.* New York, 1931.
Fitzpatrick, John C. *George Washington Himself.* Indianapolis, 1933.
Ford, Henry J. *Washington and his Colleagues* (Vol. XIV, Chronicles of America Series, edited by Allen Johnson). New Haven, 1918.
Ford, Paul L. *True George Washington.* Philadelphia, 1896.
Ford, Worthington C. *George Washington.* 2 vols. New York, 1900.
Hapgood, Norman. *George Washington.* New York, 1901.
Haworth, Paul L. *George Washington, Country Gentleman.* Indianapolis, 1925. (This volume was published in 1915, under the title *George Washington, Farmer.*)
Hughes, Rupert. *George Washington.* 3 vols. New York, 1926-1930. (The three volumes appear with different titles: *George Washington, the human being and the hero, 1732-1762; George Washington, the rebel and the patriot, 1762-1777; George Washington, the savior of the states, 1777-1781.*)
James, James A. *The Life of George Rogers Clark.* Chicago, 1928.
Johnson, Bradley T. *General Washington.* New York, 1881.

Lodge, Henry C. *George Washington.* 2 vols., American Statesmen Series. Boston, 1889.
——— *George Washington, the Man.* Boston, 1921.
Mitchell, Silas Weir. *Youth of Washington.* New York, 1904.
Moore, Charles. *Family Life of George Washington.* Boston, 1926.
Myers, Albert C. *The Boy George Washington, aged 16: his own account of an Iroquois Indian dance.* Philadelphia, 1932.
Osborn, Lucretia P., editor. *Washington Speaks for Himself.* New York, 1927.
Pryor, Mrs. Roger A. *Mother of Washington and her Times.* New York, 1903.
Ritter, Halsted L. *Washington as a Business Man.* New York, 1931.
Rush, Richard. *Washington in Domestic Life.* Philadelphia, 1857.
Savelle, Max. *George Morgan, Colony Builder.* New York, 1932.
Sears, Louis M. *George Washington.* New York, 1932.
Shreve, Royal O. *The Finished Scoundrel: General James Wilkinson, Sometime Commander-in-Chief of the Army of the United States.* Indianapolis, 1933.
Sipe, C. Hale. *Mount Vernon and the Washington Family.* Butler, Pa., 1929.
Slaughter, Philip. *Christianity the Key to the Character and Career of Washington.* New York, 1886.
Sparks, Jared. *Life of George Washington.* Boston, 1839.
Stone, William, L. *Life and Times of Sir William Johnson, Bart.* 2 vols. Albany, N. Y., 1865.
Thayer, William R. *George Washington.* New York, 1922.
Turner, Nancy Byrd. *In the Days of Young Washington.* Boston, 1931.
——— *Mother of Washington.* New York, 1930.
United States George Washington Bicentennial Commission. *History of the George Washington Bicentennial Celebration.* 3 vols. Washington, 1932.
Volwiler, Albert T. *George Croghan and the Westward Movement, 1741-1782.* Cleveland, 1926.
Walton, Joseph. *Conrad Weiser and the Indian Policy of Colonial Pennsylvania.* Philadelphia, 1900.
Whipple, Wayne. *The Story-life of Washington.* 2 vols. Philadelphia, 1911.
Wilson, Woodrow. *George Washington.* New York, 1903.
Wister, Owen. *Seven Ages of Washington; a Biography.* New York, 1907.
Woodward, William E. *George Washington, the Image and the Man.* New York, 1926.

GENERAL WORKS

Andrews, Charles M. *Colonial Background of the American Revolution.* New Haven, 1924.
Bancroft, George. *History of the United States.* 10 vols. Boston, 1879.
Bassett, John S. *Federalist System, 1789-1801.* (Vol. XI, American Nation Series, edited by A. B. Hart). New York, 1906.
Becker, Carl. *Eve of the Revolution* (Chronicles of America Series, edited by Allen Johnson). New Haven, 1918.
Beer, George L. *British Colonial Policy, 1754-1765.* New York, 1907.

Branch, E. Douglas. *Westward, the Romance of the American Frontier.* New York, 1930.
Channing, Edward. *History of the United States.* 6 vols. New York, 1912-1917.
Chitwood, Oliver P. *History of Colonial America.* New York, 1931.
Drake, Samuel A. *Aboriginal Races of North America.* New York, c1880.
Earle, Alice M. *Home Life in Colonial Days.* New York, 1899.
——— *Stage-coach and Tavern Days.* New York, 1900.
Flassan, Gaëtan de Raxis de. *Histoire de la Diplomatie Française.* 6 vols. Paris, 1811.
Garneau, Francois X. *History of Canada, from the Time of its Discovery to the Union Year 1840-1841.* Translated by Andrew Bell. 2nd ed. 2 vols. Montreal, Canada, 1862.
Greene, Evarts B. *Foundations of American Nationality.* New York, 1922.
Hassall, Arthur. *The Balance of Power, 1715-1789.* New York and London, 1896.
Kingsford, William. *History of Canada.* Toronto, Canada, 1899.
Lacretelle Le Jeune, Jean Charles. *Histoire de France.* 6 vols. Paris, 1808.
Lossing, Benson J. *Washington and the American Republic.* 3 vols. New York, 1870.
McLaughlin, Andrew C. *Confederation and the Constitution, 1783-1789* (Vol. X. American Nation Series, edited by A. B. Hart). New York, 1906.
Montgaillard, G. H. R., Abbé de. *Histoire de France, depuis la fin du règne de Louis XVI jusqu'à l'année 1825.* 9 vols. Paris, 1828-1835.
Munro, William B. *Crusaders of New France.* New Haven, 1921.
Osgood, Herbert L. *American Colonies in the Eighteenth Century.* 4 vols. Columbia University Press, New York, 1924.
Parkman, Francis. *Montcalm and Wolfe.* 2 vols. Boston, 1884.
——— *Pioneers of France in the New World.* Boston, 1897.
Roberts, Charles G. D. *History of Canada.* Boston, 1897.
Roosevelt, Theodore. *Winning of the West.* 4 vols. New York, 1889-1896.
Thwaites, Reuben G. *France in America, 1497-1763* (Vol. VII, American Nation Series, edited by A. B. Hart). New York, 1905.
Van Tyne, Claude H. *Loyalists in the American Revolution.* New York, 1902.
Winsor, Justin, editor. *Narrative and Critical History of America.* 8 vols. Boston, 1889.
Wittke, Carl. *History of Canada.* New York, 1928.
Wrong, George M. *Rise and Fall of New France.* 2 vols. New York, 1928.

LOCAL AND REGIONAL

Agnew, Daniel. *History of the Region of Pennsylvania North of the Ohio and West of the Allegheny River.* Philadelphia, 1887.
Aler, F. Vernon. *History of Martinsburg and Berkeley County, West Virginia,* from the origin of the Indians, embracing their settlements, wars, and

depredations, to the first settlement of the valley. Hagerstown, Maryland, 1888.

Alvord, Clarence W. *Mississippi Valley in British Politics:* a study of the trade, land speculation and experiments in imperialism culminating in the American revolution. 2 vols. Cleveland, 1917.

Ambler, Charles H. *History of Transportation in the Ohio Valley,* with special reference to its waterways, trade, and commerce from the earliest period to the present time. Glendale, California, 1932.

Bausman, Joseph. History of Beaver County Pennsylvania. 2 vols. New York, 1904.

Brackenridge, Henry M. *History of the Western Insurrection in Western Pennsylvania, Commonly Called the Whiskey Insurrection, 1794.* Pittsburgh, 1859.

Bruce, Philip A. *The Virginia Plutarch.* 2 vols. Chapel Hill, N. C., 1929.

Cartmell, Thomas K. *Shenandoah Valley Pioneers and their Descendants. A History of Frederick County, Virginia.* Winchester, Va., 1909.

Christian, Bolivar. "The Scotch-Irish Settlers in the Valley of Virginia," in *Washington and Lee University, Historical Papers,* No. 3, pp. 1-43. Lexington, 1892.

Conway, Moncure D. *Barons of the Potomack and the Rappahannock.* New York, 1892.

Cooke, John E. *Stories of the Old Dominion from the Settlement to the End of the Revolution.* New York, 1879.

────── *Virginia; a History of the People.* Boston, 1883.

Craig, Neville B. *History of Pittsburgh.* Pittsburgh, 1851.

────── *Olden Time.* 2 vols. Pittsburgh, 1847.

This work includes *A Memorial Containing a Summary View of Facts with their Authorities, in Answer to the Observations Sent by the English Ministry to the Courts of Europe* (Philadelphia, 1757), which was in reply to the French *Mémoire contenant le précis des faits, avec leur piéces justificatives, pour servir de répose aux observations envoyées, par les ministers d'Angleterre, dans les cours de l'Europe* (Paris, 1756).

Craven, Avery O. *Soil Exhaustion as a Factor in the Agricultural History of Virginia and Maryland.* Urbana, Illinois, 1926.

Crumrine, Boyd. *History of Washington County.* Philadelphia, 1882.

Dandridge, Mrs. Danske Bedinger. *Historic Shepherdstown.* Charlottesville, 1910.

Day, Sherman. *Historical Collections of the State of Pennsylvania.* Philadelphia, 1846.

Egle, William H. *Illustrated History of the Commonwealth of Pennsylvania, Civil, Political, and Military.* Philadelphia, 1880.

Fernow, Berthold. *Ohio Valley in Colonial Days.* Albany, 1890.

Findley, William. *History of the Insurrection in the Four Western Counties of Pennsylvania.* Philadelphia, 1796.

Hanna, Charles A. *The Wilderness Trail;* or, The ventures and adventures of the Pennsylvania trader on the Allegheny path with some new annals of the old West, and the records of some strong men and some bad ones. 2 vols. New York, 1911.

Howe, Henry. *Historical Collections of Virginia, with an Historical and Descriptive Sketch of the District of Columbia.* Charleston, S. C., 1845.

Kercheval, Samuel. *History of the Valley of Virginia.* Winchester, Va., 1833; Woodstock, Va., 1850; Dayton, Va., 1902; Strasburg, Va., 1926.

King, Grace. *Mount Vernon on the Potomac:* History of the Mount Vernon Ladies' Association of the Union. New York, 1929.

Lewis, Virgil A. *History of the Battle of Point Pleasant.* Charleston, W. Va., 1909.

Lowdermilk, William H. *History of Cumberland [Maryland].* Washington, 1878.

Lowther, Minnie K. *Mount Vernon, Its Children, Its Romances, Its Allied Families and Mansions.* Philadelphia, 1930.

Meade, Bishop William. *Old Churches, Ministers and Families of Virginia.* 2 vols. Philadelphia, 1857.

Morton, Oren F. *Story of Winchester in Virginia, the Oldest Town in the Shenandoah Valley.* Strasburg, Va., 1925.

Parkman, Francis. *Conspiracy of Pontiac, and the Indian War after the Conquest of Canada.* 2 vols. Boston, 1851.

Paxson, Frederic L. *History of the American Frontier, 1763-1893.* Boston, 1924.

Pennypacker, Samuel W. *Pennsylvania in American History.* Philadelphia, 1910.

Robins, Sally Nelson. *Love Stories of Famous Virginians.* Published under the auspices of the national society, Colonial Dames of America. Richmond, 1925.

[Rupp, Israel D.] *A Gentleman of the Bar. Early history of western Pennsylvania and of western expeditions and campaigns.* Published by Daniel W. Kauffman. Pittsburgh and Harrisburg, 1846.

Sargent, Winthrop. *History of an Expedition Against Fort Du Quesne in 1755 under Major-General Edward Braddock.* Philadelphia, 1856.

Searight, Thomas B. *The Old Pike; a History of the National Road.* Uniontown, Pa., 1894.

Sipe, C. Hale. *Fort Ligonier and Its Times.* Harrisburg, Pa., 1932.

——— *Indian Wars of Western Pennsylvania.* Harrisburg, Pa., 1929.

Smith, Joseph. *Old Redstone.* New York, 1850.

Tyler, Lyon G. *England in America, 1580-1652* (Vol. IV, American Nation Series, edited by A. B. Hart). New York, 1904.

Veech, James. *Monongahela of Old.* Pittsburgh, 1858; 1892.

Warburton, George D. *Conquest of Canada.* 2 vols. Second Edition. New York, 1850.

Wayland, John W. *German Element of the Shenandoah Valley of Virginia.* Charlottesville, Va., 1907.

Wertenbaker, Thomas J. *Patrician and Plebeian in Virginia.* Charlottesville, Va., 1910.

——— *Planters of Colonial Virginia.* Princeton, 1922.

Wilstach, Paul. *Mount Vernon, Washington's Home and the Nation's Shrine.* Indianapolis, 1916.

Winsor, Justin. *The Mississippi Basin:* the Struggle in America between England and France, 1697-1763. Boston, 1895.

——— *The Westward Movement:* the Colonies and the Republic West of the Alleghanies. Boston, 1897.

Withers, Alexander S. *Chronicles of Border Warfare;* or, a history of the settlement by the whites, of northwestern Virginia. Clarksburg, 1831; Cincinnati, 1895, edited by R. G. Thwaites; reprinted Cincinnati, 1917.

ARTICLES AND MONOGRAPHS

Adams, Herbert B. "Maryland's Influence upon Land Cessions to the United States. With minor papers on George Washington's interest in western lands, the Potomac company, and a national university," *Johns Hopkins University Studies,* 3rd series [III (1885)], No. I.

Alden, George H. "New Governments West of the Allegheny Mountains before 1780," *University of Wisconsin Bulletin* (economics, political science, and history series), II (1897), No. 3.

Alvord, Clarence W., and Bidgood, Lee. *First Explorations of the Trans-Allegheny Region by the Virginians, 1650-1674.* Cleveland, 1912.

Baker-Crothers, Hayes. *Virginia and the French and Indian War.* Chicago, 1928.

Barton, Robert T. "The First Election of Washington to the House of Burgesses," *Virginia Historical Society Collections* (new series, edited by R. A. Brock), XI (1892), 115-25.

Bassett, John S. "The Relation between the Virginia Planter and the London Merchant," *Annual Report of the American Historical Association,* 1901 (2 vols.), I, 551-75.

Beard, Charles A. *Economic Interpretation of the Constitution of the United States.* New York, 1913.

——— *Economic Origins of Jeffersonian Democracy.* New York, 1915.

Bemis, Samuel F. *Jay's Treaty: a Study in Commerce and Diplomacy.* New York, 1923.

——— *Pinckney's Treaty: a Study of America's Advantage from Europe's Distress, 1783-1800.* Baltimore, 1926.

Blackford, Harry R. *The Reconstruction of Fort Necessity.* A Pamphlet. Uniontown, 1932.

Burton, Clarence M. "John Connolly, a Tory of the Revolution," *American Antiquarian Society Proceedings,* XX (1909), 70-105.

Carter, Clarence E. *Great Britain and the Illinois Country, 1763-1774.* Washington, 1910.

Conway, Moncure D., editor. *George Washington's Rules of Civility,* traced to their sources and restored. New York, 1890.

Cook, Roy B. *Washington's Western Lands.* Strasburg, Va., 1930.

Craig, Neville B. *Washington's First Campaign, Death of Jumonville, and Taking of Fort Necessity;* also Braddock's defeat and the march of the unfortunate General explained by a civil engineer. Pittsburgh, 1849.

Darlington, Mary C., editor. *Fort Pitt and Letters from the Frontier.* Pittsburgh, 1892.
Fitzpatrick, John C. *Spirit of the Revolution,* new light from some of the originial sources of American history. Boston, 1924.
―――― *George Washington, Colonial Traveller, 1732-1775.* Indianapolis, 1927.
Flick, Alexander C. "New Sources on the Sullivan-Clinton Campaign in 1779," *New York State Historical Association Quarterly Journal,* X (1929), 185-224, 265-317.
Ford, Worthington C. *Washington as an Employer and Importer of Labor.* Brooklyn, 1889.
Frothingham, Thomas G. *Washington, Commander-in-Chief.* Boston, 1930.
Grinnan, Daniel. Review of A. O. Craven's *Soil Exhaustion as a Factor in the Agricultural History of Virginia and Maryland, Virginia Magazine of History and Biography,* XXXV (1927), 313-15.
Harrison, Fairfax. "George Washington's First Commission," *Virginia Magazine of History and Biography,* XXXI (1923), 271-73.
―――― "The Proprietors of the Northern Neck," *Virginia Magazine of History and Biography,* XXXIII (1925), 113-53, 223-67, 333-58; XXXIV (1926), 19-64.
―――― "The Virginians on the Ohio and the Mississippi in 1742," *Virginia Magazine of History and Biography,* XXX (1922), 203-22.
Haskins, Charles H. "Yazoo Land Companies," *American Historical Association Papers,* V (1891), 395-440.
Henderson, Archibald. *Washington's Western Tour, 1791.* Boston, 1923.
Hulbert, Archer B. *Historic Highways of America.* 16 vols. Cleveland, 1902-1905.
――――, editor. *Washingon and the West;* being George Washington's diary of September, 1784, kept during his journey into the Ohio basin in the interest of a commercial union between the Great Lakes and the Potomac river. New York, 1905.
――――, editor. "Washington's 'Tour to the Ohio' and articles on 'The Mississippi Company,'" *Ohio Archaeological and Historical Quarterly,* XVII (1908), 431-88.
James, James A. "Pittsburgh, a Key to the West during the American Revolution," *Ohio Archaeological and Historical Quarterly,* XXII (1913), 64-79.
Jillson, Willard R. *Land Adventures of George Washington.* Louisville, 1934.
Kemper, Charles E., editor. "Early Westward Movement of Virginia," *Virginia Magazine of History and Biography,* XII (1905), 337-52, XIII (1905), 1-16, 113-38, (1906), 281-97.
Koontz, Louis K. "The Virginia Frontier, 1754-1763," *Johns Hopkins University Studies,* XLIII (1925), No. 2.
Laub, C. Herbert. "The Problem of Armed Invasion of the Northwest during the American Revolution," *Virginia Magazine of History and Biography,* XLII (1934), 18-27, 132-44.

——— "British Regulation of the Crown Lands in the West: the Last Phase, 1773-1775," *William and Mary College Quarterly*, X (1930), 52-55.
Leffman, Henry. "George Washington as an Engineer," *Engineer Club of Philadelphia Proceedings*, XXI (1904), 277.
McLaughlin, Andrew C. "The Western Posts and the British Debts," *Annual Report of the American Historical Association*, 1894.
Mitchell, Silas Weir. *Washington in His Letters*. Philadelphia, 1903.
Pargellis, Stanley McC. *Lord Loudoun in North America, 1756-1758*. New Haven, 1933.
Phillips, Philip L. "Washington as a Surveyor and Map-maker," *Daughters of the American Revolution Magazine*, XLIV (1914).
Rives, George L. "Spain and the United States, 1795," *American Historical Review*, IV (1898), 62-79.
Root, Winifred T. *Relations of Pennsylvania with the British Government, 1696-1765*. New York, 1912.
"Selections from the Draper Collection in the possession of the State Historical Society of Wisconsin to elucidate the proposed French Expedition under George Rogers Clark against Louisiana, in the years 1793-94." *Annual Report of the American Historical Association*, 1896 (2 vols.), I, 930-1107.
Severance, Frank H. "An Old Frontier of France," *Buffalo Historical Society Publications*, I (1917), 1-436.
Shea, John G. "Daniel Hyacinth Mary Liénard de Beaujeu," *Pennsylvania Magazine of History and Biography*, VIII (1884), 121-28.
Showalter, W. J. "The Travels of George Washington," *The National Geographic Magazine*, LXI (1932), 1-63.
Stephenson, Nathaniel W. "The Romantics and George Washington," *American Historical Review*, XXXIX (1934), 274-83.
Stutler, Boyd B. "The Swords of Washington," *West Virginia Review*, IX (May, 1932), 346-47.
Toner, Joseph M. *Washington's Rules of Civilty and Decent Behavior*. Washington, 1888.
——— *George Washington as an Inventor and Promoter of Useful Arts*. Washington, 1892.
Turner, Ella May. *James Rumsey: Pioneer in Steam Navigation*. Scottdale, Pa., 1930.
Turner, Frederick J. *The Frontier in American History*. New York, 1920.
——— "The Origin of Genet's Projected Attacks on Louisiana and the Floridas," *American Historical Review*, III (1898), 650-71.
——— "The Policy of France towards the Mississippi Valley in the Period of Washington and Adams," *American Historical Review*, X (1905), 249-79.
"Washington and the Potomac: MSS of the Minnesota Historical Society [1754], 1769-1796," *American Historical Review*, XXVIII (1923), 497-520, 705-23.

INDEX

ADAMS, Herbert Baxter, quoted, 172
Adams, John, quoted, 161
Addison, Joseph, influence on George Washington, 13
Adet, Pierre-Auguste, 195
Albany, N. Y., 185
Alexandria, Va., 52, 89, 93, 97, 99, 182
Allegheny Mountains, 117, 135, 136, 138, 162, 182
Allegheny River, 39, 40
Allen, Reverend Bennett, 163
Alvord, Clarence Walworth, quoted, 38
American System, 207
Appleby School, 11
Ardmore Road Hollow, 105
Arnold, Benedict, 161, 162
Ashby's Gap, 21
Atkins, Edmund, 121
Aylett, Ann, 11

BACON'S Rebellion, 6
Ball, John, "Mad Preacher of Kent," 3
Ball, Colonel Joseph, 4, 5; letter of, to Mary Ball Washington, 15
Baltimore, Lord, 33
Bancroft, George, quoted, 86
Barbadoes, 6, 26
Barlow, Joel, 189
Batts and Fallam, explorations, 32
Baynton, Wharton, and Morgan, 135, 138, 139
Beaujeu, Daniel Hyacinth Mary Liénard de, 105, 106
Bedford, Penna., 126
Bell, Robert, 142
Belvoir, Fairfax estate, 14, 16, 18, 19, 52
Berkeley, William, 6
Berkeley Springs. See Warm Springs
Blue Ridge Mountains, 32, 117
Boone, Daniel, 33
Boston, Mass., 55, 151
"Bostonians," concern regarding the French, 55
Boston Tea Party, 150
Botetourt, Norborne Berkeley, Baron de, 146, 147

Bouquet, Colonel Henry, 128, 129; comments of, regarding Virginians, 128
Bradbury, John, and Ohio Company, 32
Braddock, General Edward, 93; arrival of, in America, 95; virtues and weaknesses of, 95-96; headquarters of, at Alexandria, 97; traits of character of, 97, 98, 102; maintains discipline, 99; leaves Alexandria, 100; Franklin's estimate of, 101; defeat of, 105-8; death and burial of, 108; grave and monument of, 109
Braddock's Expedition, 100-9; importance of, 109
"Braddock's Field," 105-10, 128, 140, 222-26
Braddock's Road, 102-4, 158
Bridges Creek, 11
Brodhead, Colonel Daniel, 165, 167, 168, 169
Brown, John, at Harpers Ferry, 205
Bullett, Thomas, 129
Bullskin Creek, 23, 26
Burd, Colonel James, 126
Burgoyne, General John, 165
Byrd, William, 31, 112, 129

CANADA, 31, 54, 198; French settlements in, 55
Capon River, 26
Carlisle, Penna., 126
Carter, Landon, 122, 165
Cassey, Peter, 22
Catawba Indians, 101, 113
Cavaliers, 19
"Ceceders," 177
Celoron, plants leaden plates, 31
"Centinel X," 122
Charleston, S. C., 194
Charlesvoix, Father, quoted, 54
Chartier's Creek, 138
Cheat River, 177, 178, 180, 182, 184
Cherokee Indians, 55, 57, 59, 96, 113, 120, 155, 190
Chicamauga Indians, 199
Churches, Catholic, 38; Protestant, 38

[261]

Clark, George Rogers, 166, 167, 169; failure of Detroit expedition under, 168
Clay, Henry, 208
Cleveland, James, 156
Clinton, George, 164
Cocke, Thomas, 100
Coldstream Guards, 95
Colonies, failure of, to coöperate, 56; differences among, 96
Committee of Safety, 202
Conestoga wagon, 191
Confederation, Articles of, 172
Congresses, Albany, 1754, 57; First Continental, 155, 159; Second Continental, 158, 160, 172, 186; Federal, 200
Congressional Committee on Indian Affairs, 172
Connolly, Doctor John, 145
"Conotocarious," Washington's Indian name, 6, 115
Contrecoeur, Captain Claude Pierre Pécaudy, sieur de, 61, 65, 71, 105
Cornwallis, Charles, 20
Cowpens, battle of, 162
Craik, Doctor James, 88, 90, 104, 140, 142, 175, 178, 181
Craik, William, 175
Crawford, Valentine, 154
Crawford, William, 7; Washington's land agent, 137-40, 142, 147, 149, 154; comments on Dunmore's War, 156; burned at stake, 170
Cresap, Thomas, 22, 141; blazed Nemacolin path, 33
Croghan, George, 142, 144, 145, 146, 148; Indian trader, 31-33; diplomat, 50; Indian leader, 59; with Braddock, 96, 100, 108
Croghan Hall, 141
Crown Point, Fort, 99, 134
Culpeper, Lord, 19
Cumberland, Duke of, 93
Cumberland, Fort, 93, 100, 101, 110, 112, 113, 114, 115, 116, 121, 128
Cumberland, Md., 175, 176
Cumberland River, 145
Currin, Barnaby, 39
Custis, Daniel Parke, 132
Custis, John Parke (Jacky), 125, 132, 133

Custis, Martha. *See* Washington, Martha
Custis, Martha Parke (Patcy), 133, 135

Dagworthy, Captain John, 115, 116
Dallas, Texas, Scottish Rite Temple of, 206
Davison, John, 43, 44
Deakins, Colonel Francis, 188
Delaware Indians, 40, 74, 77, 169
"Democratic Societies," 195, 200
Detroit, Mich., 182
Dettingen, battle of, 72
Dillon's Run, 26
Dinwiddie, Robert, 38, 46, 48, 50, 52, 54, 57, 61, 68, 70, 73, 74, 76, 93, 97, 100, 114, 115, 121, 135; names Washington county lieutenant, 20; names Washington adjutant of militia, 26, 27, 34; refuses to permit Ohio Company surveys, 34; commissioned Washington to be adjutant for the "Southern District of Virginia," 34; interest of, in Ohio Company, 35; sends messenger to French, 36; letter of, to St. Pierre, 45; publishes Washington's "Account," 48; reaction of, to Fort Necessity defeat, 50; appeal of, to Virginia (1753), 52; differences of, with general assembly, 53, 56, 96; at Winchester Indian conference, 57; resolves of, on aggression, 58; Lodge characterization of, 60; refuses "Spirit" for soldiers, 62; advises Washington, 62, 63; appoints Colonel James Innes as commander-in-chief, 74; Captain Mackay questions authority of, 76, 77; enthusiastic over contest with French, 86; resolves to strike French, 89; refuses to abide by terms of Fort Necessity capitulation, 89, 90; effort to retrieve English losses, 92; demotes Washington, 94; failure of, in Indian relations, 96; plea of, for action against Fench, 111; signs death warrant for Sergeant Lewis, 120; attitude of, toward Washington, 122, 123; threatened breach of, with Washington, 123; official contact of, with Loudoun, 124; grants Washington leave, 124, 125; proclamation of 1754, 134

"Dinwiddie's War," 51, 52, 156
Dismal Swamp, 132, 133
Dorchester, Lord, speech of, 197, 198
Douville, Dagneau, scalped, 118
Duane, James, 172
Dumas, Captain, 105, 106, 110, 118
Dunbar, Colonel Thomas, 100, 105, 112
Dunkard Bottom, 180, 188
Dunmore, John Murray, earl of, 147, 149, 150, 155
Dunmore's War, 155, 156, 158
Duquesne, Fort, 62, 78, 92, 128, 130, 132, 134; Braddock's objective, 96, 99, 104; roads to, 127; grand attack on, 129

Edmonstone, Captain Charles, 141
English, traders, 30, 31, 58, 59, 62; contest of, for Ohio Valley, 30; claims of, to the Ohio Valley, 32; claims of, to Indian lands, 36; Indian allies of, 39, 58, 61; in Ohio Valley, 43, 66; Indian relations of, 48; inroads upon, 53, 54; military failures of, 57
Ennis, Jones, 154
Epping Forest, 4
Erskine, Robert, 28
Eskridge, Major George, 3
Everard, Thomas, 163

Fairfax, Anne, wife of Lawrence Washington, 14
Fairfax, George William, friend of Washington, 16; journey of, beyond Blue Ridge, 18
Fairfax, Lord, 13, 28, 52; surveys western lands, 18; influence of, on Washington, 18; sues Yost Hite, 19; proprietor of Greenway Court, 20; death of, 20; burial place of, 20; employs Washington to survey, 23; land holdings of, 29; visits Dinwiddie, 34; interest of, in interior, 34; visited by Washington, 134
Fairfax, Sally, 98
Fairfax, William, proprietor of Belvoir, 14; makes Indian treaty, 35
Fairfax, Colonel William, 122
"Fairfax Boundary Line," 19, 21
"Fairfax Resolves," 155, 159
"Fairfax Stone," 19
Fallen Timbers, battle of, 202

Fauchet, Joseph, 195
Fauquier, Francis, 130
Fayette County, Penna., map of, 79
Ferry Farm, 7, 15
Fincastle riflemen, 161
Findley, William, 202
Fitch, John, 187
Fitzgerald, John, 187
Fitzhugh, William, 134
Forbes, General John, 28, 126; comments of, regarding Washington and Byrd, 129
Forbes's Road, 126, 127, 158
"Fort Gower Address," 155, 160
Fort Necessity, battle of, 80-83; contemporaneous newspaper accounts of, 211-16
Forts, chain of, 118, 120; on Mississippi, 41, 42
Franklin, Benjamin, 31, 36, 57, 105; aids Braddock, 101
Franklin, William, 139, 146
Frazier, John, trader, 31, 43; trading post, 47, 48, 105
Frederick, Md., 98
Frederick the Great, 205
Fredericksburg, Va., 39, 112
Freeman, Major James, 177, 178
French, arrest Howard and Salling, 16; contest of, for Ohio Valley, 30; traders, 30; Indian influences of, 33; claims of, to Indian lands, 36; on Ohio in 1753, 47; possessions of, in North America, 53; plans of, for empire, 55; in the Ohio Valley, 58, 59, 66, 67; with Indians at Logstown, 60; spy on English, 64; accounts of Jumonville skirmish of, 65, 66; capture Washington's notes, 69; occupy Gist's, 80; Canadians, 106; exultant over Braddock's defeat, 112
French and English War, 30
French and Indian War, 88; declared, 113; 139, 147, 168
French Estates General, 191
Friend, Charles, 180
Frontenac, Fort, 130
Frontier, Virginia, 1756-1758, 119, 124
Fry, Joshua, 35; commands Virginia frontier forces, 58, 74; death of, 74

INDEX

GAGE, Colonel Thomas, 100
Galpin, George, 187
Gates, Horatio, 162, 164
Genêt, Edmond Charles, 191, 192, 194-96, 197
Genn, James, 21
George II, comments on Washington, 72
George III, Washington's plea for loyalty to, 113
Germans, in Shenandoah Valley, 16, 19; Palatine, 152, 153
Gibson, George, 166
Gibson, Colonel John, 169
Gist, Christopher, agent of Ohio Company, 33; second journey of to Ohio Valley, 34; makes Indian treaty, 35; Washington's guide, 39; returns from Fort Le Boeuf, 48; crosses the Allegheny, 48; letter of, from Monongahela, 59; leads scouting party, 63; gives account of Jumonville skirmish, 70
Gist, Nathaniel, 100
Gist's. See Mount Braddock
Grant, Major James, 128, 129
Great Crossing, 62
Great Kanawha River, 142, 149, 152, 154, 155, 156, 157, 158, 163, 174, 177, 181, 182, 183, 188, 189, 204, 208
Great Lakes, 196
Great Meadows, 63, 80, 87, 88, 110, 176
Great Miami River, 33, 204
Greeley, Horace, 136
Greenbrier Land Company, 33
"Greenway Court," 19, 20, 21, 23, 24, 134
Grove, William, 7

HALE, Sir Matthew, 4
Half-King, Indian chief, 40, 41, 46, 61, 64, 67, 75, 82, 87, 90
Halkett, Sir Peter, 100, 108
Hamilton, Alexander, 201
Hamilton, Governor James, 35
Hamilton, Lieutenant Robert, 142
Hampton Roads, 95
Hand, General Edward, 167
Hanway, Captain Samuel, 180
"Happy Retreat," 175, 176
"Harewood," 32

Harmar, General Josiah, 199
Harpers Ferry, arsenal site, 207
Harrevelt, publisher, 66
Harrison, Governor Benjamin, 185
Harrison, William, 142
"Heights of Abraham," 134
Henderson, Richard, 189
Hendricks, Captain William, 161
Henry, Fort, 170
Henry, Patrick, 158, 166
Hillsborough, Willis Hill, earl of, 153
Hite, Abraham, 180, 181
Hite, Yost, 19
Hobb's Hole, 10
Hogg, Peter, 60, 100
Howard, John, 16
Howe, Sir William (General), 164
Hudson River, 55
Huntington, Countess, 173

ICE's Ferry, 180
Indians, war dance of, 22; trade of, 33; veer to English, 39, 58; at Logstown, 42, 160; accompany Washington to Venango, 43; with Jumonville, 64, 65; English allies, 68; relations of Braddock with, 96; exultant because of Braddock's defeat, 112; attack valley settlements, 117; trade with, 138; murder Logan's family, 155; defeat of, at Fallen Timbers, 201, 202
Innes, Colonel James, 74, 77, 89, 93
Iroquois Indians, 35, 57, 96, 155, 165; address of Washington to, 166
Irvine, Brigadier General William, 169, 170

"JACK the Black Hunter," Indian leader, 102
James River, 174
James River and Potomac improvement, 185, 187, 188, 204
Jay, John, 198
Jefferson, Thomas, 152, 153, 168, 172, 174, 197, 207; quoted, 195
Jenkins, William, 39
Johnson, Sir William, 121, 138
Johnson, Thomas, 187
Joncaire, Captain Philippe Thomas, 43, 44, 47
Jones, Gabriel, 181
Jumonville, Joseph Coulon de, skirmish

INDEX 265

of, 64; grave of, 64; accounts of death of, 65-72; references to, in Fort Necessity capitulation, 83-86

KENTUCKY River, 150
Kiashuta, 143, 144
King William's War, 30
King's Mountain, battle of, 162
Knights of Golden Horseshoe, 16
Knox, General Henry, 198

LAFAYETTE, Marquis de, 165, 175, 205
La Force, Captain ......, 44, 62, 64, 67, 70
Lake Erie, 92, 99
"Lake Erie and Ohio Deep Water Canal," 182
La Salle, Robert, 30
Laurel Mountain, 64, 72, 73, 78, 127
Le Boeuf, Fort, 37, 44, 47, 50, 60
Lee, Arthur, 134
Lee, Governor Henry, 201
Lee, Richard Henry, 16, 134, 173, 186, 209; quoted, 161
Lee, Thomas, and the Ohio Company, 32
Lee, Thomas Sim, 187
Leesburg, Va., 140
L'Enfant, Peter Charles, 28
Lewis, Andrew, 78, 100, 129, 163; expedition of, to Ohio River, 116; in Dunmore's War, 156
Lewis, Fielding, 3, 27
Lewis, Sergeant ...., ordered shot, 120
Lewis, Thomas, 181
Lewis, Warner, 111
Lewis, Mrs. William, quoted, 162
Ligonier, Fort, 128
Little Kanawha River, 143, 176, 177, 178
Lodge, Henry Cabot, quoted, 60, 87
Logston, Thomas, 180
Logstown, 36; treaty of, 35; visited by Washington, 40; Indian conference at, 41, 42
London Morning Post, quoted, 163
"Long Knives," 33, 135
"Lords of Trade," 196
Lost River, 26
Loudoun, Fort, 28, 113
Loudoun, John C., Earl of, commander-in-chief of King's army, 120, 121; criticized Washington, 122
Louis XIV (The Grand Monarch), 54
Louisburg, Fort, 130
Lowe, James, 154
Lower Mississippi, 150
"Lyman's Military Adventure," 150

MCCULLOCH'S Path, 180
McGillivray, Alexander, 193
McIntosh, General Lachlan, 167
Mackay, Captain James, 75, 76, 80, 89, 94
McKee, Alexander, 142
McPherson, Thomas, 154
MacQuire (McQuire), John, 39
Madison, James, 192
Map, of Washington's journey to Fort Le Boeuf, 37; of Washington's journey to the Ohio (1753), 51; of Redstone country, 79; of Braddock's trail, 103; of Washington's chain of forts, 119; of roads to Fort Duquesne, 127; of Washington's journey to the Ohio (1770), 143; of Washington's western tour (1784), 179
Marietta, settled, 188
Marin, Pierre Paul, sieur de, 39, 41, 45
Martial law, 89, 114
Marye, Reverend James, 7
Maryland, colony of, 57, 67, 92, 99, 110
Maryland Gazette, quoted, 213-16
Mason, George, 16
Masonic Lodge, 133
Massachusetts, colony of, 99
Maumee Rapids, 197
"Mecklenberg Declaration," 160
"Memoire Contenant le Précis des Faits," 65
Mercer, Captain George, 116, 147
Mercer, Hugh, 100
Mercer, Ensign John, 78
Mercer, Captain John Fenton, 117
Miller, Peter, 154
Miller's Run, 139
Miro, Governor Estevan, 193
Mississippi Land Company, 134
Mississippi River, 16, 31, 150, 182, 192; French settlement on, 55
Mohawk River, 164
Monongahela, battle of, 105-10, 128, 140, 222-26

266　　INDEX

Monongahela River, 39, 74, 138, 154, 176, 177, 184
Montague, Mary, 4
Montcalm, Louis Joseph, 134
Montour, Andrew, 100, 115
Montreal, Canada, 185
Moravian Indians, 170
"Mordington," 32
Moreau, M. de Sechelles, 66
Morgan, Charles, 142
Morgan, General D., 161, 164, 175, 176
Morgan, Zackquill, 180
Moundsville, W. Va., 173
Mount Braddock (Gist's) Penna., 39, 77
Mount Pleasant, Penna., 39
Mount Vernon, granted to John Washington, 6; named, 7; home of Lawrence Washington, 11; boyhood home of George Washington, 14; visited by George Washington, 24; inherited by George Washington, 27; Washington retires to, 93, 125; seat of Washington's activities, 132; in Washington's affections, 133; Washington returns to, 146
Muse, Colonel George, 74, 89

NAPOLEON, 30
Natchez, Miss., 168, 208
Necessity, Fort, 73, 89, 90, 91, 92, 93, 94; built, 73; battle of, 80, 83; capitulation of, 83-88; reconstructed, 86-88
Negro Slaves, insurrection of, feared, 112; sold by Washington, 132; John Posey's, 136; on Great Kanawha, 157; of Lawrence Augustine Washington, Jr., 206
Nemacolin, 33; path, 63
Neville, Colonel John, 180, 188
New Orleans, La., 135, 166, 192, 195
New River, 181
New York, city of, 116, 182
New York, colony of, 57, 77, 96, 99
Niagara, Fort, 99
Nicholas, George, 192
Nicholson, Joseph, 142
North Branch River, 180
North Carolina, colony of, 57, 92
Northern Neck, Va., 18, 19, 20, 24, 27

Northwest Territory, 166, 170, 188
Nova Scotia, 55

O'FALLON, Doctor James, 193
Ohio Company, 146, 152; organized, 32; attempts settlements, 33, 34, 53; interest of, in Ohio Valley, 93, 126; revived, 134; and Vandalia, 138
Ohio Company, Grand, 146, 155. See Vandalia
Ohio Pile (Pyle) Falls, 63
Ohio River, 16, 30, 31, 32, 35, 40, 45, 47, 52, 54, 58, 62, 130, 135, 142, 149, 155, 159, 170, 174, 177, 182, 188, 189, 196, 204
Ohio Valley, 30, 188; story of conquest of, 31; Washington's first visit to, 39; rivalries for (1752), 52; French refusal to abandon, 53; French inroads into, 58; trade of, 183
Old Town (Cresap's), Md., 22, 60
Orme, Robert, 98, 105
Ovid, quoted, 53

PAINE, Thomas, 153
Peirpoint's, 180
Pendleton, Edmund, 200
Pendleton, Fort, 180
Penn, William, 33
Pennsylvania, colony of, 31, 57, 96, 99, 110, 127, 139
"Pennsylvania Dutch," 21, 32, 101, 120, 129, 153
Pennsylvania Gazette, quoted, 54, 67, 222-26
Perryopolis, Penna., 154
"Petite Democrate," 194
Peyronie, Ensign William, 83, 107
Peyton, Colonel John L., 97
Philadelphia, Penna., 38, 116, 122, 126, 135, 138, 182, 185
Philips (Phillips), Colonel Theophilus, 178
Philipse, Mary, 116
Pitt, Fort, 28, 130, 131, 135, 138, 141, 145, 147, 148, 165, 166, 169, 170; emporium of trade, 135
Pitt, William, Earl of Chatham, 30, 125, 130
Pittsburg, Penna., 141, 182
Point Pleasant, battle of, 116, 155, 160
Polson, William, 100, 107

Posey, Captain John, 150
Potomac Falls, 28
Potomac River, 174, 175, 178, 182, 184
Pownall, Thomas, 57
Preston, Colonel William, 156
Princess Bright Lightning, 102
Proclamations (1763), 135, 137, 139; Dinwiddie (1754), 50, 140, 146

QUEBEC, Canada, 135
Quebec Act, 164
Queen Aliquippa, Indian chieftainess, 48, 74, 75

RANDOLPH, Peyton, 93, 112
Rappahannock River, 18, 27
Raystown, Penna., 128
Raystown Path, 33
Redick, David, 202
Redstone, Fort, 58, 76, 77, 78; maps of district around, 79
Reed, Colonel Joseph, 162
Repentigny, Captain Legardeur de, 45
Revolution, American, 100
Richmond, Va., 182
Roanoke River, 181
Robertson, James, 199
Robinson, Beverley, 116
Robinson, John, 116, 122, 123
Rochester, N. Y., 43
Roster, of Virginia officers and privates engaged at Fort Necessity, 217-21
Round Bottom Lands, 173
Rumsey, James, makes model boat, 175; importance of boat of, 184, 185; perfects steamboat, 187
Rutherford, John, 100

ST. CLAIR, Governor Arthur, 199
St. Clair, Sir John, 108, 128
St. Pierre, Jacques le Gardeur, sieur de, 44, 54, 71; answer of, to Dinwiddie, 45; and the Half-King, 46
Salling, John Peter, 16
Samples, Samuel, 145
Sandy Creek Glades, 180
Santo Domingo, 55
Saratoga, battle of, 162, 164, 165
Scotch Highlanders, 128
Scotch-Irish, in Shenandoah Valley, 16, 19; individualistic nature of, 120;
"Ceceders," 177; and strong drink, 200
Seneca Indians, 40, 74, 77
Servants, indentured, 152, 154, 157
Sevier, John, 199
Sharpe, Governor Horatio, 92, 93, 94
Shawnee Indians, 59, 77
Shawnee Town, 59
Sheffield, Lord, quoted, 203
Shelburne, William Petty, Earl of, 138
Shingiss (Shingas), King of Delawares, 40
Shirley, Governor William, 116
Shirley, William, Jr., killed, 116
Simcoe, Governor John Graves, 197
Simpson, Gilbert, 154, 174, 176
Six Nations, league of Indian tribes, 59, 86
South Branch River, 180, 181, 182
South Carolina, colony of, 57, 67, 75, 96
South Carolina Gazette, quoted, 67
Spaniards, on lower Mississippi and western trade, 183, 192
Spotswood, Alexander, 16, 31
Stanwix, Fort, 139
Stephen, Adam, 89, 100; gives account of Jumonville skirmish, 70; opposes building Forbes's Road, 129
Stephenson, Captain Hugh, 161
Steuben, Frederich Wilhelm August Heinrich Ferdinand von, 170
Steubenville, Ohio, 142
Stevens, William, 156
Steward, Henry, 39
Stewart, Captain Robert, 100
Stobo, Robert, hostage, 90, 110
Stroads (Strode), Captain ...., 176
Sullivan, General John, 165, 167
"Summit House," 64
Suver, Peter, 63
Swearingen, Captain Thomas, 125, 176

THOMAS, Antoine L., 66
Ticonderoga, Fort, 134
Tobacco, grown by Washington, 132, 133
Tories, 167
Trans-Allegheny, 32, 39, 50, 138, 151, 174, 175, 196, 200, 207, 208; proposed colonies in, 135
Treaties:
Basel, 195
Easton, 130

268 INDEX

Fort Harmar, 199
Fort Stanwix, 130, 139, 155; (1784), 199
Greenville, 199
Jay, 195, 198
Jay-Gardoqui, 189
Lancaster, 35
Lochaber, 155
Logstown, 35
Paris (1873), 172
Pinckney, 195
Trent, William, 36, 50, 139, 146; instructed to build forts, 58
Turtle Creek, 105
Tygart Valley River, 180

U NIONTOWN (Beason Town), Penna., 178

V AN BRAAM, Jacob, 39, 45, 47, 60; poor knowledge of French of, 70, 85, 89; hostage, 83, 90
Vandalia, 146, 147, 151. *See* Grand Ohio Company
Van Meter, Henry, 22
Veech, James, quoted, 64
Venango, Fort, 31, 43, 47, 62
Vernon, Admiral Edward, 39
Villiers, Coulon de, 81, 83, 84, 85, 86, 88
Virginia, colony of, claim of, to Ohio Valley, 31, 32, 67, 92, 96, 99, 110; executive council of, 140, 147
Virginia Assembly, mistrusts Dinwiddie, 53; authorizes volunteers, 55, 56; Dinwiddie appeals to, 92; difficulties of, with Dinwiddie, 96; aids in French and Indian War, 126; Washington a member of, 133; approved James River improvement, 204
Virginia Gazette, quoted, 67, 211-13
Voltaire, quoted, 81
Von Steuben. *See* Steuben

"W AKEFIELD," 3; Washington's birthplace, 4
Walker, Thomas, explorer, 33
Walpole, Horace, quoted, 81, 97
Walpole, Thomas, 139, 141
"Walpole Grant," 139, 141. *See* Vandalia

War of the English Succession. *See* King William's War
Ward, Ensign Edward, 60, 61, 71
Warm Springs, 26, 134, 135, 175
Washington, Anne Fairfax, 14
Washington, Augustine, father of George, 4, 5; directs George's education, 8; business interests of, 14
Washington, Augustine, half-brother of George, 3, 111; at Bridges Creek, 11; George's sojourn with, 13; promoter of Ohio Company, 32; interest of, in Ohio Company, 134
Washington, Bushrod, 180
Washington, Charles, 3, 32, 175
Washington, Elizabeth (Betty), 3, 15
Washington, George, ancestry and youth of, 3; traits of character of, 3; tribute of to mother, 5; Indian name of, 6; education of, 7-15; chain and compass drawing by, 9, 25; "Rules of Civility" of, 12; sojourns at Mount Vernon, 13; journies in 1748 beyond Blue Ridge, 18-23; describes Indian dance, 22; surveys for Lord Fairfax, 23; surveyor of Culpeper County, 25; visits Barbadoes, 26; surveys, 26; adjutant of militia, 27, 34; inherits Mount Vernon, 27; survey books of, 27; surveyor, 28; land owner, 29; returns from Barbadoes, 34; messenger to French, 36-49; *Diary* of, 39; describes Forks of Ohio, 40; at Logstown, 42; delivers letter to St. Pierre, 44; interviews St. Pierre, 46; "Account" of journey to French of, 48, 49, 50; crosses the Allegheny, 48; is commissioned lieutenant colonel, 50; map of "Journey to the Ohio" (1753) of, 51; military experience (1753) of, 52; recruits soldiers at Alexandria, 52, 56; at Old Town, 60; builds road into interior, 61; makes request for "Spirit," 62; at Great Meadows, 62; resents discriminations against Virginia militia, 63; part of, in Jumonville affair, 65-72; letter of May 29, 1754 of, to Dinwiddie, 68-69; comments on French accounts of Jumonville skirmish, 69, 70; comments on Jumonville skirmish, 72; builds Fort Necessity, 73; takes French prisoners,

73; makes efforts to win Indians, 75; disputes with Mackay, 76; negotiates with Indians, 77; sends scouts, 77, 78; at Fort Necessity, 85, 86; describes Fort Necessity, 87, 88; recruits army at Alexandria, 89; and Fort Necessity, 90; again at Alexandria, 92; patriotism of, 93; retires to Mount Vernon, 93-95; accompanies Braddock, 97, 98; finances Braddock's expedition, 100; advises Braddock, 104; in "Battle of Monongahela," 106-7; makes report of Braddock's defeat, 107-8; commander-in-chief, 111; formally declares war on France, 113; prescribes uniforms for militia, 114; defends the frontier, 114-31; visits Boston, 116; sentiments of, aroused, 117; problems of discipline of, 118; chain of forts of, 119; letter of, to John Robinson, 122; defends his administration to Loudoun, 122; writes John Robinson, 122, 123; defeated in election to House of Burgesses, 124; accused of padding pay rolls, 124; granted leave, 125; engaged to marry, 125; elected to House of Burgesses, 125; opposes building Forbes's Road, 127, 128; makes account of fall of Fort Duquesne, 131; leaves the army, 131; reflects on experiences, 131; tobacco grower, 132; administers Custis estates, 132; business activities of, 133; member of Burgesses, 133; Mason, 133; loses interest in army, 134; interested in western lands, 134; Bullskin estate of, 134; visits Warm Springs, 134, 135; advises John Posey, 136; attempts to get good lands, 137, 139; asks permission to survey land, 140; journies (1770) to West, 140; at Fort Pitt, 141; descends Ohio, 142; at mouth of Great Kanawha, 142; locates lands, 144; defends soldiers' land rights, 148; plans visit to Trans-Allegheny, 149; interest in Kentucky lands, 150; Perryopolis mill of, 154, 174; member First Continental Congress, 155; attitude of toward Dunmore's War, 157; and the Great Kanawha settlement, 156, 157; commander-in-chief of American army, 158, 160; plans to retire beyond Alleghenies, 162; at Newburg, 163; land speculations of, 163; letter of, to Landon Carter, 165; opposes Natchez expedition, 168; makes efforts to drive British from Northwest Territory, 170; western lands of, 173, 177; journies (1784) to West, 175-81; and the "Ceceders," 177, 178; "Reflections" of, 182; plans to connect East and West, 183-86; quoted on Potomac navigation, 184; letter of, to Governor Harrison, 185, 186; letter of, to R. H. Lee, 186, 187; opposes Connecticut Reserve, 188; on Mississippi navigation, 189; realizes hopes regarding West, 191; opposes O'Fallon enterprise, 193; tendency of, to Federalists, 195; and Whiskey Rebellion, 200-3; defends republicanism, 203; favors admission of Kentucky, 203, 204; western lands of, 204; heirlooms of, 205; swords of, 205; relics of, 206; Farewell Address of, 206; selects Harpers Ferry as arsenal site, 207; place in history, 208-10

Washington, Henry, 20
Washington, Jane, 4
Washington, John, 3
Washington, John, great-grandfather of George, 6
Washington, John W., 205
Washington, Lawrence, grandfather of George, 5
Washington, Lawrence, half-brother of George, 3; directs George's education, 8; George sojourns with, 13; joins Admiral Vernon, 14; death of, 26; promoter of Ohio Company, 32; president of Ohio Company, 34
Washington, Lawrence Augustine, 206
Washington, Mary Ball, mother of George, 3, 4; teaches her children, 4; influences of, on her son George, 5; refuses to let George go to sea, 15; opposes George's bent for war, 52
Washington, Martha Dandridge-Custis, wife of George, 132; supplements family income, 132
Washington, Mary Dorcas, 206
Washington, Richard, 123
Washington, Samuel, 3, 32

INDEX

Washington, Samuel W., 205
Washington, Warner, 175, 181
Washington, William Augustine, 205
Washington, William Augustine, Jr., 206
Waterford, Penna., 44
Wayne, Anthony, 198, 199
Weiser, Conrad, Indian agent, 31, 32; quoted, 86, 87
West, Hugh, Jr., 124
West, Lieutenant John, 63
West Florida, 150
Westminister Journal, quoted, 53
Wharton, Samuel, 31, 139
Wheeling, W. Va., 206
"Whiskey Boys," 202
Whiskey Rebellion, 195, 200, 203
White Mingo, Indian chief, 141
Wilkinson, James, 193
William and Mary College, 24, 34, 58
Williamsburg, Va., 39, 40, 48, 52, 73, 89, 133
Wills Creek, base for Ohio Company, 33, 39; Washington's conference at, 61, 74; Colonel Fry killed at, 74; attempt of Washington to reach, 78, 85, 88, 89
Winchester (Frederick Town), Va., 23, 24, 25, 35, 39; Indian conference at, 57; 96, 100, 112, 113
Woelper, John David, 153
Wolfe, James, 134
Wood, James, 150
Wood, John, 154
Wormley, Ralph, 175

YADKIN River, 33
Yazoo Company, 193
Youghiogheny River, 33, 62, 63, 174, 180, 182, 184

www.ingramcontent.com/pod-product-compliance
Lightning Source LLC
Chambersburg PA
CBHW021356290426
44108CB00010B/272